Global Feminist Pol

Global Feminist Politics provides a textured perspective on the diversity of women's lives and highlights the heterogeneous quality of Women's Studies. It is a sensitive and insightful study of 'gender' and activism in the developing world.

                Heather Deegan, *Head of International Studies, Middlesex University*

Global Feminist Politics examines the changing global context for feminist political action and its meaning and forms. It acknowledges the existence of dissent and debate among feminists, asserting that such debate leads to innovation in theory and practice. It comes to the conclusion that the future of the women's movement depends upon a dialogue which is unafraid to cut across perceived differences.

This book focuses on key issues raised by a feminist commitment to global political change. Subjects covered include:

- the relevance of contemporary feminist politics for younger women;
- gendered accounts of genocide and catastrophe;
- exile, migration and diaspora;
- women and the nationalist movement in India;
- gender issues in Pakistan, Australia, South Africa and the Middle East.

Featuring an international panel of cutting-edge feminist thinkers, this book demonstrates the innovative work being undertaken in the academic and professional worlds as well as in women's activism. It is an invaluable resource for students of Women's Studies and Development Studies, as well as all those interested in the development of contemporary global feminism.

Suki Ali is currently completing an ESRC funded PhD at the Institute of Education, University of London. Her work has been published in *Gender and Education* and the *Irish Journal of Feminist Studies*. **Kelly Coate** is a Research Officer at the Institute of Education, University of London. She has taught and published in the areas of Women's Studies and education. **Wangui wa Goro** is a writer, researcher and activist. She is currently completing a funded PhD at the University of Middlesex. Her main research focuses on Translation Studies, in which she also teaches and writes.

Global Feminist Politics
Identities in a changing world

Edited by Suki Ali, Kelly Coate
and Wangui wa Goro

London and New York

First published 2000 by Routledge
11 New Fetter Lane, London EC4P 4EE

Simultaneously published in the USA and Canada
by Routledge
29 West 35th Street, New York, NY 10001

Routledge is an imprint of the Taylor & Francis Group

© 2000 selection and editorial matter, Suki Ali, Kelly Coate and
Wangui wa Goro; individual chapters, the contributors

Typeset in Sabon by Taylor & Francis Ltd
Printed and bound in Great Britain by
TJ International Ltd, Padstow, Cornwall

All rights reserved. No part of this book may be reprinted or
reproduced or utilised in any form or by any electronic,
mechanical, or other means, now known or hereafter
invented, including photocopying and recording, or in any
information storage or retrieval system, without permission in
writing from the publishers.

British Library Cataloguing in Publication Data
A catalogue record for this book is available from the British Library

Library of Congress Cataloging-in-Publication Data
Global feminist politics: identities in a changing world/
edited by Suki Ali, Kelly Coate, and Wangui wa Goro.
   p. cm.
Includes bibliographical references and index.
1. Feminism. 2. Women's rights. I. Ali, Suki, 1962– II. Coate,
Kelly, 1967– III. Wangui wa Goro.
HQ1121. G56 2000
305.42–dc21   99–054583

ISBN 0–415–21469–6 (hbk)
ISBN 0–415–21470–X (pbk)

Contents

Notes on contributors   vii
Acknowledgements   x

Introduction: trying to connect you   1
SUKI ALI

1 The women's movement revisited: areas of concern for the future   5
NIGHAT SAID KHAN

2 Despite diversity: women's unity in Western Cape, South Africa (1980–94)   11
GERTRUDE FESTER

3 Political thoughts and domestic lives: women activists in North India   28
SURUCHI THAPAR-BJORKERT

4 Gender, ethnicity and 'the community': locations with multiple identities   49
TIJEN UGURIS

5 Is there a space for gender in modernist planning?   69
TOVI FENSTER

6 The feminisation of catastrophe: narrating women's silences   92
RONIT LENTIN

7 Gendered diaspora identities: South African women, exile and migration (c. 1960–95) 107
ELAINE UNTERHALTER

8 No fixed abode: feminism in the 1990s 126
DEBBIE EPSTEIN AND DEBORAH LYNN STEINBERG

9 Who knows best? Politics and ethics in feminist research into 'race' 133
SUKI ALI

10 Fast capitalism, fast feminism and some fast food for thought 154
JANE KENWAY WITH DIANA LANGMEAD

Conclusion: reflections on global feminisms 176
KELLY COATE

Index 181

Contributors

Suki Ali is currently undertaking an ESRC-funded PhD at the Institute of Education, University of London. Her research focuses on gendered 'mixed-race' identities in children between the ages of 8 and 11. She has also worked on a project on teenagers' use of slang. She has taught several units on Sex and Gender, Sexualities, and Families at the University of Greenwich. Her main research interests are family relationships and their impact upon identities, sexualities, multi-ethnic identities, cultural hybridity, and the effectiveness of anti-oppressive policies in primary schools.

Kelly Coate is a Research Officer at the Institute of Education, University of London. She is currently completing a PhD (funded by an ESRC studentship) on the history of Women's Studies in the UK. Her research interests are in the areas of feminist pedagogies, the higher education curriculum, and the development of Women's Studies as an academic subject area. She has taught and published in the fields of Women's Studies and the sociology of education, and has been an active member of the Women's Studies Network (UK) Association since 1994.

Debbie Epstein is a Reader in Education at the University of London Institute of Education, where she teaches Women's Studies and Cultural Studies. Her research is about the co-construction of sexuality, race and gender in education and in popular culture. Recent publications include *Schooling Sexualities* (co-authored with Richard Johnson, Open University Press), *A Dangerous Knowing: Sexuality, Pedagogy and Popular Culture* (co-edited with James T. Sears, Cassell) and *A Question of Discipline: Pedagogy, Power and the Teaching of Cultural Studies* (co-edited with Joyce E. Canaan, Westview).

Tovi Fenster is a Senior Lecturer at the Department of Geography and Human Environment, Tel Aviv University, Israel. She is the editor of *Gender, Planning and Human Rights*, (Routledge, 1999) and has published articles and chapters on ethnicity, citizenship and gender in planning and development. Currently she is writing a book entitled *Gender, Space, Culture in Planning and Development* (Pearson).

Gertrude Fester has been a long-standing member of grassroots women's organisations in Cape Town, South Africa. She has published some fiction and non-fiction, mainly focusing on women's lives. She has written and performed a one-woman play based on her experiences as a political prisoner under the apartheid regime. She is currently registered at the Gender Institute, London School of Economics, where she is doing her PhD.

Jane Kenway is the Director of the Deakin Centre for Education and Change, Geelong. She teaches Educational Administration and Policy Studies at Deakin University. Her research expertise is in cultural change, educational policy and change in schools. She has published widely in international and national refereed journals, in books and in professional journals for the education profession. She has a successful record of building cross-institutional and state research teams and also regularly provides consultancy services to governments, keynote addresses to the education community, guest lectures and professional development programmes for other universities and the education profession. Her most recent book, *Answering Back: Girls, Boys and Feminism in Schools*, was published by Allen and Unwin in 1997.

Nighat Said Khan is an activist based in Pakistan. She recently helped establish the Institute of Women's Studies in Lahore.

Diana Langmead is a BLitt (Hons) student, currently working as a research assistant with Professor Kenway at the Deakin Centre for Education and Change, Deakin University, Geelong. She previously undertook research with Professor Robyn Rowland in the area of reproductive technology. She has been actively involved in the women's movement, in the community and the university. Her research interests centre around women, work and education.

Ronit Lentin is course co-ordinator of the MPhil in Ethnic and Racial Studies at the Department of Sociology, Trinity College Dublin, where she also lectures in Sociology and Women's Studies and where she did her doctoral research on the gendering of the relationship between Israel and the Shoah. She is the editor of *Gender and Catastrophe* (1997) and of two volumes of *In from the Shadows: The UL Women's Studies Collection* (1995, 1996). She has published articles on gender and Shoah commemoration, citizenship and minority Irish women, gender and racism, feminist research methodologies, and Israeli and Palestinian women's peace activism. Her latest novel is *Songs on the Death of Children* (1996).

Deborah Lynn Steinberg is a Senior Lecturer teaching feminism and cultural theory in the Department of Sociology, University of Warwick. Recent publications include: *Bodies in Glass: Genetics, Eugenics, Embryo Ethics* (Manchester University Press); *Border Patrols: Policing the Boundaries of Heterosexuality* (co-edited with Debbie Epstein and Richard Johnson, Cassell) and *Mourning Diana: Nation, Culture and the Performance of Grief* (co-edited with Adrian Kear, Routledge).

Suruchi Thapar-Bjorkert researches on gender, colonialism and nationalism in India. She has published earlier in *Feminist Review* (1993), *Manushi* (1993), *Women's Studies International Forum* (1997), *Women's History Review* (1997) and made contributions to various edited books (1995, 1996).

Tijen Uguris trained as an architect in Istanbul, Turkey. She has investigated gender and ethnic divisions in the built environment as her PhD research at the University of Greenwich in London. She is also involved with research into 'diasporic space' and Kurdish women living in diaspora. She has participated in anti-racist and anti-sexist campaigns as well as campaigns for democratic rights among migrants, immigrants and refugees in general and women in particular.

Elaine Unterhalter was born and grew up in South Africa and did her first degree at the University of the Witwatersrand. She came to the UK in the mid 1970s, initially as a student, but remained and joined the ANC. She was active in the ANC Women's Section in the 1980s and was a researcher and later the director of the RESA (Research on Education in South Africa) project, which undertook policy research and training for a post-apartheid South Africa. She has taught Gender and Ethnic Studies at the University of Greenwich and from 1994 has been a member of the Centre for Research on Education and Gender at the Institute of Education, University of London. She is currently teaching and researching in the area of education, gender and international development. She has published widely in the area of gender and education policy change in South Africa.

Wangui wa Goro is a writer, researcher and activist. She is currently completing a funded PhD at the University of Middlesex. Her main research focuses on Translation Studies, in which she also teaches and writes. Her previous work includes equal opportunities in education, devising and implementing new practice in London primary schools. Wangui is also a writer of fiction and a writer and performer of poetry. Her current interests are translation, feminist theory and activism, education, and African women's sexuality.

Acknowledgements

This book would never have come about without the tremendous response to the Women's Studies Network (UK) Association tenth annual conference, 'Women, Policy and Politics'. Thanks to our colleagues at the Institute of Education and to the members of the WSN Executive Committee who offered support and advice throughout the conference organisation and the process of editing this collection. Diana Leonard, Val Hey and Debbie Epstein provided continual encouragement and shared their experience and knowledge with us, for which we are very grateful. Thanks also to all the women who volunteered to help out on the site and to the delegates who contributed to the lively debates at the sessions and afterwards. It was this enthusiasm and positive atmosphere that helped us to get a book off the ground and believe that there would be a considerable interest in it. Most importantly, we would like to thank all the contributors for their hard work, patience and understanding while we have been putting together this collection. The quality of their work has been the motivation to produce it, and we hope that their efforts will inspire many others.

Suki Ali, Kelly Coate and Wangui wa Goro

Introduction

Trying to connect you

Suki Ali

In July 1997, Women's Studies Network (UK) Association held its tenth annual conference entitled 'Women, Policy and Politics'. The aim of the conference was to bring together women from all over the world and from as many different professional backgrounds and disciplines as possible with special emphasis placed on reaching women from both inside and outside academia. The conference attracted an international array of delegates – nearly two hundred papers were given over three days – and it was from this wide range that the chapters for this book were drawn.

Both formal and informal discussions with women who attended the conference and during the following months revealed several key themes. These are not necessarily new concerns, rather they are things that women continue to struggle with at the level of the everyday as well as the discursive. The future of feminism and what the next millennium will bring for women fighting oppression is a subject that concerns us all. The chapters in this book reflect the political focus of the conference and show the continued engagement of feminism with existing theoretical problems while creating or utilising exciting new intellectual and empirical endeavour in order to push forward the definitions and applications of 'feminist theory'. It is this ability to think creatively and to transgress intellectual and political boundaries that marks out the extreme achievements being made by women on a global scale and provides a response to those who repeatedly asked whether there is still a recognisable women's movement.

In the international context we see developments which provide a clearer answer to such a question. The opening chapters of this volume chart the continuing changes that are being wrought on a global scale as a result of women's activism. Whether this takes the form of resistance in the 'domestic' sphere, like that of the women Suruchi Thapar-Bjorkert found, or the more 'public' political arena of grassroots women's groups in South Africa documented by Gertrude Fester, women are 'out there'. For many women the word 'feminist' still evokes a problematic hegemonic 'white imperialist feminism' which imposes a limited and unhelpful view of what feminist politics is, who can be a feminist and what kind of actions should

2 *Suki Ali*

be deemed feminist. The chapters in this book all call for new ways of thinking about feminism in one way or another, whether in theory or in praxis. Ongoing critical analysis of the ways organisations can become complacent is essential, and Nighat Khan does not shy away from the difficult task of demanding that feminists in positions of power be sure that they retain their political sharpness.

For many modern Western women, feminism is an outdated concept. It harks back to the 'old days' of 'women's libbers' and militant politics, a few women who fought for changes that are now in place. A major concern of the conference was how to draw in new young women when they are unaware of or uninterested in the idea of a women's movement. In the case of academia, recent trends mean that Women's Studies courses are decreasing, women-only classes are no longer the norm, and the radical edge of early feminist courses has in some cases been blunted. There are those who would argue that inclusion in the mainstream has brought Women's Studies out of the 'ghetto', while others regard the postmodern slant of contemporary 'feminist theory' to be a sell-out. Many younger women feel that the concerns of a radical movement are not *their* concerns, and for them 'girl power' is far more attractive than 'feminism'. Some believe that they do live in a post-feminist world where if they truly want it they can have it all. In other areas of society and other parts of the globe, the renaming of academic courses and the debates over lifestyle choices could not be further from the minds of women activists.

The problem of racism within institutions in Europe and North America remains at the centre of much of our discussions, and the continuing concerns about the lack of sustained critiques which centralise ethnic and 'racial' oppression and which lay claim to the label 'feminist'. Black women and women of colour remain marginalised at both the material and discursive levels, as do women with disabilities. Lesbians have become slightly more visible, but the institution of heterosexuality is still oppressive. How we might deal with these silences and absences when engaging in feminist theory and research remains problematic, and often produces ethical and methodological dilemmas for those in the academy (see Ali, this volume). Tijen Uguris critiques the construction of communities in spatial and conceptual terms and reveals the failure of planners and architects in Britain to engage with these issues. Tovi Fenster, in her unique work with Bedouin women, gives an insight into the quotidian struggles for mobility within spatial constraints.

One of the ways in which the resistance to oppression may be advanced is by the sharing of ideas. The need to be open to new ideas, or to engage with those that may be at odds with our own, is crucial to healthy dialogue. A common complaint is that there is very little genuine conversation between women in the northern and southern hemispheres, and in spite of continued debates about the relationships between feminist academics and activists, there is need for further committed effort for a cross-fertilisation of ideas at micro, macro and global levels. A central theme of this book is the importance of listening as well as talking, and, again, it is more explicit in chapters which utilise some form of narrative analysis. Elaine Unterhalter and Ronit Lentin found women's narratives to be rich sources of inspiration, as did Suruchi Thapar-Bjorkert.

The politics of location, of where one chooses to fight one's battles and with whom one forms political identifications, is also central to the papers. Underpinning that are the concepts that are the cohesion for all the papers, that is belonging and identity. Whether one believes in the future of a women's movement also rests to an extent on the reworking of allegiances that cross the divides within the term 'women'. Even if one is not located within the same geographical or political location as another, we must strive to communicate. The fact that identities are dynamic also plays a significant part in the way in which we understand our belonging to a place, a time, a movement and so on. For those who are relocated through economic, political and social imperatives, the search for belonging has a particular significance, yet that search can still be a powerful force for those who have not moved geographical place, but are travelling social and intellectual planes. Epstein and Steinberg have engaged with this theme to produce a light-hearted yet thought-provoking piece about the feminism of the academy and its lack of a 'home'. Movement of information and knowledge are also themes that Jane Kenway and Diana Langmead tackle within the Australian university, but they are also relevant to many working in the business-driven cultures of education and development as well as government.

The future of feminism is uncertain. Women continue to discuss the meaning of the term and whether they wish to claim the label 'feminist' for themselves or not. There are ongoing debates raging across theoretical boundaries, across geographical and spatial boundaries, and across lines that are marked by shared beliefs. Before we lower our heads in defeat in the face of such disagreement, we should reflect that this is also how the future strength of feminism may be assured. These women who are working full time for and on behalf of women and other oppressed groups still have the energy left to argue and discuss and demand that the women's movement continues to evolve and transform. It would appear that there is an ongoing commitment among feminists to some kind of women's movement even if there is dissent about what form it currently takes and what form it may take in the future. The movement is not an amorphous whole, it may even be fragmented, but in each of the fragments the idea of a political project is alive and well. In some parts of the globe there is no questioning of whether there is a women's movement: it is visible and strong, and focused on struggles of life and death, against poverty and exploitation.

Perhaps one of the keys to a strong future feminism is finding a way to make women more aware of connections from local to global. The need is for women in the north to take up struggles with southern sisters, to look at the impact of their work upon them, or simply for the next generation of young women to see such connections and want to act upon them. Globalisation used to be seen as a buzzword, but its reality has profound effects on women, and a global awareness needs to be incorporated into all of our feminist politics. In sharing our ideas, arguments and political beliefs we will ensure that the future is feminist!

1 The women's movement revisited
Areas of concern for the future

Nighat Said Khan

While the women's movement is today acknowledged by the United Nations, by governments and other institutions, the negative aspect of this support has been that the women's movement itself has lost its political edge and, in some cases, its commitment. This trend has led not only to some more powerful groups becoming part of the establishment, but to these groups taking on the very male norms that they were earlier challenging.

The last two decades for Pakistani women have been of particular significance. In 1975, the state was encouraging women into the mainstream and many women were taking advantage of these spaces. Soon after, however, with the Islamisation/militarisation process resulting from the military take-over in 1977, the state actively tried to push women into the *chadder* and *chardevari* (seclusion) and promulgated several ordinances and directives that made women more vulnerable than they had been earlier. Women in Pakistan have been fighting back ever since, and the 1980s saw the emergence of a dynamic, innovative and committed women's movement in Pakistan. Of these, Women's Action Forum is the most significant. Unfortunately the movement all over the world has been taken over by the NGO establishment, and even in Pakistan one has seen the commitment and the politics of the movement increasingly subsumed by ahistorical and apolitical discourses and actions.

While the women's resource centres and organisations that grew out of the women's movement in Pakistan have worked with dedication, the movement itself has lost its political sharpness and its energy. What is even more unfortunate is that the women's movement has begun to be defined only by a few women-centred groups, mainly in the urban areas. This has tended to exclude and to overlook the efforts that women have been making all over Pakistan in their own areas of work or expression, and this in turn has meant that the media, the government, international agencies and even these organisations believe that it is only they who give legitimacy to the movement.

There is, however, little validity in the assumption that the interests, issues, understanding and, in some cases, sophistication of urban/professional groups are different from those women not considered part of the movement. If anything, experience shows that women from different class, ethnic, religious, and professional backgrounds are much more able and willing to understand and grapple with issues of their own subordination. For example, it is often said by urban/professional or women's rights groups that the women's movement cannot be very political, or confrontational, or secular, or conceptual, or feminist, because the 'average' woman is not yet ready for any of these. Yet we have often found that these women are much more willing and able to understand and identify with these notions than middle-class urban women, and that these women (and some men) are more willing to travel long distances, put up with uncomfortable situations, take leave from their jobs, stay away from their families, and even take enormous personal risks, to be a part of something that they believe in. To them the issues of class contradictions in society, the patriarchy inherent in all religions, militarisation, poverty, unemployment, suppression of creativity, etc., are not only concepts or objective realities, but what they deal with on a daily basis. They are therefore much more interested in why this happens and how it may be resolved. In the National Assembly/Conference of Development Activists organised by the ASR Resource Centre in April 1995, there was little disagreement, for example, on the nature of the state, on political economy and the hegemony of a particular class, on religion, on provincial rights and on patriarchy.

The question then is: what is the women's movement in Pakistan? The tendency, as said above, is to see it as either Women's Action Forum in itself, or as WAF and a few other 'known' women's rights groups. This is unfair even on these organisations, since they are then put in the position of constantly explaining what they are doing and why they are not doing what other movements and groups expect them to do. In many cases the demands on them in terms of what they should be doing, or should have done, are too enormous for the movement to handle in any circumstances. For example, women's groups are often asked, 'Why are women in Pakistan still exploited?', or 'Why has WAF not stopped violence against women?', or, worse, 'What is Women's Action Forum doing about the situation in Karachi, and why can't it do something about electricity failure?'! These questions, however absurd, are not asked rhetorically. There is a genuine expectation from the women's movement, or specifically from a few women's groups, that far outweighs its size or capacity. This leads not only to considerable stress, since women then take on more than they can handle, but also gives a sense of failure and a feeling of being depleted. In many ways, however, these groups, by being high profile and perhaps exclusive, bring this upon themselves.

Feminists are also criticised for not living up their own principles of feminism. To some extent this criticism is justified, since many feminists and women's groups replicate male norms and mainstream organisations. The problem, however, also lies in the fact that the women's movement has not attempted to make a distinction between the feminist movement and the movement for women's rights. There is a difference. The women's movement is a struggle for democracy and equal rights for women within the liberal feminist tradition. Feminism, on the other hand, is the recognition of patriarchy as a system of male oppression and domination which has a material (that is, economic) base. Feminists therefore seek a more holistic and structural transformation of society and a transformation of all relationships, including the personal. The women's rights movement is a necessary stage towards this transformation, just as a democratic, liberal stage may be necessary for social and economic structural transformation in general, but as far as feminism is concerned equal rights within the existing system is not an end in itself. If the women's movement were to make this distinction, it could be much more inclusive, since it could include and mobilise all those women struggling for women's rights. This would in itself make the movement larger and stronger. Feminists who struggle for a more profound transformation would also be a part of this movement. In this sense, the movement would not only include all those struggling for equality in the public and private sphere but also those struggling in their individual capacities, such as writers, poets, artists, etc., quite apart from women's and human rights groups, development NGOs and the like.

This would not only give strength to the movement but would limit the criticism that the women's movement is simply the aspiration and articulation of a small group. Recently there have been attempts at redefining the movement by including development activities and projects. In many cases, however, projects, programmes and action plans have subsumed and/or negated the very activism and the commitment on which the movement is premised. These initiatives have in a concrete sense depleted much of the dynamism, energy and flexibility of the movement. For instance, in most cases these activities are financially supported, and this invariably brings with it the constraints of paperwork, proposals, reports, accounts, etc., quite apart from the fact that often activities also get defined by the agendas and the constraints of funding agencies. This also leads to professionalism, since management and efficiency become important, and to a competition for resources and financial support. In the case of funded activities and the responsibility of 'keeping the office operational', continuity of the issue and the activity becomes a further problem, since the group must end the programme once the project period is over, and it goes into another programme without seeing the first one to its logical and necessary conclusion.

Paid political and social activism, whether it is in NGOs or the press or other institutions that supposedly work in the public interest, also gives a false sense of commitment and fulfilment. If, for example, one is spending several hours a day doing 'good works', there is a tendency to switch off when one is 'free'. Activism in this sense has increasingly become a job or a task, and the issues and actions not necessarily internalised. This not only leads to a further fragmentation of the self and to a false consciousness, but, by reinforcing the separation of the public and the private, it negates what the women's movement is trying to struggle for.

Although the debate on the pros and cons of funding is rare in Pakistan, and most NGOs are simply content that it is there, what is or should be clear is that these funds are public funds and given in the name of the people of Pakistan. The responsibility of using these funds must therefore be more holistic and should require more of a commitment from those handling these funds to change themselves as they set out trying to 'change society'. At the same time there must be a greater transparency and accountability to the people of Pakistan for the management and use of these funds. Further, given that all political and progressive movements are increasingly being subsumed by funded/professional activity, and since the 'business' side of development has become confused with development activism, there is a need to identify and accept the development professional as a new professional category. This category should then be subject to the same ethics, rules and norms as other professional groups. In other words, development professionals, especially those in consultancy work, should not be confused with development/social/political activists. A distinction should also be made between activism and action plans. Action plans do not necessarily lead to activism and do not necessarily produce social and political activists. Much of the confusion on these issues in development initiatives and processes has also played a role in diffusing the politics and energy of the women's movement.

The area that has, however, diffused the political edge of the movement the most is the issue of 'gender', especially the positing of 'gender' as opposition to 'feminism'. Gender is a complex, and even profound, concept which came out of the socialist feminist tradition. Unfortunately it has been trivialised to the point of losing not only its original meaning but also its history. It is increasingly promoted by the World Bank, the United Nations, bilateral aid agencies and governments, all of whom link this concept to development assistance; it has therefore become an integral part of the jargon and the activities of development groups and of the women's movement. In real terms, in most cases the word 'gender' has simply replaced the word 'woman' and has become a euphemism for it. However, there are inherent dangers in the use of this word and the concept (as it is understood), because the word 'gender' is encouraged as supposedly neutral, apolitical and not as threatening or divisive as 'woman'. This has had the effect that was intended. Feminism and the women's movement have been subsumed by this concept and both have consequently lost their political edge and are increasingly also losing their autonomy.

The most detrimental aspect of this concept, as it is understood in many development circles, is that it takes the position that women are oppressed because of male and female socialisation, and that therefore, if one can sensitise men and women to their own processes of socialisation, this oppression will cease to exist. Even feminists who use this concept to understand women's oppression and subordination often simply posit the concept of socialisation versus the biological fact of sex. This is a crude simplification of a concept that sought to enrich the debate within socialist feminism, especially since, used in this way, it shifts the focus and the debate away from understanding patriarchy as a system, and shifts the movement from challenging the structure of patriarchy and class to one that seeks to 'sensitise' women and men.

The women's movement has moved from being a movement to becoming institutionalised and becoming a part of the establishment. In other words, the anti-thesis has been through a process of synthesis and is increasingly becoming the new thesis. Women's groups are now institutions; feminists are members of the establishment; Women's Studies is rapidly being incorporated in many universities; women's lists are carried by mainstream publishers; women's issues are being addressed by governments; and 'key' women are being included in decision-making in state structures. This is the success of the women's movement. However, if one understands history as a dialectical process, this thesis or establishment will produce its own new anti-thesis to challenge it. The women's movement (in most countries) is not necessarily responding to the challenge within itself with an openness and a flexibility that would allow it to move to a higher stage of development and a higher stage of politics. The question is: how do we get out of this stagnation and out of the apathy that funding and the ideology of postmodernism inculcates? or, where do we go from here?

There is still space within the women's movement to respond to this challenge, but the tendency has been to move away from the principles of feminism such as 'consciousness raising', 'speaking out', 'the personal is political', 'holistic', 'non-hierarchical', 'collective', etc. Challenge and reflection are often dismissed as divisive or a 'waste of time', and, in any case, too painful. Many of these principles are also considered no longer valid, and in many cases, flawed. While there may be some truth to this, there is a need to re-examine and redefine these principles rather than to dismiss them out of hand. The process will be painful, but perhaps less painful in the long run than the conflicts, splits and misunderstandings have been. This residual pain is what a lot of feminists are afraid of, but perhaps the intensiveness of the pain was inherent in a movement which built itself on interpersonal relationships that transcended public and private barriers. In other words, the very intensity and passion that women brought to their struggle played itself out in the intensity with which they fell apart. This intensity, passion and commitment is, or should be, a source of pride for the movement, and feminists should make every effort to bring it back into the struggle. It is this lack of personal support, understanding and sharing, this lack of personal space and personal expression, this tendency of objectifying the issues and the actions, that depletes the members of the movement, and this that deters new members from identifying with it. Re-creating the dichotomy of the public and the private, and encouraging the fragmentation of the self, also negates the struggle of the women's movement, and particularly feminism, to remove the false barriers of the public and the private.

The women's movement is being challenged from within to heal itself, especially by younger women. It is not enough for those of my generation to say that the younger generation does not join the movement because it is not interested or committed or political enough, or that 'we don't want to go over the same ground that we have been through'. The women's movement must reflect upon itself, otherwise it will be forced to tread the path again, and it must once again try and integrate its own principles into itself. This is its greatest challenge. If this challenge is not addressed or confronted or resolved, there is a danger that the trappings of the movement's issues and struggles will be co-opted by patriarchy and capitalism, while the substantial changes that it seeks get lost in the process.

2 Despite diversity
Women's unity in Western Cape, South Africa (1980–94)

Gertrude Fester

Much is being said about the achievements that South African women have gained since the new government came to power in 1994. There is an average of 30 per cent women at all government levels, a Commission for Gender Equality, a gender-sensitive constitution, an office on the status of women in the deputy-president's office and a climate in which there seems to be a commitment to improving the quality of women's lives.

Many writers refer to the challenging atmosphere in the country since the unbanning in 1990 of the African National Congress, the Pan-Africanist Congress and the South African Communist Party, and the return of exiles. Others again credit the Women's National Coalition (WNC) for its intervention in creating a gender-sensitive atmosphere in South Africa. It had a high-profile campaign, collecting women's demands for the new South Africa.

I agree that the WNC has made a big impact nationally and politically. However, I'd like to stress the preparation made for its work by small grassroots women's organisations.[1] Although I will focus on the women's organisations in the Western Cape (i.e. Cape Town and environs), women's organisations flourished in various parts of the country in the 1980s to 1990s and decidedly influenced the political sphere, and their history also needs to be written. I will focus on the following themes: unity despite diversity; women's and national liberation; and particular forms of feminisms in South Africa.

Unity despite diversity

The historical and legal separation and exploitation of peoples in general and women in particular in South Africa are well known.[2] It is important to emphasise that there was not only a black vs. white polarisation and exploitation, but also degrees of oppression, and differential oppression and identities of women. So even though it was theoretically contradictory to use the term 'black', it was politically pragmatic at the time. Because of the Coloured Labour Preference Act, coloured people were privileged in terms of job opportunities. Even though UWO emphasised unity, it wasn't blind to the truth. One undated UWO pamphlet states: 'Bosses and government say "Jobs for Coloureds only! We say: JOBS FOR ALL!"'

Coloureds and Indians, although oppressed, did not suffer the iniquities of having to carry passes. Figures from the African National Congress Women's League (1993) indicate that Indian women had lower levels of employment than coloured women, and that 86 per cent of domestic workers were African women. White women were more likely to be employed as managers and professionals than African, Indian and coloured women. In the new South Africa there is still an urgent need to deal with race and class issues.

Although the system benefited whites, there were a minority of working-class whites. However, the situation of whites is very underdocumented as most writers focus on the situation of black people and women.

Some writers claim that South African women's organisations were used by the liberation movement. The issue of gender complicity and resistance is quite central to this. At what stage do we say that women comply or resist? Moore argues that 'gender identity is both constructed and lived' (Moore 1994: 49). She traces the intricacies of individuals' personal histories and

> the intersection of this history with collective situations, discourses and identities that the problematic relationship between structure and praxis, and between the social and individual, resides. Thus, resistance and complicity are not only types of agency, they are also forms ... of subjectivity ... and as types of agency and forms of subjectivity they are marked through structures of differences based on gender, race ... and so on.
>
> (Moore 1994: 50)

The range of differences is enormous, but it is important to understand that differences arise within a particular context. 'At one moment the racial may take priority over sexual, and in another ethnicity may act as the defining difference' (Butler 1990: 50). For instance, during the Black Consciousness period, race was prioritised. However, because of the 1980–90s context and of women's multiple and contradictory subjectivities, formations emphasising gender emerged.

It is against this background that I wish to explore the South African situation. The UWO was launched in April 1981. Some pioneers of the organisation had been active in the ANC Women's League since 1950. The organisation was a response to the increasing repression in the country as well as mobilising 'mothers' around the torture of youth since 1976. The invitation to the meeting spelt out that the organisation aimed 'to unite all women' and to eradicate political, economic and social discrimination of women. It said: 'We strive for women to obtain: the right to vote; the right to full opportunities to work; equal rights with men in relation to property, marriage and children; and the removal of all laws that discriminate against women.' When the audience was invited to participate, they emphasised unity. 'Here we are all one colour,' said the eleventh speaker.³ I assume that within the context of the period, it was strategic to emphasise unity: in other words, that all were united against apartheid. UWO had a unitary structure with branches in various areas. According to organisational policy each branch focused on issues which members chose.

Triple oppression

In most organisational rhetoric, there was reference to the 'triple oppression' of women. Walker comments that the triple oppression of women has become a 'rhetorical commonplace' (1990: 2), and Wells (1991) has even argued that the term is 'theoretically vacuous'. Yet according to our analysis at that time, women were oppressed as workers, as women and as blacks. Race, class and gender oppression intersect. The term 'gender oppression' was only used from about 1985 when 'gender' was introduced as being theoretically more comprehensive. The 'triple oppression' analysis meant that African working-class and/or rural women were the most oppressed. On the one hand there was a consciousness of the different race and class positions women had, while on the other hand we were building unity and 'non-racism'.

Despite the objections by academics to 'triple oppression' it has, however, been useful for the United Women's Organisation and later the United Women's Congress members actively organising women at grassroots level. To members it highlighted the fact that all women are not oppressed equally. Organisational literature always referred to the interaction of race, class and gender. This was quite clear from our everyday practices. For instance, it was a common routine that after each meeting of UWO/UWCO a lift scheme was in operation, to help women from the poorest areas with an unreliable public transport system. This was preceded by a direct comment and later discussions on class, privilege and power. Another discussion was whether it was ethical for middle-class members (or white and coloured members) to employ unemployed/African and/or working-class members.

The 'triple oppression' of women meant placing a particular way of working firmly on the agenda, i.e. taking cognisance of differences. UWO/UWCO had unitary structures with branches in various areas. It has led to policy statements of the UWO/UWCO: 'Each branch will work on a programme of action to suit the needs, demands and interests of the women in that particular area.' Because of the Group Areas Act, each branch had a particular 'racial and/or class identity'. There were also attempts to link activities. 'Partnered' branches would take up joint or similar issues. The Wynberg branch (coloured middle-class) and the KTC branch (an African informal housing or 'squatter' area) established a crèche as joint project; the Observatory branch (middle-class white area) workshopped plays dealing with current issues; the Surrey Estate branch (working-class and middle-class coloured area) supported 'youth on the run'; the KTC branch campaigned for taps; the New Cross Roads branch (comprising working-class and some unemployed people) had a rent boycott; the Mitchell's Plain and Guguletu branches helped to build the civic organisations. These efforts once again illustrate the demands of women's needs and the differences between communities. Branches in rural areas had priorities which were vastly different to those in metropolitan areas. There were tensions between gender issues in branches and the needs of the national struggle (Kemp *et al.* 1995). Branch dynamics and character, given the vicissitudes of race and class, varied immensely.

The state of emergency placed new pressures and demands on organisations. Venues for meetings were kept secret and systems devised whereby venues were made known. Middle-class academics had easier access to venues, and on one occasion tensions arose when the leadership were not informed of the venue. A response by a senior member was that the organisation would not be dominated by intellectuals. This reference to the problem of 'intellectuals' may have been an attempt not to be racist: we were trying to build a *non-racial* movement.

There were other areas of tension around the intersection of race and class. The Education and Training Sub-Committee appealed for greater representation, and it was women with tertiary education who attended (Education and Training Sub-Committee, 22 July 1985). When women were fasting for specific demands, such as 'Troops out of the Township' and the ending to the state of emergency, this entailed being based in churches for a week's duration. Few 'non-township' members participated fully, ostensibly because most of them were employed. The UWO/UWCO choir was mostly township based. Finally, some middle-class/white members did not participate in the 'unity talks' between UWO and Women's Front, as they 'did not want to get involved with township dynamics'.

Building unity

In order to break down the apartheid barriers there were central themes in which all members could participate. There was a realisation of different interests and needs as well as a joint organisational programme of action 'to build unity'.

What is important to note, however, is that although there was this awareness of the different positions of members, the focus of the organisational theme was always to concentrate on the problems of the most oppressed and marginalised. Hence Hassim's comment that 'there is a prioritization of African women's racial oppression' (Hassim 1991: 68). I would qualify that to 'African *working-class* women's racial and class oppression' as the main focus of UWO/UWCO. The decision to concentrate on the problems encountered by working-class African women was a strategically political one. In doing this, women from more middle-class and 'more privileged races' were politicised by the realisation of their class positions and where and how they fitted into the apartheid/capitalist hierarchy.

Hassim and Walker (1993) maintain that white members of these non-racial organisations did not make use of the opportunity to articulate their positions in the organisation. They say this without any substantiation. However, in my experience in the Western Cape, many white women played crucial roles. There were always white members on the executives. Observatory and Woodstock branches (in middle-class white areas), especially in UWO, were very dynamic, and the Gardens branch (UWCO) had a joint project with the South African Domestic Workers' Union (SADWU). In most cases there was an awareness among the middle-class group of women not to dominate, although I do not think they would have been allowed to dominate by grassroots women.

Broadening out – the Federation of South African Women (FSAW)

UWO and UWCO were part of discussions with women's groups nationally. A national meeting on 9 August 1956 decided that the Federation of South African Women (FSAW) should be revived in order to protest against passes being extended to women.[4] Although FSAW was not banned, it slowly stopped functioning. When the ANC was banned in 1961 many of the FSAW were among them. Some went into exile whereas others were imprisoned or placed under house arrest. But when the FSAW (Western Cape region) was relaunched in August 1987, it immediately succeeded in 'broadening out the struggle'. Some of the organisational affiliates were Rape Crisis (mostly white middle-class), Bellville Gemeenskaporganisasie (a coloured, mainly religious community) and coloured working-class organisations like Atlantis Women's Group.

Because of our different political perspectives, we focused on what was common to us all, such as the issue of violence against women. A night 'candle march' against violence against women took place in 1988. When the state of emergency was declared, organising became difficult. The police had enormous power. Any group of more than ten people constituted a 'riotous assembly', and the group members could be arrested. Executive members of anti-apartheid organisations, including the women's organisation, UWCO, or any leadership figures, were either detained or 'on the run'. As a response, FSAW had a campaign to release women political prisoners. Linked to this was a women's religious service with liturgy composed from a woman-centred perspective, a very novel experience for most Western Cape women.

16   *Gertrude Fester*

The highlights of FSAW activities were the annual cultural festivals celebrating women's culture and creativity. From 1988 to 1990, FSAW held two-day festivals with fêtes, poetry, plays, songs and dance, speeches and *gumbas* (dance parties). The festival was a way of enhancing working relationships among affiliates and popularising FSAW. It also served as a means of circumventing state of emergency regulations which prohibited political gatherings. One negative aspect was that the planning group was not always broadly representative because of the political violence and repression in African townships.

The organisation of the festivals raised further issues of diversity among women. It was at a festival planning meeting in November 1987 when lesbianism was first discussed.[5] Butler argues that '(t)he internal coherence or unity of either gender, man or woman ... requires a stable and oppositional heterosexuality' (Butler 1990: 23). Throughout the history of these organisations, the hegemonic discourse was that of heterosexuality, although there was no obvious homophobia expressed or intimated on that occasion.

A strength of the Federation was the amount of rural work done. A sign of this was obvious because of languages used. Most UWO/UWCO meetings were either in Xhosa with English translations or vice versa. However, because of the large rural constituency, Afrikaans had to be used as well. An innovation was conducting a council meeting in Atlantis in Afrikaans with English and Xhosa summaries. It was an interesting experience to note the different power dynamics. The link between language and power will also be alluded to in a discussion of the Women's National Coalition.

Affiliates brought along new skills and creativity. Some of the protests included women chaining themselves to the ferry that took prisoners to Robben Island, to demand the release of political prisoners, and nailing a copy of the Freedom Charter on to the door of the Houses of Parliament. FSAW dissolved in 1991 as the national mandate called for a broader alliance.

The Women's Alliance (WA)

As the other regions had not yet relaunched FSAW and the repression intensified, the national decision to revive FSAW was altered. An even broader front was required, based on principles of non-racism, non-sexism, democracy and a unitary South Africa. As a result, the Women's Alliance was launched on 24 November 1991. For the first time parliamentary politics joined grassroots women's movement in the form of the Democratic Party. A range of new organisations joined. New and different skills and resources were acquired.

The changes in working altered immediately. Meetings were held in English only. Minutes, pamphlets and other media now had a professional and polished look. However, despite the above and other contradictions, there was an air of celebration that we had succeeded in coming together. New friendships and relationships developed. We were always aware of our different political positions but there was an understanding that we would agree to disagree on certain issues. Race and class contradictions inevitably emerged.

Campaigns around reproductive rights, sexuality and violence against women were consolidated. In spite of these common goals, there were differences between women which needed to be overcome. The planning of venues and times, for instance, presented problems. The South African Domestic Workers' Union (SADWU), despite their enthusiasm, found meeting times difficult because of their schedules. Because of the repression and violence in the township, meetings were not held there, which meant that the poorest women had to travel furthest, using unreliable public transport. Lift systems were sometimes arranged.

Initially some affiliates never thought political change was necessary. They were politicised and exposed to the lives of oppressed and exploited black women. However, many white women and some coloured women saw African townships for the first time.

Women's National Coalition

If all is going well in your coalition, it is not broad enough![6]

'Apartheid' or legal segregation was introduced over a period of time by the National Party when they came to power in 1948. In Natal at that time there were intense conflicts, often fatal, between the Inkatha Freedom Movement and the United Democratic Front who supported the banned African National Congress.[7] At that time it was speculated that a 'third force' (whites), or the South African police were involved in fuelling the tension. Through the testimonies to the Truth and Reconciliation Commission, these speculations have been found to be true.

There was an atmosphere of jubilation in the country when the African National Congress and other organisations were unbanned in February 1990, but also some apprehension for future challenges. Because of the negligible participation of women in the negotiations for transformation, the African National Congress Women's League (ANCWL) proposed a broader front (irrespective of political or ideological positions). Despite misgivings, the majority felt that if women's demands were to be taken seriously, we had to have maximum intervention.

In 1992 the Women's National Coalition (WNC) was launched. The aim was to consult all South African women and to document their demands for the new South Africa. WNC united more than fifty-five national organisations and hundreds of regional organisations as affiliates. This was a major challenge because women with polarised political positions, and even (former) 'enemies', were working together: for instance, ANC women sat next to women from the National Party, which had earlier imprisoned them. The tension between ANC and Inkatha Freedom Movement in Natal had often resulted in fatalities. Now these women were deliberating together.

The initial atmosphere of distrust gradually disappeared as we worked. Similar problems were experienced in the Coalition as in the Alliance in terms of race and class. That the Coalition had a definite mandate and a two-year timespan during which to collect demands helped to facilitate work. I see this limited time-scale as both a strength and a weakness. It was a strength in that this strategic alliance could constructively work together as it was goal-directed, and simultaneously a weakness because of the fast pace – sometimes at the sacrifice of empowering marginalised women.

Workshops were held on various topics like culture and religion, women's reproductive rights, women and the constitution, and violence against women. One successful campaign was the 'shopping mall' canvassing. Volunteers, outside supermarkets, collected demands from women for the new South Africa.

To return to the link between language and power, it is significant that within the Alliance only English was used. For some professionals 'time' was always a problem and many did not want to spend more than two hours at a meeting. This meant that there was not enough time for translations. I see this as disempowering and excluding women whose English was not fluent from full and meaningful participation.

I have highlighted some difficulties and challenges women in Western Cape experienced in order to unite. Bringing together women from diverse backgrounds, diverse women's groups and political parties was crucial in establishing a women's lobby – to overcome apartheid and to establish democracy, a gender-sensitive constitution and a state with national machinery to promote the quality of women's lives.

Women's liberation and national liberation

How does one understand women's issues and liberation when legislation prevented the majority of families from living together? African men were allowed as workers into 'white cities' while women remained in rural areas. While radical Western feminists were critical of the family, South African women were demanding the right for families to live together. When all black women and men, however differentially, were oppressed, it was not always possible to separate women's issues from people's issues.

I have mentioned earlier that UWO/UWCO branches and conferences decided on activities. However, there were sometimes criticisms from middle-class women on why we were not taking up 'women's issues'. But this question did not only come from outsiders. At the 1984 annual conference a branch from a middle-class area raised the concern that our programme should include more women's issues. A long debate then followed on what precisely we understood by 'women's issues'. It concluded that: 'these problems of women – childcare, contraception and so on – are part of a bigger system. The passes hit women first.'[8] One could deduce that often tension around women's and national liberation could be influenced by class, race, gender privilege and/or oppression.

The tension between women's and national liberation is sometimes equated with race and gender loyalty, and there were times when some African and coloured women prioritised national liberation. Different positions around this emerged: one was that with the socialist revolution women would automatically be liberated, while others saw national liberation as the primary struggle and believed that once this was achieved the secondary one of women's liberation could be tackled. However, it is interesting to note that in the funeral brochure (December 1984) of a well-known leader, Dora Tamana, reference was made to the violence she endured during her short marriage. As part of branch education in 1985, Rape Crisis offered a tape and slide presentation looking at violence against women. In the UWO documents both these incidents were contextualised by the unemployment and frustration that people experienced. This could be interpreted as not confronting patriarchy directly. Formulation of statements also depended on who wrote them. Budlender *et al.* (1983) raise the issue of members not always agreeing with the content of organisational documents. In reading through the organisational documents it was obvious to me how documents reflected the various secretaries' positions. However, one of the more successful joint projects with Rape Crisis in 1986 that UWCO was involved in was the Campaign Against Sexual Abuse. The contents contextualised violence against women in general as well as particularly during apartheid repression.

The establishment of UWO also procured women the position of leaders in the male-dominated political struggle. Most of UWO literature demanded that the government resign.[9] At our first conferences, men did the catering and childcare. When prices of bus fares (1984) and bread (1985) increased, UWO initiated boycotts. Important political education accompanied this.

Formation of the United Democratic Front

One could say that the UDF, a broad anti-apartheid front formed to oppose the state's tricameral reforms, symbolised the national struggle, whereas the women's organisations stood for women's liberation and national liberation. As part of the South African government's attempt to 'reform' apartheid, a new constitution was drawn up. This implied the creation of three 'separate' chambers for parliament: one each for whites, coloureds and Indians. However, the majority of the population were left out. The Coloured and Indian Houses (Representative and Delegates respectively) together were less than the White House (Assembly). This effectively still meant white majority rule. Because the majority Africans were left out and there was no substantial power for coloureds and Indians, progressive organisations and people boycotted this new system. The major UDF campaign was focused around campaigns for boycotting these 'racist' elections for coloureds and Indians.

There was a good working relationship between UWO/UWCO and UDF. However, minimal tensions could be interpreted as the tension between national liberation and women's liberation. A characteristic of the women's organisations was that we worked 'shoulder to shoulder with our menfolk'. Members were instrumental in forming mixed organisations like parent–teacher associations (1981), the Western Cape Civic Association (1982) and the UDF (1983).

The relationships within these organisations revealed the contradictions women experienced as regards women's and national liberation. Theoretically, women's and national liberation are complementary, but not always in praxis. Apart from tensions around which issues were prioritised, the reality was demanding for many women as they worked in all these structures. Even though women initiated the Civics, men were the leaders. Typically, it was mostly the women who carried the burden of domestic labour. Some branches ceased to function as their members were leaders in the civic while others prioritised UDF activities.[10] Other members took up leadership positions in the trade unions.

Because of our existing infrastructure, UWO members were central in the formation of UDF area committees. The three women on the UDF executive were all UWO members. For the first few months of its existence UDF shared our office.

The effect of UDF on UWO was in general positive. However, UWO had to adapt to working within a male-dominated organisation with a very fast pace. In UWO General Council, the UDF representative raised this issue: 'UDF must be led by its affiliates, not the other way around.'[11] In order to affiliate to UDF, UWO was advised to amalgamate with the township-based Women's Front (WF) as we had similar constitutions. This amalgamation took place on 22 March 1986.

However, even though the UDF focused on building non-racialism, democracy and non-sexism, there did not seem to be as committed a programme of non-sexism as there was to building democracy and non-racialism. Or it often seemed as if sexism was accepted theoretically and the reality was different. There were often examples of male leaders articulating aims of non-sexism on public platforms. However, their personal relationships with partners/wives indicated a different reality. At a UDF assessment workshop in the Cape Town region, a key question was: to what extent did we promote non-racialism, non-sexism and democracy? A male comrade stated that it was women's own fault that they were oppressed. During the plenary session the chairperson cut the discussion on sexism as there were 'time constraints'. However, immediately afterwards the issue of democracy was discussed without any time problems.

Nationally, women were not at all complacent within UDF. The UDF Women's Congress was launched on 25 April 1987 in Cape Town because of the need for UDF women to assert themselves within UDF. Its formation and resolutions are important statements. The resolutions on the role of women in UDF and leadership indicate the problems women have encountered with male comrades and within progressive structures. Some of the clauses were:

> Noting that: Sexual harassment of women comrades by male comrades is not unheard of; Believing that: The national struggle against racism and exploitation will not be a victory unless it is also a victory against sexism; We therefore resolve: to eradicate sexism from the ranks and to promote a vision of a non-sexist future South Africa amongst progressive organisations. We believe that the future emancipation of women is dependent on the level of participation of women in the struggle as a whole.
> (Extract from UDF Women's Congress Resolutions, Cape Town, 1987)

Despite the good working relationship among the various affiliates, there were subtle tensions around a more Eurocentric/Western feminism and what the grassroots women saw as priority – that there cannot be women's liberation without national liberation. A concrete example of this was the discussion around the Convention on the Elimination of All Forms of Discrimination Against Women (CEDAW). Although most women felt it was important that it be ratified, the question was: when? For some of us the present government was illegitimate and we argued that democracy was the first aim. Others wanted it ratified immediately. The majority decided that a democratic government should ratify it. In January 1996 the South African government ratified CEDAW without reservation as part of its commitments to the Beijing Platform of Action.

Women's Charter for Effective Equality

In the drawing-up of the interim constitution, a highly emotive and sensitive case was that of customary law versus the equality clause. The CONTRALESA (Convention of Traditional Leaders of South Africa) was a strong and vociferous lobby for the retention of traditional law which in some cases would mean continued minority status for women. The WNC, the Transvaal Women's Movement and various other women's groups formed a formidable force in opposing the proposal of CONTRALESA. As a result, in both the interim constitution and the final constitution, traditional law is subjected to the Equality Clause.

The WNC had workshops throughout the country in order to collect demands from women. In February 1994 the Women's Charter for Effective Equality was accepted by the WNC national conference. The Charter has demands around all aspects of women's lives. It is obvious that it is a compromise document, as the clauses around reproductive rights and culture are vaguely phrased. However, it is still a major achievement that women from a polarised and antagonistic South African society could come up with a joint Charter. On National Women's Day, 9 August 1994, the state president and each of the premiers of the nine provinces were presented with a copy of the Charter to use as guidelines for legislation.

Emergence of South African feminisms

In many Third World struggles, there are often condemnations from sectors of the liberation struggles, usually males, who condemn feminism as being divisive or imperialist, or argue that women's emancipation should be focused on after the 'primary or major contradiction'. McClintock (1995) outlines the implications of nationalism and nation-states. According to her, they are not fixed but are constantly under contest. She argues that all nationalisms, national-states and citizenship are male. But just as there are various forms of nationalisms, there are also various forms of patriarchy. She argues that there are various forms of feminisms to respond to these forms of patriarchy. 'Neither nationalism nor feminism is transhistorical. Our history too has many examples of the different types and forms of feminism' (McClintock 1995: 9). She provides examples of the well-known tension between women of colour and Western and/or privileged feminists who do not confront their own power, class and race positions:

> Hazel Carby who issued her famous call to white feminists to listen, Egyptian feminist Nawal El Sa'adawi who accused certain Western women of 'maternalism' and Marnea Lazreg, an Algerian feminist who warned Western feminists to be wary of the borrowed, imperialist power of academic interpretation.
> (McClintock 1995: 120)

She warns that it may be calamitous for Third World women to brand feminism imperialist as they/we will be eradicating our long history of women's resistance to local and imperialist patriarchies.

Kumari Jayawardena also makes this clear:

(M)ovements for women's liberation and feminism flourished in several non-European countries well before Western Feminism emerged ... Feminism was not imposed on the Third World by the West, but rather historical circumstances produced important material and ideological changes that affected women.

(Jayawardena 1986: 11)

In South Africa the word 'feminism' conjures up mixed responses: from Benjamin's appeal 'Don't call me a feminist' to Kadalie's assertion of the immense contributions feminists have made (Benjamin 1995; Kadalie 1995). This ambivalence about feminism is a result of the hegemony of Western imperialist feminism. Most members of our organisations did not identify with the various Western feminisms which some white and middle-class South African women ascribed to. But just as there are many different forms of patriarchy and nationalisms, so too are there various forms of feminisms.[12]

Much attention has been given to the fact that South African women organise on the basis of motherhood (see Charman *et al.* 1991; Gaitskell 1990; Gaitskell and Unterhalter 1989; Hansson 1991; Hassim 1987, 1991; Hassim and Walker 1993; Horn 1991, 1994; Walker 1982, 1990, 1995). Wells (1991) refers to this as 'motherism', which she sees as unfeminist and politically immature. I agree with Drew's statement that female consciousness becomes politically activated into feminist consciousness under certain conditions (Drew 1995: 19). I want to emphasise that women's resistance arises out of their particular historical contexts, and that motherism and working 'shoulder to shoulder with our menfolk' could be seen as a form of South African feminism. Motherist movements which defy oppression of all kinds, including patriarchal oppression, are more likely to inspire a feminism which will be effective in South Africa than would be the liberal feminism espoused by First World feminists (Fouche 1994: 94).

I want to contest that the feminism Horn and Charman *et al.* were promoting, and not finding in any South African women's organisations, must be Western-inspired. They assessed local organisations with imperialist criteria. Of course, it does not follow that women involved in women's organisations will develop a critical understanding of gender relations among women, nor that the organisations will be a vehicle for gender struggle in society. On the contrary, women's organisations can be important institutions in the conservation of women's subordination (Charman *et al.* 1991: 59). But due to the absence of strong grassroots feminist organisation in South Africa, the ANC works 'with very little strongly-directed guidance from militant democratic women's organisations' (Horn 1991: 25). It is not clear what Horn means by feminist, although she does plead that women should 'work out what progressive feminism means in practice in the present-day South African context' (Horn 1991: 27).

On examining the South African women's movements, five distinct aspects arise:

- women stood 'shoulder to shoulder with their menfolk' in the fight against apartheid and exploitation;
- there was a strong motherist appeal;
- campaigns focused on what affected the most oppressed women, i.e. African working-class women;
- national liberation was an integral if not determining issue;
- race/class alliances were made at particular historic junctures.

Conclusion

I have quoted some examples of women in the Western Cape coming together despite their very stark differences. It has not always been easy – tensions around race and class abounded – but if we as women wanted to change our situations there were and still are times where we have to form these 'uneasy but strategic' alliances. I do not want to give the impression that we in South Africa have solved all our problems. Even though we have formed alliances at strategic times, there are many challenges. There should always be an awareness of power relations and how to confront them. How do we create spaces for diverse women with different skills and energies? What is the difference between making spaces and being liberal? There were times when the balance was uneven. We have impressive legislation and policies in place but the real challenge for us as South African women is that we translate the theory into praxis.

There are strategic times when fostering alliances is imperative. These alliances should not be concentrated at a high-profile level only, but should start with ordinary grassroots women in their areas. From this local level, women will take up issues that are important to them. In the short term, some of the issues may not seem radical or capable of transforming the status quo, yet these issues are important in transforming women's feminist consciousness. For instance, many women joined UWO in order to support their children. Through their everyday confrontation with the state, they realised that as women and black women, they too are oppressed.

A different politicisation occurred for many women in the UWO/UWCO who wanted votes for women. In their campaigns for democracy they realised that all black people, both men and women, could not vote. There was therefore no way in which women could campaign for the franchise without general enfranchisement. In many ways, black men were oppressed, and therefore women in the 1980s adopted the slogan 'working shoulder to shoulder with our menfolk' from women in the 1950s.

The 'working shoulder to shoulder with our menfolk' sometimes made middle-class women feel uneasy. There have been accusations of women colluding with patriarchy. However, as I have tried to point out above, there is not one form of feminism. Women respond to their respective material and ideological conditions. Thus I want to emphasise that women in South Africa had to organise in such a way that they could address their uniquely South African problems within their own material and historical reality. It is for this reason that I want to advocate various forms of feminisms that are influenced by local conditions in private and public realms. We now need to concentrate on how women's movements in their diversity can move forward in order to positively enhance the lives of women everywhere.

Notes

1 In this discussion I will refer to the following mass-based women's organisations: United Women's Organisation (UWO) 1981–6; United Women's Congress (UWCO) 1986–91; Federation of South African Women (FSAW) 1987–91; Women's Alliance (WA) 1991; and the Women's National Coalition (WNC) 1992–4.
2 In apartheid South Africa, the population was divided into Africans, who were in turn subdivided into specific language/cultural groups like Xhosa, Zulu, Pedi, etc.; coloureds (people of mixed heritage), whose ancestors were Khoisan, Bantu, Indonesian or Malaysian slaves and European settlers; Indians whose ancestors were brought as indentured labour; and whites (whose ancestors were mostly European settlers). African people were most oppressed, while coloureds and Indians, although oppressed, had certain privileges. However, with the advent of the Black Consciousness Movement (late 1960s), many oppressed people saw themselves as black. Hence I will use 'black' to refer to all disenfranchised people (prior to 1994) and the apartheid labels of African, Indian and coloured.
3 Minutes of first conference, 5 April 1981.
4 FSAW was launched in April 1954. The main affiliates were the African National Congress Women's League, trade unions such as the Food and Canning Workers' Union, the South African Indian Congress, Congress of Democrats (whites and the Coloured People's Congress). It was the FSAW that organised the 20,000-strong women's march to the Union Buildings.
5 See my chapter, 'Lesbian lobby: apartheid's closet' (1996) in *Amazon to Zami: Towards A Global Lesbian Feminism* edited by Monika Reinfelder (London: Cassell). The South African constitution has a non-discriminatory clause against people on the basis of their gender, geographic orientation, sexual orientation, etc. This does not mean that South Africa is any less sexist or homophobic than other societies. The challenges lie ahead for all South Africans to promote the gains made by the constitution.
6 This was said by Bernice Reagon Johnson of *Sweet Honey in the Rock* and director of Smithsonian Institute, Washington, DC, in discussion with some of us from the Gender Advocacy Project while we were lobbying (September 1992).
7 The Inkatha Movement was initially a cultural movement promoting Zulu culture and traditions. It became the Inkatha Freedom Party when it registered as a political party to contest in the first democratic elections in April 1994.
8 Minutes of Fourth Conference of UWO (June 1984) held at Samaj Centre, Rylands.

9 Pamphlet and general council minutes (10 December 1984).
10 Athlone, Mitchell's Plain, Macassar and Kensington branches became defunct as most members worked in the UDF area committees. The number of core activists of some branches decreased as well. However, branches ceased to function because of a complexity of reasons.
11 UDF General Council Representative, minutes of UWO General Council (3 August 1984).
12 For arguments on nationalist or Third World feminisms see Basu 1995; Fouche 1994; Jayawardena 1986; Kemp *et al.* 1995; McClintock 1990; Ghose *et al.* 1995; Soiri 1996; Drew 1995; Kaplan 1982, 1997.

References

African National Congress Women's League (1993) *Status of South African Women*, Marshalltown: South Africa: ANCW.
Basu, A. (1995) *The Challenge of Local Feminisms: Women's Movements in Global Perspective*, Oxford: Westview Press.
Benjamin, J. (1995) 'Don't call me a feminist', *Agenda* 27: 90–4.
Budlender, D., Sheila, M. and Schreiner, J. (1983) 'Women and resistance in South Africa: review article', *Journal of Southern African Studies* 10: 1.
Butler, J. (1990) *Gender Trouble: Feminism and the Subversion of Identity*, London: Routledge.
Charman, A., De Swardt, C. and Simons, M. (1991) 'The politics of gender: negotiating liberation', *Transformation* 15: 41–64.
Drew, A. (1995) 'Female consciousness and feminism in Africa', *Theory and Society* 24: 1–33.
Fouche, F. (1994) 'Overcoming the sisterhood myth', *Transformation* 23: 78–95.
Gaitskell, D. (1990) 'Devout domesticity? A century of African Women's Christianity in South Africa', in C. Walker (ed.) *Women and Gender in Southern Africa to 1945*, Cape Town: David Philip Publishers.
Gaitskell, D. and Unterhalter, E. (1989) 'Mothers of the nation: a comparative analysis of the nation, race and motherhood in Afrikaner nationalism and the African National Congress', in N. Yuval-Davis and F. Anthias (eds) *Women–Nation–State*, London: Macmillan.
Ghose, S., Menezes, S. and Panneerselvan, A.S. (1995) 'Indian feminism: coming of age women', *Outlook* 20 December: 62–7.
Hansson, D. (1991) 'A patchwork quilt of power relations: a challenge to South African feminism', paper presented at the International Conference on Women, Law and Social Control, Montreal, Canada.
Hassim, S. and Walker, C. (1993) 'Women's Studies and the women's movement in South Africa: defining a relationship', *Women's Studies International Forum* 16 (5): 523–34.
Horn, P. (1991) 'Post-apartheid South Africa: what about women's emancipation?' *Transformation* 15: 19–30.
Horn, P. (1994) 'Whither the WNC?' *Agenda* 23: 64–6.
Jayawardena, K. (1986) *Feminism and Nationalism in the Third World*, London: Zed Press.
Kadalie, R. (1995) 'The F-word', *Agenda* 25: 72–7.
Kaplan, T. (1982) 'Female consciousness and collective action: the case of Barcelona', *Signs* 7 (3): 545–66.

Kaplan, T. (1997) *Crazy for Democracy: Women in Grassroots Movements*, New York: Routledge.
Kemp, A., Madlala, N., Moodley, A. and Salo, E. (1995) 'The dawn of a new era: redefining South African feminism', in A. Basu and C. E. McGrory (eds) *The Challenge of Local Feminisms: Women's Movements in Global Perspective*, Oxford: Westview Press.
McClintock, A. (1990) 'Maidens, maps and mines: King Solomon's Mines and the reinvention of patriarchy in colonial South Africa', in C. Walker (ed.) *Women and Gender in Southern Africa to 1945*, Cape Town: David Philip Publishers.
McClintock, A. (1995)*The Imperial Leather: Race, Gender and Sexuality in the Colonial Contest*, London: Routledge.
Moore, H. L. (1994) *A Passion for Difference*, Oxford: Polity Press.
Soiri, I. (1996) *The Radical Mother: Namibian Women's Independence Struggle*, Uppsala: Nordiska Afrikainstitutet.
Walker, C. (1982) *Women and Resistance in South Africa*, London: Onyx Press.
Walker, C. (1990) *Women and Gender in Southern Africa to 1945*, Cape Town: David Philip Publishers.
Walker, C. (1995) 'Conceptualising motherhood in twentieth-century South Africa', *Journal of Southern Africa Studies* 21 (3): 25–39.
Wells, J. (1991) 'The rise and fall of motherism as a force in black women's resistance', paper presented at 'Women and Gender in Southern Africa', at University of Natal, Durban.

3 Political thoughts and domestic lives

Women activists in North India

Suruchi Thapar-Bjorkert

Introduction

The nationalist leaders of India, particularly those in Gandhi's non-violent programme, provided the opportunity for women to make contributions to the nationalist movement from the public sphere.[1] Not only did this participation deny the West's claims that Indian women and gender relations were backward, it also allowed the nationalist movement to create a form of resistance which was demonstrably superior (to Western movements and violent struggles) in terms of its respect for human life and its reliance on persuasion rather than force.

However, for many women the social constraints of the period did not allow any form of public activity. Yet women's lives within the domestic sphere were being affected by changes in the public sphere. It was not just the individual but the whole household which got involved in the movement. In these circumstances, *purdah*-bound women were compelled to take cognizance of the movement, since members of their family were participants in it.

I will argue that the domestic site underwent changes as a consequence of developments in the public (political) world and became a significant location of women's nationalist activities. Women had to adapt to the changes brought about by the nationalist movement as well as adhere to certain role-models constructed by nationalist leaders. They had to face the hardships and the traumas of an uncertain domestic existence while remaining good wives, nurturers and mothers. In retrospect, the domestic sphere, for these women, was a centre of political activity and involvement with the public world. These women now see their support for their family members as their contribution to the nationalist movement. If some women could not participate in the public sphere, their activities within the domestic sphere facilitated the process of its politicisation. This article draws on the oral life accounts of middle-class male and female activists in Uttar Pradesh. Newspapers, vernacular magazines and proscribed literature have been additional sources of information.

I have interviewed seventy men and women but still feel that all of them are in some respects incomplete. Most of the respondents are Hindu men and women, mainly from the Brahmin caste. Family wealth, ownership of property and a high standard of living defined their middle-class status from those of lower-class women.

Domestic voices

In most writings on women and nationalism in India, women's political involvement is implicitly defined as an activity undertaken in the public sphere (Kaur 1968; Agnew 1979; Basu 1976; Jayawardena 1986; Rao and Devi 1984; Rao 1994) and concepts such as political activity, public participation and active role are associated with women 'coming on to the streets'. A recent article, 'Narratives that never surfaced', by Jagdish Prasad Gupt Jagesh in a special Independence Day feature of the Kanpur newspaper *Dainik Jagron*, made me aware that though women's achievements in taking out processions and demonstrations, holding meetings and giving speeches were important, they have been overemphasised in academic history in relation to their activities within the domestic sphere (particularly as mothers and nurturers).

> The tears of *pativratas* [a woman whose love for her husband is unchanging and who serves her husband throughout her life] do not fall on their motherland without any significance. In our long nationalist struggle for independence, the widows and companions of nationalist men have shouldered extraordinary pain without a sigh, without complaining. However, the nation has not realised it, neither has anybody remembered it. The names of men who sacrificed their lives for the nation have been recorded in books, in memoirs and biographies, inscriptions and writings on slabs of stones. However, those wives, mothers and nurturers who agreed with their husbands and who transformed the oil of their tears to light the paths of their husbands – their names are never mentioned.
> (Jagesh 1992)

A number of issues were raised from this article. First, a woman marching in a street demonstration is typically taken as an example of a politically active woman, but while demonstrating she may not have been thinking of the nationalist movement. We need to reconsider whether the heroic portrayal of women leaving their homes and coming out on the streets really provides an adequate view of the movement. A few respondents mentioned that they participated in the movement because 'everybody else was doing it' or because it was 'fun to be out on the streets with the crowds'. Second, the article suggests that the definition of 'political' has always been constructed around men's political activities in the public sphere. I propose that the political nature of the public sphere cannot be understood without reference to the importance of the domestic sphere for both men and women.

In the last few decades, however, women's roles have at last gained recognition in vernacular literature and newspapers. After independence, articles containing reminiscences of the nationalist movement were published. Examples include 'There were dreams in our eyes' (*Saptahik Press* 29 January 1984), 'The struggle for independence gave birth to the murmur of women's independence' (*The Times of India* 28 August 1985) and 'True Grit' (*The Week* 30 May 1993).

This chapter seeks to understand women's politics of this period as a dialogue between feminist ideas and nationalist feelings established through acts which conventionally have not been seen as forms of political activity. For example, writing poetry and prose, reading nationalist literature, giving support to another male or female activist, were political acts undertaken by women in the domestic sphere. I understand a political act as one which supported the nationalist cause or expressed nationalist feelings, irrespective of whether it was located within the domestic or public sphere. Furthermore, I have identified the domestic sphere as a dynamic site of contradiction and ambiguity, a site where women were subjected to oppressive practices but also resisted those same practices.

In the following sections I will identify five domestic values that helped women to contribute politically from within the domestic sphere as well as engage emotionally with the movement. These activities were:

1 spinning *khadi*;
2 keeping fasts;
3 being supportive wives, mothers and nurturers;
4 being pillars of support to friends and neighbours;
5 conducting secret activities.

Women utilised their existing roles in the family not only to contribute politically to the movement, but also to bring about changes in their own lives.

Domestic values

The idea that women could contribute to the nationalist movement from within the domestic sphere has a long history in India. It first surfaced in the first decade of the twentieth century at the time of the partition of Bengal in 1905. An important act of protest by women was to conduct the ritual of *arandhan*, whereby women did not light the hearth for cooking food on a publicly named day (Basu 1976: 17). Women identified with the political decision of partition by focusing on an important activity in the domestic sphere.

During the non-co-operation movement (1920), the first organised mass campaign against the British Raj, Gandhi was acutely aware of the social status of women. Though direct participation of women in the public sphere was not significant during this movement, women were encouraged by nationalist leaders to make their political contributions from within the domestic sphere (Rao 1994: 33).

Women's public activities were more pronounced during the civil disobedience movement (1930). However, many upper-caste women were still confined to the domestic sphere. In these circumstances family dynamics were important in encouraging women to express themselves politically.

A broad generalisation can be drawn from my interviews with women in Uttar Pradesh who had been active in the domestic sphere. Strict *purdah* (physical incarceration) was practised in these households, though the degree of restrictions could vary across households or was affected by the contradictions within the joint family. For example, some women did not come out because the elder women (grandmother, mother-in-law, old aunt, sister-in-law) in the household objected to younger women discarding *purdah*. On the other hand, women were able to enjoy the company of other women (sisters, aunts, sisters-in-law) in a joint household, and it was possible for them to organise and conduct activities as a group. The element of solidarity and sisterhood was stronger in a joint household. One activist, Avadh Rani Singh, commented:

> I do not remember my mother either encouraging or discouraging me. *Purdah* prevailed in *sasural* [the husband's house] and I could only go out with my mother-in-law. However, there was lots of conversation between the womenfolk about the prevailing political atmosphere.

Where the father opposed any nationalist activity within the house, women conducted activities clandestinely. For example, my own grandmother paid no heed to her civil servant husband's pro-British stance and continued with her activities. Occasionally, men tried to persuade their womenfolk to participate or encouraged them to leave the *purdah*. Often, when this happened, women refused to come out of the domestic sphere because, as Kishori Devi said, '*Us samay aache khandan ke aurate khar se bahar nahin nikalti* (in those days women from good families did not come out).' Within this broad social context I will discuss the first activity that demonstrates the political significance of the domestic sphere.

The constructive programme

The concept of *swadeshi* (national independence) was aligned with the political liberation of the country. The nationalist leader Mahatma Gandhi politicised and popularised domestic objects like the *charkha* (spinning wheel) at both national and local levels. Spinning *khadi* (coarse hand-spun

Plate 1 Avadh Rani Singh

cloth) on the *charkha* was a powerful nationalist statement, which showed that not only could domestic values be associated with nationalist activities in the public sphere, such as in the picketing of foreign cloth shops, but also that nationalist activities could be taken into and performed within the domestic sphere. Men and women wore *khadi* in the public domain as a mark of national pride. The *charkha* was the 'symbol of the unity of the people and their respect and dignity as a nation' (Agnew 1979: 37). Women's roles were significant in this constructive programme because they were expected to be responsible for spreading both the message for *swadeshi* and emphasising its importance in India's struggle for independence. Ideas about spinning and weaving *khadi* were propagated through the literature. For example, it was said by Shri Yatindra Kumar in the magazine *Chand*:

> Delicate sisters of ours are wearing coarse *khadi*. The modern Indian woman has sacrificed all means of luxury and old archaic rotten traditions into the sacrificial fire of freedom. This is an absolutely new fact in the history of the world.
>
> (Kumar 1930: 72)

By spinning, weaving and selling *khadi*, women, especially of the lower classes, could help in their own liberation by gaining a modicum of economic independence.

> Womankind, it's time to be alert,
> Wake up from your slumber,
> Leave your laziness behind,
> Call Swaraj to the household yourselves,
> In your free time move the *charkha*.
> Make your clothes yourselves.
> (Hin. B. 3121, 1922)

The self-sufficiency achieved through producing *swadeshi* (indigenous) cloth also helped the struggle for national liberation. Women could bring *swaraj* to the household. Individual women respondents spun on the *charkha*. Dr Kusum Agarwal said, 'When I was 12 years old my father's elder brother used to tell us to spin on the *charkha*. Even at 12 years, I was very conscientious about my nation. Every day we used to spin after school.' Another respondent says that she spun on the *charkha* every day and the *khadi chadars* (sheets made from coarse cotton) that she made were given away to revolutionaries in hiding.

To support and co-ordinate the efforts of women involved in spinning and weaving, local organisations were formed, which encouraged constructive work and also had access to *purdah*-bound women. For example, the Mahila Mandal (women's association) in Benares was established in 1934 by Smt Ratneshwari Devi when she was 27 years old. The first agenda of the Mandal developed gradually into a small organisation. Its first agenda was to introduce *purdah*-clad women into some sort of social and economic activity. Ratneshwari had a strong belief that if women were to become educated and economically independent, they would be able to be of greater help to the nation. The initial committees within the organisation were formed primarily to educate women, and to develop their consciousness towards both their position in society and the broader political situation. For example, there was a *charkha* centre, a home nursing centre, a music department, a painting school, a rifle club and the magazine *Vidhusi* (literate woman). Women who joined this organisation, were, as Srimati Sulbha Gupta, managing director of Mahila Mandal, said, 'enlightened towards the notion of loving one's nation' and made monetary contributions towards the Azad Hind Fauj (Army for India's Independence).

Symbols of nationalism were also popularised through cultural themes. The political situation was illustrated by cartoons in magazines and newspapers. Plays were staged in public places, often based on nationalist themes associated with the domestic sphere, such as spinning and weaving of *khadi*. The nationalist symbolism associated with domestic objects like the *charkha* was made of public interest.

Familial sacrifice

The domestic-based qualities of sacrifice, the good nurturer, strength of will and fortitude were linked by the key concept of 'service (*seva*) to the nation'. The vernacular literature acknowledges some of these qualities. In one article, Vidyavati Sahgal quotes from an Indian Mahila Sangh's magazine, *Stree Dharm*, and states that 'the weapons of the movement like truth, patience, sacrifice, purity of soul are only of women and it is thus no surprise that women are taking the main part in the movement' (Sahgal 1930: 4).

The best example of sacrifice within the household was fasting. In their own homes, women fasted and conducted nationalist religious prayers. Fasting is associated with the Hindu religious beliefs of purification of the body, mind and soul. Gandhi advocated fasting for men and women to enable them to have greater control over their bodies and the senses that generate pleasure:

> Gandhi viewed the body as inextricably linked to the soul and spirit, and also as a microcosm of the social. It is thus not surprising to find that his political campaigns were often intimately linked with bodily functions. He used fasting as a weapon in his political armoury.
> (Caplan 1989: 277)

Fasting for self-purification as well as for the general prosperity of one's own family is still practised in India on a wide scale. For example, a popular fast, Karvachot, is still kept by married women for the well-being and long life of their husbands. Thus, it is not surprising that during times of political upheaval women fasted for the well-being of their own husbands, sons and brothers who were serving jail sentences, and then extended this to the idea of fasting for the nation. Fasting was associated with the Hindu concept of *dharma*. *Dharma* can be interpreted as a doctrine of righteousness, sacred law or a general code of conduct which is appropriate to each class and each stage in the life of an individual. Through fasting women were completing their essential religious duties (*dharma*).

I will illustrate the importance of fasting through an interview I conducted. Dhirendranath Pandey says that his mother died in 1930 after fasting for an extended period of time. He was 1 year old at the time and does not remember his mother. However, his father, Surendranath Pandey, had told him that he, along with other associates, was accused in the Lahore conspiracy case and imprisoned in the Lahore Borstal jail. During this time his mother fasted 'and the day she died, all the accused in the jail wore black bands and did not eat for the whole day'. In this particular example, the wife, in *purdah*, fasted within the confines of the domestic domain as a way to identify with her husband's suffering in prison. His mother was also aware that her husband was repeatedly undergoing hunger-strikes, and her own fasting enabled her to support his struggle.

However, in the context of current feminist debates, it could be argued that fasting raises contentious issues about the female body as a site of self-inflicted violence. There were other examples of violence on women such as *lathi* (stick) slashes on women's bodies by the police, and going to prison, a site of imprisonment of the body. The question that often remains unanswered is whether nationalist activity within the domestic sphere called for sacrifice beyond what would now be considered as feminist. However, it can be argued that women's conceptualisation of their roles as wives was inscribed within a particular historical moment and a specific cultural context. Death through fasting (for her husband) elevated the woman to the status of a *devi*, or goddess, and most Indian women aspired to this respect, accorded by society.

Women also conceptualised their roles as wives in accordance with political demands. Separation from her husband increased a woman's social burden and her political responsibility was reorganised by the necessity of her assuming the place of absent men. Women were left to manage the household finances and to raise children when their menfolk were active in the nationalist movement. Since most of these women were in *purdah*, they felt they could not seek employment outside and had to manage as well as possible. However, circumstances forced a few women to step out into the public domain. Another male respondent's narrative about his grandmother illustrates this.[2] Mr P.C. Mitra's grandmother, Sharad Kumari Sinha, was an ordinary housewife. In 1925 her eldest son, Raj Kumar Sinha, was imprisoned in the Kakori case.[3] Soon after, her husband, Markhandya Sinha, died from depression due to his son's arrest. The respondent gives an insight into the changes in his grandmother's life:

> My grandmother kept strict *purdah*, so much so that when she visited *Balika Vidyalaya* [educational institution], she used to hang a *chadar* [sheet] on the *tonga* [horse-driven carriage]. But once her sons [the second son was arrested for the Lahore conspiracy case] were imprisoned, she left her *purdah*. She mortgaged her house and struggled financially. She had never travelled alone on a train, but now she started travelling to Lahore for her son's *mukadma* [criminal case]. Political circumstances and difficult times changed my grandmother.

The respondent suggested that in difficult social circumstances women were allowed to discard their *purdah*.

Adverse circumstances rendered these women vulnerable but not less patriotic. I will illustrate this through the experience of a particular respondent whose father, Chail Bihari Cuntack, spent most of his life serving jail sentences. The respondent, Sushila Devi, narrated an incident when a woman supporter of the British Raj tried to draw them away from nationalist activities:

> Lady Kailash, wife of Sir Srivastava and a supporter of British rule, brought to our house expensive clothes made of *malmal* [silk] and *poplin* [fine cotton]. Her intention was to brainwash my mother, so that she would become a supporter of British rule. My mother refused to entertain them.

Lady Kailash, a resident of Swarup Nagar in Kanpur, was held in awe by the residents because of her title and wealth. Her visit to the respondent's house indicates that Chail Bihari Cuntack was considered a dangerous political prisoner, and that the authorities thought that social pressure on his family would deter him from nationalist involvement. It was clear that the visitor tried to use the adverse circumstances of the family to her own advantage. She realised that if she could convince the mother, she could also influence the opinion of the father.

Women respondents said that the stability of their domestic lives was wrecked during the course of the movement. Many did not see their husbands for long periods of time, and the most unfortunate of them became widows when their husbands were hanged or died after contracting diseases in jail. However, these women were expected to keep up the nationalist spirit. They did not complain, but accepted widowhood as a nationalist sacrifice. Left with no other choice, women faced their widowhood alone.

Fasting, facing domestic instability and forgoing or losing their life companions without complaint were unparalleled sacrifices made by women in the domestic sphere as forms of resistance to colonial oppression.

Women as mothers and nurturers

British attempts to 'liberate' Indian women was accompanied by the parallel development of Hindu revivalism. The latter highlighted the positive Hindu qualities of motherhood which were given political significance by leaders, reformers and writers (Engels 1989: 430).

In the Indian tradition the mother has always been deified. For example, goddesses like Durga, Saraswati, Sita and Vaishno were regularly represented as mothers. This sanctified image of the mother was now considered an important vehicle for symbolising a strong civilisation inherited by the nation. An ideal wife and mother was described in most Hindi tracts as 'a Hindu woman who considers her husband as a god and in his welfare considers her own welfare' (Shukla 1938: 212).

A poem in a magazine, *Maharathi*, redefines the qualities of Indian mothers. This particular poem is entitled 'Matra Puja (Worship of Mother)':

> May the womankind of India be the ideals for the world
> May India worship its mothers
> May our minds be full of knowledge
> May our bodies be full of strength and devotion
> May we gain happiness from serving our pure husbands
> May India worship its mothers
> May we fight with anti-nationalist people
> May we crush enemies of religion within the homes
> Let mothers transform from being weak to strong, and help our nation
> May India worship its mothers.
> (Suri 1927: 624)

This poem exhorts women to change themselves from 'weak' to 'strong' individuals. They should be devoted to their husbands and should protect their religion and society from dissent and desertion. Through acquiring moral, physical and emotional strength, women would help themselves and their nation. This poem links the role of women as mothers with women's support for the nationalist movement.

Mothers were the sole guardians of children, especially when their menfolk were busy in nationalist activities or serving long jail sentences. They acquainted their children with popular nationalist vocabulary and with the important goal of becoming the enlightened future citizens of the nation. The family was seen as an integral part of national life and without children or their mothers, the nation would lose its glory (Thapar 1993: 84).

Motherhood was closely associated with the qualities of women as nurturers. I will illustrate the representations of the nurturer through the example of a Hindu middle-class activist, Sushila Devi. She had strong feelings about the importance and responsibilities of the mother, towards both the nation and the domestic sphere (the husband and children). Sushila Devi had been confined to the domestic sphere and expressed no displeasure about this, but used her educational qualifications as a teacher once her husband started his jail sentence. However, her employment was terminated because of the revolutionary activities of her husband (the late Brahmdutt Misra) and her own revolutionary ideas. In relation to her burgeoning political consciousness, she said:

> In 1928, I was influenced by the political environment. Before marriage, I was influenced by Gandhi and after marriage, Brahmdutt [her husband] influenced me with communist ideas. My husband used to bring home revolutionary material and I read a lot on Russian

history. At this time I had mixed feelings for both the Gandhian movement and the revolutionary movement. In 1929, I was a revolutionary. I realised that non-violence was not effective.

Despite the influence of revolutionary ideas, it was implied by the respondent that being a good housewife not only gave her personal satisfaction, but was also of political support to her husband, who was active in the public sphere: 'I never went to jail, I never led a procession. I was actually a housewife and would prefer to serve my husband.'

To my enquiry on the influence of ideas of women's emancipation articulated by male and female leaders, she said, 'It did not affect me. The idea of emancipation was impossible for me because then and still now my home is very important.' Sushila Devi linked emancipation with the neglect of domestic duties and expressed displeasure at words like 'emancipation' and 'equality'. Her husband was a participant in the public sphere and she wished to support his nationalist goals by supporting him. During the movement, her husband had remarked that 'Because of you my life has become successful. You are managing the house and my children.'

The imagery and symbolism associated with mothers and nurturers enhanced their significance for the nation and the struggle for independence. However, what becomes more important is to understand that discourses that relegated women in symbolic roles as mothers and nurturers further reinforced gendered social roles, and to some extent explain why the majority of women went back to the domestic sphere after independence. Symbolic representations, I argue, facilitated the nationalist project, and the construction of a non-violent and asexual 'nationalist woman' contained women's activities. Women exercised their agency on behalf of the 'nation'. However, most women found it an appealing identity, and the honour and respect associated with it enhanced their confidence. It can be argued that by adopting these symbols, women exercised agency on behalf of themselves. Thus, Indian women were negotiating their roles: their agency was expressed within a symbolically constituted national imagery.

Women as sources of strength and support

The nationalist movement created a stressful period for many activists' families. Political upheavals shook domestic stability and comforts in the lives of many activists. If a woman went out demonstrating in the streets, then someone had to be at home to support her family.

Children and elderly people were the primary responsibilities within families. Children were perceived to be especially vulnerable, since it was more difficult to explain to them the reasons for the disruptions in the family. The circumstances were different for each family. For example, in nuclear families, if both the husband and the wife went out to participate in the movement, the responsibility for the children had to be shouldered by neighbours or relatives. I will illustrate this through an example where the movement was a traumatic experience for the whole family. A particular activist narrated events from the movement through her experience as a young child. Both her parents were politically active in the public sphere. In 1931 Bhagat Singh and Sukhdev Thapar, Hindu male activists, were hanged by the British government. Hindu and Muslim riots broke out in Kanpur City. Uma Dixit's mother, along with other Hindu women, was shifted to a safer site in the Kallu Mal building in Begumgang locality, Kanpur. The father was busy defending people from the riots. Uma Dixit was looked after in a nearby neighbour's house in the area named Sisa Mau. When I enquired about a particular incident that had left an impression, she said:

> When I was very young, my mother was locked in the building [mentioned earlier]. In the night, I used to get up and enquire from my aunt [neighbour] if my father had come back. When I did not find him, I used to cry. I wanted my mother back but could not understand

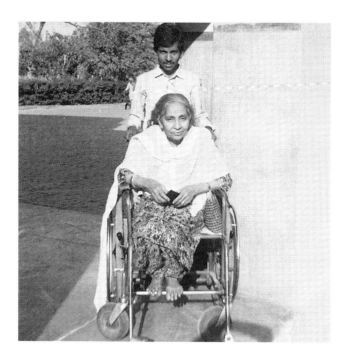

Plate 2 Uma Dixit

what was going on. When I asked my father, he used to say, 'She will come back, she has gone for some work.'

At other times, the neighbours took upon themselves the responsibility of feeding and clothing the children. For example, in Tulsa Devi's family, the father served long jail sentences. The mother shouldered the responsibility for the family's livelihood. However, once she was arrested, the children were looked after by a family friend, who was not a public activist herself. The respondent commented:

> I was present when my mother was arrested after addressing a meeting. We children came back home and were fed by our father's friend, Narayan Prasad Arora. His wife used to buy *aata* [flour], *dal* [lentil] and *chawal* [rice] for us.

On being asked about her feelings towards the help rendered by the neighbour, she responded: 'Participation in the nationalist movement does not have to be "on the streets" only. Krishna Arora [the wife] was serving the nationalist cause by helping another family.' Mutual help enabled women in gaining confidence and the momentum of their collective force further sharpened their political consciousness.

Some women saw involvement in nationalist activities more as a way of supporting and encouraging the male members in jail, while facilitating at the same time their desire to stay close to the husband. The emotional loyalty of women towards their husbands and sons was an expression of commitment to the movement as well. I will illustrate this through the experience of an activist.

Uma Dixit, a Hindu woman, is the daughter of the famous poet, the late Chail Bihari Cuntack mentioned above. Chail Cuntak was a member of the Congress Committee in Uttar Pradesh. He had been married to Kishori Devi (Uma's mother) when he was fourteen, before the civil disobedience movement started. Disagreements with his father over his involvement with the Congress Party forced Chail Cuntak and his young family to resettle in Kanpur where there was no family income and the financial condition of the household deteriorated. Chail 'would barely come out of the jail for a few months before going back again'. Kishori Devi, however, was too scared to object to her husband's activities because she feared that he would send her back to her in-laws in Itawah. She told him, 'You could do something that will at least give food to the children.'

The Nationalist Movement called for upheavals and readjustments in Kishori Devi's life. She herself did not want to leave *purdah*, but wanted to give as much support as she could to her husband. She once said to him, 'I will bear all hardships but will not leave you alone.' In her account, Uma Dixit stated that her 12-year-old brother died during the Quit India movement:

> My father was in the prison. When he was informed he sent a message: 'The whole of India is full of boys. So what happens if one does not exist any more?' It was my mother's courage that she faced it bravely. She often used to cry silently but never in front of us.

Though this appears to be a cruel remark from her father, the respondent herself did not express any resentment or regret. On the contrary, she implied that during the movement the fever of patriotism governed everybody's heart and her father had made this particular statement to instil her mother with courage. It was to remind her mother that the nation was like a big family, and that all the boys were her sons, too.

The anguish and the sadness of a wrecked domestic life and a husband who was always in jail affected Kishori Devi more than did the colonial crisis. What was remarkable was her ability and courage to conceal it, while still being a source of moral and emotional support to her husband. On this issue the respondent remarked, 'Was not so much support itself a contribution to the movement?' She tried to explain through her own experiences that it was possible to make sacrifices for the nationalist movement without taking on public activities, for example, through activities such as looking after the children of another activist's family, facing economic adversities and long separations while the husband was in prison, or offering support and assurance to others who were involved in public activities. At no point did the respondent see this as a form of constraint on women's activities or an indication of lack of power.

Women told their husbands that they would face all kinds of hardship in their absence, as in the following words: '*Chahe hum barbad ho jaye, par maphi mang kar khar na aana* (we might get destroyed but never ask for forgiveness and come back home).' The respondents were aware that deteriorating domestic conditions could put a moral strain on men and force them into seeking pardons.

Women formed support networks to help each other through difficult times. There were instances where, if one family member was in prison, the police would come looking for other family members, break into their houses, sell their animals, burn their crops and fine them. In such circumstances the neighbours were ready to offer support. As one activist, Kamala Seth, remembered:

> Other women would come and praise me for supporting my husband. They used to say, 'Don't lose hope. We will all eat together and if we die we will do it together.' Women from all castes used to be present in such moments of crisis.

The help from neighbours was often spontaneous and unconditional. *Mohallas* (neighbourhoods) organised themselves to give nationalist support. The nationalist consciousness of a particular neighbourhood burgeoned at moments of crisis and created an environment of neighbourhood nationalism. I will illustrate this through two examples.

A particular activist recalled an incident in Lahore. The deputy commissioner was passing through a street with his entourage when his car was hit by a boy's wooden ball.

> Immediately, the commissioner ordered his car to be stopped and he sent the accompanying policemen to bring the boy for punishment. The boy panicked and fled into the narrow bylanes. Some women who were peeping through the doorways had seen what had happened. They secretly took the child and hid him in a *tandoor* [a domestic oven for roasting food] which was situated on one of the rooftops. They then placed a *ghada* [a round pan] on the mouth of the *tandoor*.

Plate 3   Kamala Seth

The policemen searched everywhere but could not find the child and the commissioner left.

According to the activist, the women in the *mohalla* realised that if the child had been caught, his parents would have been jailed. Women were also aware of British brutality, and they sought both to resist it and to save other families from being unjustly imprisoned. My mother remembers being told by her mother and other women in the locality that 'the British are very strict. They are a heartless race and the punishments they give are harsh. They are *jalim* [ruthless] and think that they are the greatest. If caught by them, one was definitely tortured.'

A second example reflects on another aspect of neighbourhood feelings in other parts of India. A Bengali revolutionary described how she and her companions hid from the British in villages near Chittagong: 'We used to hide in Khirod Prabha Biswa's [a woman's] house. Other people in the village used to make tea in large cauldrons and call us over. They used to call us *athiti* [special guests].'

Such sacrifices called upon women's greatest talents. Although it could be argued that women were compelled by their situation to support the movement, in retrospect they see it in terms of their own nationalist contribution.

Clandestine activities within the domestic sphere

If the family dynamics did not permit such activities, then women who were politically aware tried to circumvent the constraints without challenging the familial norms. These women relied on their own willpower and determination to serve the nationalist cause.

The domestic sphere was a useful location for secret activities since women were sometimes more effective than men in this respect. Police were less suspicious of women's activities and were wary of encroaching on the privacy of the domestic sphere, especially since it was seen as the woman's space. In a politically sensitive environment, any encounter between the police and women was widely publicised by the media and could lead to further disturbances. Women were primarily involved in holding secret political meetings, shifting people and proscribed literature and passing information to men in hiding.

Urmilla Goorha and her mother, Ganga Devi, Hindu middle-class women from Kanpur district, were both involved in the nationalist movement. As a 13-year-old, Ganga Devi had married an 18-year-old, Triveni Shah Johari, who was literate in both English and Hindi, while Ganga Devi had received no formal education. They lived in a joint family of sixty-two people, all relatives of her husband. The household was so large that, as Urmilla Goorha remembered, 'Food was cooked in a large cauldron which needed more than two people to lift it off the fire.' She observed *purdah* and was confined to her room for most of the day. No part of her body could be exposed, especially in front of male cousins. A maid-servant who had come with her from her parent's house looked after her needs. A new bride was expected to stay in her own room and only come out when some form of domestic help was required of her.

Mr Triveni enforced strict discipline over his wife and children, and did not encourage any nationalist activities. However, Ganga Devi reacted against her husband's authoritarianism and encouraged her son, daughter and nephews to support the movement. Once, when her son made a donation to the Congress Committee, the receipt was mistakenly drawn in his father's name, and the father, a government employee, was reprimanded at work: 'His salary was cut by seventy-five rupees (Indian currency) and he was nearly suspended.' He thrashed his son. The mother, who witnessed this, advised her son to be cautious but not to give up his activities.

Ganga Devi avoided confronting her husband, trying to work her way around the familial constraints. She realised that all nationalist activities had to be undertaken clandestinely while maintaining a united domestic façade. For example, her husband was given no opportunity to complain when he wanted his food on time. Her daughter recalls her father's attitude:

> My father wanted his food on time. At the same time, he did not want the name of his family to be associated with the movement. When my father came back at four o'clock and realised that my mother had gone outside the house in relation to nationalist activities, he would get angry and not eat food at all.

In Indian households, the eldest earning male member of the family is supposed to be revered, especially by the women. His domestic needs, especially for food and clothes, are well looked after by his wife, sister or daughter. For example, his clothes for the next day will be washed and ironed and his food prepared on time. For the husband to deny the women the privilege of looking after him by refusing food is taken as a serious protest. Even today, women who are financially dependent on their husbands find it rewarding to prepare and serve food. Often they prepare special dishes of interest to their husband. In this light, the protest of Ganga Devi's husband was important. This quotation demonstrates that not all women accepted the restrictions imposed on them by men in the family. Ganga Devi's consciousness of the political situation and her desire to support the nationalist cause led her to get round these domestic constraints. She started to organise secret meetings with people in hiding when the husband was away at work. Her daughter remembered: 'Sometimes my cousins held a meeting in the house from 2 to 4 p.m., when my father was away. My mother used to sit in these meetings and was always ready to help.'

She contributed *khadi chadars* (sheets made from coarse cotton) and money in these meetings. For example, Ganga Devi gave ten rupees to one of the activists in hiding from the money she had received from her husband for household expenses. She then managed the household with the remaining money since she could not ask her husband for more. She also prepared food late at night for activists in hiding. The daughter said:

> The people who visited our house were 'wanted' by the police. Swatantra Bhai Sahib[4] came to our house and told my mother that he needed food at three o'clock in the morning for the other inmates in hiding. When my father was asleep, my mother cooked *chappatis* worth five kilograms of flour. After that she cleaned everything so that the *Mahri* [the woman who cleans domestic utensils] did not realise the night activities. My mother gave the *gahtari* [a sort of bundle] to Swatantra and said to him, 'God bless you, but I should not see you again in the *mohalla* [locality].'

She did not want him to come to the house again because the police would get suspicious and this would jeopardise the domestic order.

Ganga Devi also spun on the *charkha* and she encouraged her daughter to wear *khadi* sarees. An understanding between daughter and mother facilitated clandestine activities so that everything in the house would appear to be normal.

In their role as messengers, women, who were less suspect than men, kept people in hiding informed of political developments. This was especially the case with women whose husbands were in hiding from the British authorities. Tulsa Devi used to keep *purdah* in the joint family of in-laws, and her mother-in-law was specifically opposed to any political activity on the part of her son. However, he continued, in secret, to be politically active. He used to go into hiding in the jungles near their village and emerge when it was safe. Tulsa Devi used to sneak out of the house late at night disguised as a man, a beggar or a religious mendicant, and she would give her husband news of the developments of the day, concerning (for example) whether the police were looking for him or whether there was any message from his compatriots. Tulsa Devi was aware of the political upheaval and was a strong pillar of support to her husband's political practices. She said that the constraints at home did not stop her from moving outside the household. She was also aware that her movement at night was more dangerous for women than was participation in daylight: 'Near the village there were jungles. I used to sneak out at night without informing my in-laws and disguise myself.'

Often households were used as hideouts by political suspects or political prisoners on the run, and usually in these cases both male and female members were politically involved. Since women were less suspect, they were responsible for moving people in hiding from one domestic space to another. Women effectively used their domestic roles as wives, mothers and sisters for such clandestine activities. For example, Tara Devi Agarwal describes the activities at her residence in Kanpur City and her role in facilitating the movement of a political prisoner. The incident occurred during the festival of Rakshabandan, when the sister ties a symbolic thread of protection on her brother's wrist.

> My house in Latouche Road was called Azad, because Chandra Shekhar Azad used to come and stay there. Once Azad was in my house and the police surrounded the house. Consequently, I pretended that I had to visit my brother to put *rakhi* on him. I disguised Azad as my servant and with my *thali* [a plate decorated with sweets] went out.

Azad, as Tara's escort to her brother's home, was transferred from one household to another and escaped arrest. Azad was also hidden by another respondent, Sharad Kumari Sinha.

Women hid proscribed literature for the menfolk, and it thus became difficult for the police to confiscate this literature. As Uma Dixit said, 'My mother [Kishori Devi] used to hide my father's books and pamphlets regularly. There were difficult times because sometimes my mother used to keep the books with her women friends.'

Sometimes the literature had to be moved from one hiding place to another (usually another house). At times certain menfolk of families in the neighbourhood objected to the hiding of proscribed literature. These men would tell their wives that they would also get caught and asked their wives to return the material, which they would then proceed to do.

Some women also hid ammunition, pistols and other kinds of arms for revolutionaries. A particular respondent would hide pistols in the mud near a house well, and bring them out when they were required by her husband or his friends.

Through the activities described above (for example, informing, shifting people and hiding contraband literature), the domestic sphere emerged as a site of both resistance and subordination. For some Indian women, their domestic status enhanced rather than inhibited their ability to play a vital role.

Conclusion

Changes in the public sphere are always potentially reflected in the domestic sphere and the nationalist movement introduced changes in most urban middle-class homes. Women's roles within the domestic sphere were shaped by changes in the public sphere.

Many women could not cross the boundaries of the domestic sphere to be 'political'. 'Political' did not mean the same for everybody. Yet most women had to take cognizance of the movement and, looking back, see their domestic activities as an integral part of their nationalist contribution. When women were asked to realign their domestic roles with the nationalist cause, their political consciousness was sharpened. The domestic sphere underwent a steady politicisation.

More outstanding than women's overt political activities was their determination and fearlessness, facing ridicule from other women relatives, dealing with loss of income and shortages of food. The awareness that they had to survive without inhibiting their husband's commitment to the nationalist cause helped in the development of their own nationalist consciousness. When women lost their family members, not only did they suffer the grief and sorrow that accompanied this, but also their previously routinised normal domestic lives were altered.

Women did not see these activities of support as restricting their individual development, although we might see it that way now. Rather, these women saw their lives extended to encompass activities in both public and domestic spheres. The importance of respect for their domestic roles actually increased in this period, through popular nationalist symbols, which legitimised and privileged women's contribution. The domestic sphere became such an important category in nationalist political thought, raising awareness of new dimensions in the relationship between gender and political life.

Acknowledgements

I am grateful to Joanna Liddle and Carol Wolkowitz for their comments on earlier drafts of the paper. An earlier version of this paper was presented at the 'Women, Policy and Politics' conference, Institute of Education, London in July 1997.

Notes

1   Women were urged to carry over values from the domestic sphere into their new public roles. I have called this process the domestication of the public sphere.
2   The details of the narrative were provided to the respondent by his mother, Asha Lata Misra.
3   A train robbery by revolutionary terrorists near Kakori, Lucknow, in 1925. The four accused were sentenced to death (Pandey 1978: 93).
4   The word *Swatantra* means independence. Revolutionaries who concealed their identity from the police adopted a patriotic pseudonym. This prevented the police from easily tracking down the family of the activist.

References

English sources

Agnew, V. (1979) *Elite Women in Indian Politics*, Delhi: Vikas.
Basu, A. (1976) 'The role of women in the Indian struggle for freedom', in B.R. Nanda (ed.) *Indian Women: From Purdah to Modernity*, Delhi: Vikas.
Caplan, P. (ed.) (1989) *The Cultural Construction of Sexuality*, London: Routledge.
Engels, D. (1989) 'The limits of gender ideology: Bengali women, the colonial state, and the private sphere, 1890–1930', *Women's Studies International Forum* 12 (4): 429–36.
Jayawardena, K. (1986) *Feminism and Nationalism in the Third World*, London: Zed Press.
Kasturi, L. and Mazumdar, V. (eds) (1994) *Women and Indian Nationalism*, Delhi: Vikas.
Kaur, M. (1968) *Role of Women in the Freedom Movement: 1857–1947*, Delhi: Sterling.
Nanda, B.R. (1976) *Indian Women: From Purdah to Modernity*, Delhi: Vikas.
Pandey, G. (1978) *The Ascendancy of the Congress in Uttar Pradesh, 1926–34: A Study in Imperfect Mobilisation*, New Delhi: OUP.
Rao, U. (1994) 'Women in the frontline: the case of U.P.', in L. Kasturi and V. Mazumdar (eds) *Women and Indian Nationalism*, Delhi: Vikas.
Rao, U. and Devi, M. (1984) 'Glimpses: UP women's response to Gandhi, 1921–1930', paper presented at the Second National Conference on Women's Studies, Trivandrum, India.
Thapar, S. (1993) 'Women as activists; women as symbols: a study of the Indian Nationalist Movement' *Feminist Review* 44: 81–96.

Hindi sources

Jagesh, J.P. (1992) 'Dastaye Jo Darjit Nahi Hui', *Dainik Jagron*, October.
Kumar, Y. (1930) 'Urmilla Devi Shaastri Ke Yad Me', *Chand*, November.
Sahgal, V. (1930) 'Samphadak', *Chand*, November.
Shukla, D. (1938) 'Rashtra Mata Kasturbai', *Saraswati*, September.
Suri, R. (1927) 'Matra Puja', *Maharathi*, April–May.

Proscribed book collection (IOL)

PP. Hin. B. 3121 (1922) *Striyan aur Samaj*.
PP. Hin. B. 462 (1923) *Ankhon Ka Kata*.

4 Gender, ethnicity and 'the community'
Locations with multiple identities

Tijen Uguris

This chapter looks at the relationship between the so-called 'community' and the social divisions of race, ethnicity and gender on the one hand and space and place on the other. It examines the notion of 'the community', which assumes collectivities as homogeneous and overlooks the conflicting interests among their members (Yuval-Davis 1994). The chapter takes up the concepts of space and place as social constructs and discusses their links to the notion of 'the community'.

In conditions of modernity, the effects of globalisation and space/time compression have resulted in immense changes to the lives of vast numbers of people and local 'communities' in highly unpredicted ways. Locales are permeated by social events taking place quite distant from them, while the local 'communities' are influenced and shaped by changes taking place on a much wider scale, e.g. migration, dislocation, etc. These processes and their effects on the locales are, however, highly gendered, ethnicised and classed. So are the responses by the local institutions to the emerging issues and problems (Massey 1994; Giddens 1990).

In the search for an alternative solution to the problems in housing, notions such as 'the community', race and gender have been on the agenda of planners in most of the industrialised countries since the late 1960s. In Britain, for instance, projects tried to involve the existing and future inhabitants as attempts to offer participatory processes, in order to solve housing problems exacerbated by mass-produced housing and their management bureaucracies widely used as a response to housing shortages. I am concerned with the housing policies in Britain and their implications in terms of gender and ethnicity as a result of my own social positioning, in that I am an ethnic minority woman (of Turkish origin) who has trained as an architect and lives in Britain. I have explored the extent to which tenants (particularly in London) are able to participate in decision-making as well as the ways in which gender and ethnicity configure in these processes.

In Britain a wide range of initiatives has been tried, namely 'community planning', 'tenant participation', 'user participation', 'popular planning', etc. The common aim of these projects is to offer people the means to be positively involved in affecting their surroundings and to enable them to gain power in making decisions about their environment. These projects, however, have major flaws since they make implicit and explicit assumptions regarding the notions of 'the people', 'the community', 'empowerment', etc. These notions homogenise social groupings and draw a fixed boundary around these collectivities, constructing a sense of 'us' and 'them', and dismiss the existing internal differences of power and conflicting interests.

On the other hand, urban planners and architects designing for 'the local communities' make assumptions about the notions of space and place. They treat production of space and place merely as physical enclosures – products – assuming homogeneity in the use of the built environment. They also treat concepts of space and place as neutral – homogeneous rather than social constructs which are the results of social processes, therefore highly heterogeneous and dynamic. However, class, race, gender, sexuality, disability and age are among the many other factors which clearly influence our experience in the use of the built environment. Women, for instance, have different experiences, needs and uses in relation to the built environment than men, resulting from different gender roles in our society. Furthermore, women of different cultures will have varying notions of space in the same locality as a result of different gender relations in different cultures (Matrix 1984; Massey 1994; Greed 1994; Wilson 1991). In the following discussion the notions of 'the community' and 'empowerment' and their relation to divisions of race, ethnicity and gender are examined for their hidden assumptions of homogeneity, neutrality, and so on. Then concepts of space and place are taken up as social constructs and their links to the notion of community are discussed.

The first part of this chapter explores concepts such as 'the community' and 'empowerment' which homogenise and naturalise social groupings, assuming a fixed boundary around a given collectivity. Their members are assumed to have common interests and goals. These closely linked notions deny the highly heterogeneous nature of these collectivities with differential power relations among their members and their ever-shifting boundaries. It is argued that people have multiple identities and thus occupy different positions in terms of ethnicity, gender, class, etc., within any community (Yuval-Davis 1994).

The following section of the chapter argues that the conceptualisation of ethnic, gender and class divisions in the society reflects dichotomous thinking on which policies such as housing and town planning are based. While dichotomisation is used as a tool to make the reality more manageable, belief in dichotomies such as public/private is enforced by land-use zoning policies and maintained by spatial division. In dichotomous thinking, places are conceptualised as having a boundary around them, resulting in the construction of a counterposition between 'us' and 'them', excluding as 'the other' all those perceived as different (Greed 1994; Duncan 1996; Massey 1993; Anthias and Yuval-Davis 1992; Yuval-Davis 1994; Collins 1990).

Hence, the last section of the chapter argues that personal experience of space is based on the specificities of individual's social positioning. Space is not an independent dimension; instead the spatial is created and re-created out of social relations and needs to be thought of in the context of space–time. When space is seen in terms of social relations, it follows that space can be neither neutral nor homogeneous; instead it contains differential power relations and conflicts of interest as well as relations of support and solidarity. Therefore, design of the built environment reflects the existing social inequalities based on ethnicity, gender and class. What is more, it can also further contribute towards it. The process has a reciprocal nature. The urban space is the outcome of existing social relations, yet it also has an impact upon it. The chapter suggests that since space mirrors social relations, and social change and spatial change are intrinsic to each other, then social change needs to produce new spaces which appreciate the multiple identities of the inhabitants (Massey 1993; Greed 1994; Duncan 1996).

The community

The concept of community, as Margaret Rodman (1993) argues, is usually perceived to be a positive thing. She refers to the observation of Raymond Williams:

> Community is unusual among the terms of political vocabulary in being, I think, the one term which has never been used in a negative sense. People never, from any political position, want to say that they are against community or against the community ... I think on the one hand we should be glad that this is so, on the other hand we should be suspicious. A term which is agreed among so many people, a term which everybody likes, a notion which everybody is in favour of – if this reflected reality then we'd be living in a world very different from this one. So what is the problem inside the term, what is it that allows people to at once respond very positively to it and yet mean such very different things by it?
>
> (Williams 1973: 112–13)

Indeed, the term 'community' has always meant different things to different people and has also changed its meaning with the changes in the society.

The community is often perceived in relation to a place. Rodman (1993), for instance, links community to place and claims that community 'grows out of and is expressed in the experience of place'. Doreen Massey, however, suggests that persistent identification of place with 'community' is in fact a misidentification. 'Communities can exist without being in the same place – i.e. networks of people/friends with similar interests, major religious, ethnic or political communities' (Massey 1994: 153).

Rodman makes a distinction between *rural* community and *industrial* community. The former is seen as based on mutual responsibility that grows out of living in the same place and sharing a sense of identity. Industrial community, on the other hand, is 'forged in common struggle and conflict' (Rodman 1993: 135). The emergence of industrial capitalism meant the emergence of a new concept of community.

David Harvey examines the construction of community in relation to the urban experience. In the new industrial society, he argues, a new tradition of community had to be invented by the ruling class to counter or absorb the class antagonisms. This was done on the one hand by taking the responsibility for reproduction of the labour force, e.g. health, education, welfare and housing provision for the working class. On the other hand, it was achieved by employing open force as well as more subtle means of social control such as through the police, relative democratisation, ideological control through religious establishments and mass media, and controlling space as a form of social power. The pursuit of the working class of a new definition of community for itself as a way of survival helped industrial capitalism forge new traditions of urban community out of conditions of social disintegration and class conflict (Harvey 1994: 31).

Examining the class practices and the construction of community, Harvey argues that there is a profound disparity in the ways different classes construct their sense of territory and community. He points out the striking contrast between community construction in the low-income and disempowered, as against the affluent and empowered strata of the population. Low-income groups lacking the means to command space often find themselves trapped in space. Their constant pursuit of sharing use-values for their survival results not only in co-operation but also in highly conflicting interpersonal social attachment in private and public spaces. In order to remain in control over space, an exact sense of boundaries is constructed and unwanted elements are excluded from it. Such a process of community construction involves resorting to ethnic, religious, racial and status discriminations. Affluent groups, on the other hand, can control space through spatial mobility and ownership of basic means of reproduction (houses, cars, etc.). They are not dependent upon community-provided use-values for their survival. Having abundant exchange-values, their construction of community is geared to the maintenance or augmentation of exchange-values. It is money that provides access to the community. At the same time, it makes it less exclusionary on other grounds. Harvey claims that residential segregation on the grounds of ethnicity and even race tends to get weaker the further up the income scale one goes. He agrees that the agencies of class, gender or other social practices give specific meanings to spatial practices. These meanings are put into motion and spaces used in a particular way through them. He also believes that the gender, racial, ethnic and religious components of spatial practices have to be contemplated in any full description of community formation and the production of social spaces in urban settings (Harvey 1994).

Discussing the concept from a feminist perspective, Sue Brownhill (1997) underlines the problematic nature of the term 'the community', owing on one hand to the existing variety of definitions and interpretations, and on the other hand to the fact that particular views about women are embedded in the term. She points out that the concept originates from the harsh realities of urbanised, capitalist society as opposed to an imaginary protected, warm and humanised place – the community. Thus the notion implies specific 'traditional' gendered roles. Community relates to the social space associated with the whole notion of home: the private sphere involving intimacy and caring relations and a protection from the outside world. 'This is women's sphere and a "women's place",' maintains Brownhill, '– in both social and spatial meaning of the phrase – comes to rest on the naturalisation of women's roles within society' (Brownhill 1997: 2).

In her feminist critique of the ideal of community, Iris Marion Young (1990a, 1990b) points out that critics of welfare capitalist society, including socialists and feminists, frequently appeal to community as an alternative to the alienation and individualism of modern Western society. Feminist groups impelled by a desire for closeness and mutual identification view community as an expression of a desire for transparency and social closeness. Community, however, argues Young, denies and represses difference by positing fusion rather than separation as the social ideal. This desire for the fusion of subjects with one another in practice operates to exclude 'the other' – e.g. those who have characteristics with which the group does not identify. Furthermore, by privileging face-to-face relations, the ideal of community seeks a model of social relations that are not mediated by temporal and spatial distancing. Rejecting the idea that social groups can be unitary in the sense of having members with a singular identity, Young calls for the recognition of group differences. She argues that, to achieve political equality, formal mechanisms for representing group difference are needed. Stressing the fact that some groups are privileged while others are oppressed, she notes that existing mechanisms provide dominant groups with power. This way the suppression of any marginalised, disadvantaged voice is maintained. She thus calls for institutionalising forms of group representation.

Other theorists argue that although recognising difference and differential power relations is important, Young's position is problematic. Institutionalising forms of group representation may put more emphasis on constructing boundaries around these groups which exclude as 'the other' all those perceived as different, and contribute to the conceptualisation of these boundaries as fixed with no possibility of shifting. This consequently strengthens the divide and blocks further development and change (Yuval-Davis 1994, 1997; Phillips 1993; Shapiro and Kymlicka 1997). Responding to criticisms, Young expresses her agreement with the view that treating gender or racial groups as fixed and unitary in their interest is problematic, for it 'inappropriately freezes fluid relational identities into a unity and can create oppressive segregations' (Young 1997: 350). She claims that while members of oppressed or marginalised groups are rarely unified in their interests or opinions, they often do share a certain perspective which emerges from their experience as group members. Her position, however, remains problematic, for it separates social perspective from the interests and opinions in an essentialist way.

In her feminist approach to town planning issues, Clara Greed (1994) suggests that, with the development of capitalism, urban problems and, in particular, the housing problem have been seen in terms of class and capitalism. In order to legitimate their power, planners have claimed they are planning for the good of working-class communities. However, she stresses, 'the construction of the class, of what is considered wrong with capitalism and what is perceived to be the right solution to meet the needs of the worker, are all highly gendered' (Greed 1994: 10). She refers to the existing debate around patriarchy and capitalism and the relationship between the two, particularly as to which has precedence as the causal factor. Among the existing positions on the issue, some give class-based explanation to urban problems while others look for explanations by theorising patriarchy. Some look at the relationship between capitalism and patriarchy. There are, however, those who are of the opinion that reductionist discourses based around gender or class cannot accommodate their life experiences, especially those from minority ethnic groups and other 'minorities'. They suggest that race should be viewed as a key element, alongside class and gender, in attempts to understand urban spatial structure (Smith 1989; Cross and Keith 1993 quoted by Greed 1994). The latter views are increasingly gaining support. Indeed, in Western countries in recent years the ideology of the community has become popular with regard to planning issues, with an increasing emphasis on gender, race and ethnicity.

Yet there are inherent problems within the notion of community that are common to all formations. It implies certain implicit assumptions and remains problematic. As Yuval-Davis (1994) argues, the community is perceived as a 'natural' social unit. Its 'naturalness' assumes the existence of boundaries around a given collectivity. It exists in its own right, so that one can either belong to it or not. There is an assumption, for instance, that there exists a commonality of interests and goals among people living in a particular locality or among those who belong to certain collectivities, such as working-class, ethnic or cultural minorities. According to the ideology of community, the so-called community is a more or less egalitarian and homogeneous grouping. There are, however, conflicts and differences of interests among its members as a result of the differences in the power attached to the different identities of people. Many individuals are members in more than one collectivity and they occupy different positions in terms of ethnicity, class, gender, etc., within any community. As a result, some projects are better suited to certain members of the collectivity than others. Yet in the notion of community there is an assumption that there is a single sense of community which everyone shares. Through 'the community' a sense of belonging is constructed which develops bonds between individuals and groups as well as between people and places. These perspectives of 'the community' construct boundaries which exclude as 'the other' all those perceived as different, for example ethnic and cultural minorities. They also assume these boundaries as being fixed with no possibility of shifting – in other words, they have the potential to become extremely conservative and racist (Yuval-Davis 1994; Massey 1994).

All ethnic groups are characterised by a notion of 'community' (Anthias and Yuval-Davis 1992: 8). Expressions such as 'the Asian community' and 'the Bangladeshi community' are used to define the spatial concentrations of these ethnic groups or their presumed lifestyles and values. Again, there is an assumption here that these ethnic communities are homogeneous. The Commission for Racial Equality (CRE), for example, established by the Race Relations Act in 1976, looks at ethnic communities as homogeneous – with fixed boundaries. It talks about harmony within the community, therefore seeing these communities as non-problematic. Implicit in notions of multi-culturalism and harmony is the stereotypical view of what a community is and what a 'typical' member of a community is. Equal opportunities policies assume that the interests of all the oppressed and disadvantaged are automatically shared and reconciled – as if everyone is disadvantaged at the same level. They do not see the existing conflicting interests within these communities.

It is women who have suffered most from these assumptions of unified and homogeneous collectivities. Women have different experiences and needs from men in relation to the built environment. However, despite the fact that women form the majority in Britain (women constitute 52 per cent of the population) their different needs and experiences are rarely expressed, their voices are not heard during decision-making processes. Furthermore, they are still considered by many men planners as a minority, and are planned for accordingly (Greed 1994; Brownhill 1997). Cultural conflicts between minority groups are also overlooked. It is important to recognise that the black and ethnic minority community is not a homogeneous group but has a number of particular interests and a range of views on issues. Values, beliefs and traditions may vary from group to group resulting in differences of opinion and lifestyles. The so-called 'neutrality' of the planners in their approach to planning, and concepts like 'neutral planning' and 'equal standards' may lead to indirect discrimination, as 'identical treatment almost guarantees discrimination because people are different in their characteristics ... because people vary ... policies should always vary according to their different impact' (RTPI/CRE 1983: 15).

'Empowerment' and identities

In order to address the problems of the segregated, oppressed and impoverished populations found in all urban areas, Harvey (1994) calls for ways to address the question of spatial empowerment. The notion of 'empowerment' is closely connected with the notion of 'the community' with a commonality of interests and goals. Incorporating collectivities into decision-taking processes is linked with the notion of 'empowerment' (Jacobs 1992). 'Empowerment' is taking more control of one's life. It is not something that a collectivity can be given. Rather, it is a process that they go through (Karl 1995). The notion of 'empowerment' of 'the community' assumes common interests and goals among its members. Community is unified by a single idea of common good. There is an automatic assumption that no inherent conflicts of interest can arise during the process of people gaining empowerment. Dylis Hill, for instance, states that 'the key to empowerment is a notion of the public ... with shared concern for the common good' (Hill 1994: 24). She further points out that:

> While empowerment ... means different things from different standpoints, there is a common emphasis on community, on a variety of definitions of localism, and on the need to generate the will to engage in action. Such motivation arises both from enlightened self-interest and from shared values and common loyalties.
>
> (Hill 1994: 28)

Indeed, the emphasis on a community with 'shared values and common loyalties' is problematic, for communities are not homogeneous. They have internal structures, and involve differentiated power relations through which a wide range of power positions are produced and reproduced. Within a community, such as on a housing estate, 'the otherness' may be constructed in terms of ethnicity, culture, sexuality or employment status, revealing the multi-dimensional nature of power and powerlessness. It also underlines the diversity of ways in which the disadvantaged experience oppressions, which has ramifications for the notion of 'empowerment'.

Black and ethnic minority people's housing experiences may be different from the majority ethnic people living in the same locality, in terms of access to public housing, overcrowding and access to amenities in the locality. In Britain, for instance, there exist major differences between the housing needs of minority ethnic groups and their white counterparts (Clarke 1994). The average size of minority ethnic households is larger than the average white household, and there are proportionately more black households with young children, all of which underlines the issue about the design and location of housing projects, size of dwellings, and play facilities for children. Local authorities do not have a sufficient number of larger dwellings, therefore overcrowding is more common among ethnic minorities (Morris and Winn 1990; Ginsburg 1992).[1]

Recently, new and radical approaches to planning and the housing problem have emerged, with the aim of empowering 'the people' and giving them greater control of their homes and environment. Thus popular planning aims:

> to democratise decision making away from the state bureaucrats or company managers to include the workforce as a whole or people who live in a particular area ... empowering groups and individuals to take control over decisions which affect their lives, and therefore to become active agents of change.
> (Montgomery and Thornley 1988, quoted in Cullingworth and Nadin 1994: 247)

There can be no *political* disagreement with the above statement. It is, however, based on a specific theoretical understanding with certain hidden assumptions that are problematic. There is an assumption of a pre-given, non-problematic definition of the boundaries of 'the people'. 'The people' to be empowered are the local working-class population who are usually perceived to be white male workers. As a result of stereotyping, as Greed (1994) argues, some planners (most of them male)[2] perceive men as workers and all women as non-workers, forever fixed as housewives or young mothers in spite of the fact that only 15 per cent of households consist of a male breadwinner, a wife not in paid employment and dependent children. Ethnic minorities are also left out of the working class by planners since they often occupy part-time jobs or are unemployed, despite the fact that certain industries in Britain are based on the cheap labour of migrant workers, i.e. catering, garment and cleaning industries. The highly gendered and racialised nature of class is often not recognised, and the range and diversity among the local population is not taken into account. Black and ethnic minority women are often absent in these processes. Popular planners often fail to acknowledge the specific needs and interests of black and ethnic minority women, partly because they assume these women have other identities (i.e. 'woman' or 'black') and therefore belong to other collectivities (i.e. ethnic minority groups or women's groups), which they also assume are homogeneous. Identity, however, 'is a slippery concept', as Kum-Kum Bhavnani describes, 'for it is not fixed, it is never closed and it is created through difference' (Bhavnani 1993: 37). People have multiple identities which may be internally defined or externally imposed, or both. As a result, individuals become part of collectivities which are social constructs with no fixed boundaries. Their boundaries, structures and norms are the result of constant processes of struggles and negotiations. They can also be the result of more general social developments (Yuval-Davis 1994).

Dichotomous thinking

There can be no such thing as value-free 'neutral planning' as it is claimed, nor should there be. The thinking, beliefs and assumptions of agents are reflected in the planning processes. Planning, as Greed argues, is all about creating realities – or reorganising existing reality – and 'imposing these on space, often obliterating other realities and needs in the process' (Greed 1994: 11; Department of the Environment 1972). Phenomena such as capitalism, patriarchy and racism are reflected in the space. Urban planners, through their plans and designs, transmit on to space the existing ethnic, gender and class divisions of the society. Conceptualisation of these divisions as fixed is often expressed in dichotomous perceptions. In dichotomous thinking, separation is made and barriers kept between concepts such as us/them, us/the other, private/public, work/home, physical/social, spatial/aspatial, breadwinner/homemaker, majority/minority, professional/personal, suburb/city, users/providers, male/female. Ethnic and gender divisions are built not only into houses and public buildings, but also the whole structure of the urban system. As Judy Wajcman observes, it is the 'architecture and urban planning that have orchestrated the separation between women and men, private and public, home and paid employment, consumption and production, reproduction and production, suburb and city' (Wajcman 1991: 110).

People do not live according to these binary oppositions. Nevertheless, the existing pervasive belief in them has an ultimate influence on decisions and policy formulations, and has a major impact on the lives of those who have no say in these decisions, such as women and minority ethnic groups. A range of dualisms that exist in dichotomous thinking are related to the political processes that construct ethnic collectivities and 'their interests' as well as the distinction between genders in society. However, terms such as 'man' and 'woman' and key dualisms and concepts such as equality and difference, the public and the private, power and dependence, need to be questioned and re-examined. They all have specific meanings at different times and in different places (McDowell and Pringle 1992: 50).

The public and private dichotomy

One of the dichotomies that affects gender relations in our societies is based on the distinction between the public and the private. As Nancy

Duncan argues, this distinction is embedded in political philosophy, law, everyday discourse and continual spatial structuring practices (Duncan 1996: 127). Through these practices, a private domain where domestic and embodied activity takes place is produced. This private space is further separated and isolated from a political sphere which is perceived to be disembodied and predominantly located in public space. The public and private dichotomy is closely linked to the mind/body dualism. That being so, traditional patriarchal and heterosexist power structures are maintained through the constant use of the dichotomy 'to construct, control, discipline, confine, exclude and suppress gender and sexual difference' (Duncan 1996: 128). Yet, Duncan argues, women's confinement (voluntary and forced) in the private sphere undoubtedly has an impact on the public sphere as a political site by reducing its vitality. Moreover, it hampers the ability of marginalised groups to claim a share in power. She states:

> It is clear that the public–private distinction is gendered. This binary opposition is employed to legitimate oppression and dependence on the basis of gender; it has also been used to regulate sexuality. The private *as an ideal type* has traditionally been associated and conflated with: the domestic, the embodied, the natural, the family, property, the 'shadowy interior of the household', personal life, intimacy, passion, sexuality, 'the good life', care, a haven, unwaged labour, reproduction and immanence. The public *as an ideal type* has traditionally been the domain of the disembodied, the abstract, the cultural, rationality, critical public discourse, citizenship, civil society, justice, the market place, waged labour, production, the polis, the state, action, militarism, heroism and transcendence.
>
> (Duncan 1996: 128)

The private and the public dichotomy is based on the assumption that these spaces are homogeneous, whereas both of them are highly heterogeneous and no definite distinction can be made between the public and private space. As Duncan puts it: 'Both private and public spaces are heterogeneous and not all space is clearly private or public' (Duncan 1996: 129).

Furthermore, as Patricia Hill Collins (1997) observes, the public and private are given new meanings through racialised and classed processes. In the United States, as the public sector becomes more democratic, the public and the private are redefined in terms of the value attached to each one of them and the boundaries between the two domains. The public increasingly becomes associated with lack of privacy and overcrowding. The public space is devalued, as it is perceived to be populated by the underclass – e.g. black men making it dangerous – and all of a sudden becomes privatised, and thus heavily surveyed, while the private gains an increased value. Privacy is equated with safety, and on the whole implies racial homogeneity. Thus new definitions of public and private spaces emerge through highly classed and racialised processes, resulting in an increased subjection of racialised minorities to public scrutiny.

Dichotomous thinking is reflected in space by agents of design and planning processes, such as town planners and architects, through their methods of 'zoning' according to perceived dichotomies. Among these agents, there exists a firm conviction that dichotomisation is a tool to make the reality more manageable. Division has been widely used in order to control and solve a range of urban problems. Belief in public/private dichotomies, for instance, is enforced by land-use zoning policies and maintained by spatial division. Town planning, especially zoning of industry and the creation of separate residential neighbourhoods, is a way of enforcing divisions spatially between male and female. The spatial separation of work and home is based on the assumption that work takes place outside the home. Enormous distances between zones, however, make it very hard for women to combine work inside and outside the home (Greed 1994).

The notion behind the design of urban space is that of separation of various aspects of life. Homes, shops, workplaces and leisure places are all in separate areas. The creation of residential areas and the distances between homes and workplaces reflects the stereotyping of women's and men's work and reinforces the assumption that men work away from the home with no responsibility for its day-to-day running or for childcare. It is also assumed that women, having the responsibility for looking after homes and children, do not work outside the home (Matrix 1984; Massey 1994; Greed 1994; Fraser 1996). In Britain, just a small number of households, however, conform to this pattern. Around a third of households consist of a husband, wife and dependent children (Matrix 1984; Quiney 1986). As argued by Matrix, in more than half of the existing households the mother has a paid job outside the home. 'About one in nine of all households consists of a man with a paid job, a woman without one, and children under the age of 16' (Matrix 1984: 4). Women, as Greed notes, who might need to move between home, childminder, school, work and shops, may be prevented from doing this because of the distance between zones (Greed 1994: 42). It is clear that this separation has affected women more than men, since there are no neat divisions between women's lives at work, leisure and home in the way that men have. Hence, many women's confinement in private space, the isolated nature of their lives and their exclusion from the public sphere, has been reinforced through zoning practices. Zoning restrictions in the suburbs, on the other hand, may operate to separate different kinds of housing development, which may be a way of maintaining class and race segregation (in South Africa, for instance, black people are limited to certain parts of the city through urban planning) (Wajcman 1991: 119).

Space and place

In dichotomous thinking, places are conceptualised as having a boundary around them. Such a boundary differentiates between an inside and an outside, which is yet another way of constructing an imagined opposing position between 'us' and 'them' (Massey 1994).

Place is perceived as having a single, uniform and essential identity. Subsequently, in planning the built environment there has been a false assumption that there is a single sense of place everyone shares and that all sections of the population use their environment in the same way and expect their environment to do the same things for them (Matrix 1984; Massey 1994). Yet people not only have a different sense of the same place, but they all use it differently, too. One of the key factors, Greed suggests, in understanding why people with the same class or gender characteristics have different life experiences in the same physical space, is their 'belief' (Greed 1994: 9): that is, the way people 'see' the world. She argues that people occupy different social and ideological space. Their differing characteristics, such as the individual outlooks and lifestyles, ethnicities, states of health and age, as well as the subculture they adhere to within and across classes, all need to be considered to understand the specificity of their experiences of urban life (Healey 1992; Greed 1994).

If it is recognised that people have multiple identities, the places they relate to will have different identities and their sense of place will vary accordingly. In other words, a sense of space/place is not the same for everyone, and because of the multiplicity of their identities people will have a different sense of space depending on their identity in a specific situation. Sense of the same space/place of a particular person varies also according to her/his specific identity at a particular time, since space is not an unequivocal independent dimension. Instead, the spatial needs to be thought of in the context of space–time. It is formed out of social relations at all scales. Place is then a specific articulation of those relations, 'a particular moment in those networks of social relations and understandings' (Massey 1994: 5).

In societies where ethnicity, race, gender roles and class are strongly differentiated, members of these collectivities, e.g. black and white, women and men, working-class and middle-class, will have diverse values and attitudes towards their environment. Their experience and perception of the same environment will be different. Not only do women use the space differently from men, but women of a specific ethnic minority group also use the space differently from other minority and majority women. Spatial experiences of individuals vary profoundly even within the same environmental setting, resulting from the combined effect of their race and ethnicity, gender and class, as well as factors such as their state of health, stage in the life cycle, etc. Thus, an individual's experience of space is based on the specificities of their social positioning. Women's relationship to domestic space is not similar to that of men because of their differently valued gender roles and the social power attached to each. Women of a minority ethnic group will also have a different relationship to the domestic space, not only from the men of minority and majority ethnic groups, but also from women of the majority ethnic group. In other words, the private is not only gendered but ethnicised, too. bell hooks, for instance, argues that as a result of the hostility African Americans (both men and women) experience in public space, the home can serve as a crucial site of resistance. Underlining its radical political dimension, hooks describes home as a place where 'we could restore to ourselves the dignity denied us on the outside in the public world' (hooks 1990: 42).

Furthermore, the private can also be a space which represents autonomy for those people who are not dependent on the welfare state, whereas those with low income who rely on the welfare state are often subject to unnecessary intrusion and scrutiny (Duncan 1996). Thus the private space that is ethnicised, gendered and classed represents disparate meanings to people with diverse social positioning.

The same is true for public buildings and public spaces. Women, for instance, do not have equal access to streets and parks to use free from fear for their safety, although they are alleged to be open to all people. Some racial and ethnic groups are even denied access to certain residential areas. Elizabeth Wilson (1991), describing the lives of women in the metropolis, portrays how some groups of the population who are denied access to the public spaces in the city have nevertheless adapted:

> although women, along with minorities, children, are still not full citizens in the sense that they have never been granted full and free access to the streets, industrial life drew them into the public life and they have survived and flourished in the interstices of the city, negotiating the contradictions of the city in their own particular way.
>
> (Wilson 1991: 8)

The way buildings are designed and used reflects the social purposes they are meant to serve. Through the design of the built environment, the existing social inequalities are reflected. Design of the built environment in general, for example, rests on stereotypical views about the roles of women and men and assumptions about their 'proper' places. It is assumed that men have no domestic responsibility and work away from the home. Women are perceived to look after homes, with caring responsibilities towards children, the elderly and the sick, and therefore do not work outside the home. Thus gender is regulated through the arrangement of urban space.

'Like gender,' Duncan argues, 'sexuality is often regulated by the binary distinction between public and private' (Duncan 1996: 137). While heterosexuality is universalised and naturalised and therefore made invisible, 'the other' – homosexuals – are expected to be restricted to private spaces. Valentine argues: 'It is usually assumed that sexuality is (and should be) confined to private spaces. This is based on the naturalisation of heterosexual norms. Naturalised heterosexuality makes sexuality in public spaces nearly invisible to the straight population' (Valentine 1993, in Duncan 1996: 137). The heterosexing of space that is invisible to heterosexuals but excludes lesbians and gays as 'the other' calls for denaturalisation of the sexuality of public places.

Therefore, the design and use of public spaces, public buildings and domestic architecture inevitably reflects the existing social inequalities, whether of gender, race, sex, class or any other. But it is a two-way process and the built environment in turn contributes in reinforcing and maintaining the existing inequalities (Matrix 1984; Weisman 1994; Greed 1994; Massey 1994).

Until recently, the meaning of the term 'space' was strictly geometrical: the idea it called forth was simply that of an empty area, and hence to speak of social space would have sounded strange (Lefebvre 1992). In recent years, however, there have been attempts to formulate concepts of space and place in terms of social relations.

Lefebvre (1992) argued that a 'unitary theory' was needed in order to discover or construct a theoretical unity between 'fields' which are apprehended separately: first, the *physical* – nature, the cosmos; second, the *mental*, including logical and formal abstractions; and, third, the *social*. There are now an increasing number of people from various disciplines (geography, anthropology, town planning and architecture, etc.) who have been treating space as a concept that is socially constructed and contested.

Massey, for instance, discusses the importance of regarding space not as some absolute independent dimension, but as constructed out of social relations. 'The spatial' is social relations 'stretched out' and it can be envisaged as 'constructed out of the multiplicity of social relations across all spatial scales' (Massey 1994: 2–4), from the global scope of finance and telecommunications to the social relations in the locality, e.g. the town, the neighbourhood or the household. In the conditions of modernity, the geography of social relations is changing, and increasingly they are stretched out over space. 'Economic, political and cultural social relations, each full of power and with internal structures of domination and subordination, stretched out over the planet at every different level, from the household to the local area to the international' (Massey 1994: 155). In conditions of modernity, the effects of global space–time compression have resulted in immense changes to the lives of vast numbers of people and local 'communities' in totally unexpected ways. Thus locales are thoroughly permeated and shaped by distant social influences (Massey 1994; Giddens 1990).

Alfred B. Parker (1965: 16) describes architecture as enclosing space so that beauty and utility become one. He, too, thinks that it is an accurate image of our society: 'Whatever we are is reflected by our buildings,' he says. 'There is no escaping the disconcerting fact that architecture mirrors society.'

Robert Rotenberg (1993a), on the other hand, underlines that people do not merely act in the world but try to understand it. They are in a constant effort to give meaning to their world, and this process is socially constituted which transforms space into place. People in cities impel the spaces around them to take on meaning. Thus no space is allowed to remain neutral – or homogeneous (Rotenberg 1993a: xiii; Kuper 1992: 421).

Indeed, once it is accepted that social life unfolds in space and it is seen in terms of social relations, it follows that space can be neither neutral nor homogeneous. People have different life experiences in the same space. Ethnicity, gender, class divisions and such factors as differences in lifestyles, beliefs, personal outlooks, state of health and stage in the life cycle all influence a particular person's experience of a particular place. Places are full of conflicts as a result of their multiple identities. When place is conceptualised in terms of social interactions, then it is not static: 'Space is not static, nor time spaceless' (Massey 1993: 155). It is dynamic and it is a *process*. And by its very nature it is full of power and symbolism, a complex web of relations of domination and subordination, of solidarity and co-operation as well as of conflicting interests (Massey 1994). Housing, for instance, is not a motionless 'end-product', e.g. frames standing apart from social life. They are contested, created processes, not simple products of plans. The process of public housing involves continuous decision-making in terms of design and management (allocation, repairs, transfers, etc.) which are based on experiences and beliefs of individual architects and planners, and the policies of institutions such as local authorities, housing associations and co-operatives. Housing process takes place within urban space. And urban space is constantly created and recreated as the spatial expression of economic, political and social processes at a level wider than the local. Composition of urban space reflects social relations such as those of class, gender, ethnicity and race and those inequalities embedded in them therefore can be exclusive and discriminatory. Design of the built environment not only mirrors the existing social inequalities based on differences of gender, ethnicity and class but can further contribute towards it.

Greed (1994) points out the duality of the process:

> It is a two-way process. The city is the product of the reproduction over space of social relations but, once built, the physical structure can, in turn, feed back its influence onto its inhabitants, by acting as a constraint on the nature of future societies living in that city because of the restrictions of its layout, street pattern, design and subculture.
>
> (Greed 1994: 87)

Policies keep such divisions reflecting unequal relations of power in the policy-making process and reinforce them in terms of spatial outcomes. Planning policies serve to reflect and influence the way societal divisions are reflected in space. In the existing built environment, social and cultural values are already embodied; the challenge is how to change them through policies and replace them with the social and cultural values we wish to see embodied in the built environment.

Conclusion

Those initiatives that attempt to democratise housing processes in an urban setting use notions such as 'the community' and 'empowerment', which have hidden assumptions. They homogenise social categories and groupings, fix boundaries and deny internal power differences and conflicts of interests. A range of dualisms resulting from dichotomous thinking keeps existing barriers between concepts and their spatial expressions. Often, however, the two sides of a dichotomy interrelate and overlap in daily life, while their shifting boundaries are denied by dichotomous thinking. Lefebvre (1992) calls for the reconstruction of a spatial 'code', that is of a language common to inhabitants and architects, as an immediate task. The first thing such a code would do, he suggests, is to break down such barriers as that between private and public.

If space reflects social relations, then it follows that social change needs to produce a new space, since social change and spatial change are intrinsic to each other. Intermeshing of constructs such as race, ethnicity, gender, class, sexuality, ability and age determines a particular person's experience of a particular place. Policies need to be developed that acknowledge and appreciate the multiple identities of the inhabitants and aim to produce places whose full identity is a complex mix of all the multiple identities.

Acknowledgements

I would like to thank my supervisors, Nira Yuval-Davis, Professor of Ethnicity and Gender, and Anthony Quiney, Professor of Architectural History, at the University of Greenwich for their support and helpful comments in my PhD research on which this article is based.

Notes

1 Recent research into the issues of social exclusion in London points out that 2.5 per cent of white households live in overcrowded conditions, whereas the figure is 16.9 per cent for black African households, 22.8 per cent for Pakistani households and 53.8 per cent for Bangladeshi households. See *Barriers: Social and Economic Exclusion in London*, London Pamphlet 2, London Voluntary Service Council (LVSC), 1998.
2 In Britain the planning profession is predominantly white and male. According to a 1988 profile of the Royal Town Planning Institute, only 18 per cent of

planners are women. Women members are not evenly spread over the age groups while men are. Women comprise a third of all members in the age group 25–34, whereas they comprise one in ten in the age group 40–50 and just one in twenty of those over fifty years of age. Women are under-represented at the higher levels in that only 1.6 per cent of chief planning officers are women. The percentage of disabled members is less than 1, and relatively few members are from minority ethnic groups (Greed 1994; Nadin and Jones 1990; Cullingworth and Nadin 1994).

References

Anthias, F. (1996) *Rethinking Social Divisions: Or, What's So Important about Gender, Ethnicity, 'Race' and Class?*, inaugural lecture, London: University of Greenwich Press.

Anthias, F. and Yuval-Davis, N. (1992) *Racialized Boundaries: Race, Nation, Gender, Colour and Class and the Anti-Racist Struggle*, London: Routledge.

Bhavnani, K. (1993) 'Towards a multi-cultural Europe?: "race", nation and identity in 1992 and beyond', *Feminist Review* 45: 30–45.

Brownhill, S. (1997) 'Regen(d)eration: women and urban policy in the UK', paper presented at the 'Women and the City' conference, Oxford Brooks University, Oxford, England.

Clarke, V. (1994) *Getting Black Tenants Involved: A Good Practice Guide*, London: Co-operative and Tenant Controlled Housing (Catch).

Collins, P.H. (1990) *Black Feminist Thought: Knowledge, Consciousness, and the Politics of Empowerment*, London: Unwin Hyman.

Collins, P.H. (1997) 'The more things change, the more they stay the same', special lecture given at the University of East London, London, England.

Cross, M. and Keith, M. (eds) (1993) *Racism, the City and the State*, London: Routledge.

Cullingworth, J.B. and Nadin, V. (1994) *Town and Country Planning in Britain* (11th edn), London: Routledge.

Department of the Environment (1972) *How Do You Want to Live? A Report on Human Habitat*, London: HMSO.

Duncan, N. (1996) 'Renegotiating gender and sexuality in public and private spaces', in N. Duncan (ed.) *Bodyspace: Destabilizing Geographies of Gender and Sexuality*, London: Routledge.

Fraser, N. (1996) 'Gender equity and welfare state: postindustrial thought experiment', in S. Benhabib (ed.) *Democracy and Difference: Contesting the Boundaries of the Political*, Princeton, New Jersey: Princeton University Press.

Giddens, A. (1990) *The Consequences of Modernity*, Cambridge: Polity.

Ginsburg, N. (1992) 'Racism and housing: concepts and reality', in P. Braham, A. Rattansi and R. Skellington (eds) *Racism and Anti-racism: Inequalities, Opportunities and Policies*, London: Sage in association with the Open University.

Greed, C. H. (1994) *Women and Planning: Creating Gendered Realities*, London: Routledge.

Harvey, D. (1994) *The Urban Experience*, Oxford: Blackwell.

Healey, P. (1992) 'Town planning in the 21st century', paper presented at South Bank University, London.

Hill, D. M. (1994) *Citizens and Cities*, London: Harvester Wheatsheaf.

hooks, b. (1990) *Yearning: Race, Gender and Cultural Politics*, Boston: South End Press.
Jacobs, B.D. (1992)*Fractured Cities, Capitalism, Community and Empowerment in Britain and America*, London: Routledge.
Karl, M. (1995) *Women and Empowerment: Participation and Decision Making*, London: Zed Books.
Keith, M. and Pile, S. (1993) *Place and the Politics of Identity*, London: Routledge.
Kuper, H. (1972) 'The language of sites in the politics of spaces', *American Anthropologist* 74: 411–24.
Lefebvre, H. (1992) *The Production of Space* (2nd edn), Oxford: Blackwell.
McDowell, L. and Pringle, R. (1992) 'Introduction: recognizing difference', in L. McDowell and R. Pringle (eds) *Defining Women, Social Institutions and Gender Divisions*, Cambridge: Polity/Open University.
Massey, D. (1993) 'Politics and space/time', in M. Keith and S. Pile (eds) *Place and the Politics of Identity*, London: Routledge.
Massey, D. (1994) *Space, Place and Gender*, Cambridge: Polity.
Matrix (1984) *Making Space, Women and the Man Made Environment*, London: Pluto.
Morris, J. and Winn, M. (1990) *Housing and Social Inequality*, London: Hilary Shipman.
Mouffe, C. (1988) 'Radical democracy: modern or postmodern?', in A. Ross (ed.) *Universal Abandon? The Politics of Postmodernism*, Minneapolis: University of Minnesota.
Nadin, V. and Jones, S. (1990) 'A profile of the profession', *The Planner* 76 (3): 13–24.
Parker, A.B. (1965) *You and Architecture: A Practical Guide to the Best in Building*, New York: Delacorte Press.
Phillips, A. (1993) *Democracy and Difference*, Cambridge: Polity.
Quiney, A. (1986) *House and Home. A History of the Small English House*, London: BBC.
Rodman, M. (1993) 'Beyond built form and culture in the anthropological study of residential community spaces', in R. Rotenberg and G. McDonough (eds) *The Cultural Meaning of Urban Space*, London: Bergin and Garvey.
Rotenberg, R. (1993a) 'Introduction', in R. Rotenberg and G. McDonough (eds)*The Cultural Meaning of Urban Space*, London: Bergin and Garvey.
Rotenberg, R. and McDonough, G. (eds) (1993b)*The Cultural Meaning of Urban Space*, London: Bergin and Garvey.
Royal Town Planning Institute/Commission for Racial Equality (1983) *Planning for a Multi-Racial Britain*, London: RTPI/CRE.
Shapiro, I. and Kymlicka, W. (1997) *Ethnicity and Group Rights*, New York: New York University Press.
Smith, S. (1989) *The Politics of Race and Residence*, Oxford: Polity.
Valentine, G. (1992) '(Hetero)sexising space: lesbian perceptions and experiences of everyday spaces', *Environment and Planning: Society and Space* 11: 395–413.
Vincent, N. and Jones, S. (1990) 'A profile of the profession', *The Planner* 76 (3): 13–24.
Wajcman, J. (1991) *Feminism Confronts Technology*, Cambridge: Polity.

Weisman, L.K. (1994) *Discrimination by Design: A Feminist Critique of the Man-Made Environment*, Chicago: University of Illinois Press.

Williams, R. (1973) *The Country and the City*, New York: Oxford University Press.

Wilson, E. (1991) *The Sphinx in the City: Urban Life, the Control of Disorder and Women*, London: Virago Press.

Young, I.M. (1990a) *Justice and the Politics of Difference*, Princeton: Princeton University Press.

Young, I.M. (1990b) 'The ideal of community and the politics of difference', in L.J. Nicholson (ed.) *Feminism and Postmodernism*, London: Routledge.

Young, I.M. (1997) 'Deferring group representation', in I. Shapiro and W. Kymlicka (eds) *Ethnicity and Group Rights*, New York: New York University Press.

Yuval-Davis, N. (1994) 'Women, ethnicity and empowerment', in K. Bhavnani and A. Phoenix (eds) *Shifting Identities, Shifting Racisms*, London: Sage.

Yuval-Davis, N. (1997) *Gender and Nation*, London: Sage.

5 Is there a space for gender in modernist planning?

Tovi Fenster

Introduction

This chapter challenges the underlying assumption of modernist planning that space is neutral and absolute by exploring how space is constructed culturally on a gender base. The chapter shows how ignoring these meanings in modernist planning negatively affects women of cultural minorities.

To highlight these points the chapter analyses gender as a cultural construction and reconstruction of space among Bedouin society in the Negev Desert in southern Israel. It focuses in particular on changing meanings and boundaries between 'forbidden' and 'permitted' spaces, a definition which came about in discussions held with Bedouin women in the Negev. These meanings and perceptions are critically analysed in the light of the 'modernity planning project' which has gradually moved Bedouin from spontaneous settlements to seven government towns in the last forty years.

The chapter explores how spaces are culturally and gender constructed so that for Bedouin women there are 'forbidden' and 'permitted' spaces. In addition, the chapter explores how these Western modernist planning assumptions serve as a double or an increased control over Bedouin women which is expressed in boundary reformulating between 'forbidden' and 'permitted' spaces in the towns. The chapter concludes with looking at how cultural constructions of space should become the very first topic that planners should look at when planning for cultural minorities.

The Bedouin in the Negev

Fifty thousand of the 100,000 Bedouin in the Negev live in seven government towns: Rahat, Tel Sheva, Kasifa, Aruer, Segev Shalom, Hura and Lakia. According to the authorities, these towns were established so that modern infrastructure and social services could be provided for the Bedouin population in concentrated areas. The remaining 45,000 live in some 108 spontaneous settlements scattered over the area and are considered 'illegal' by the authorities (Ministry of Housing 1995).

Spontaneous settlements are considered far more successful than professionally designed environments in their response to the cultural needs and socio-economic priorities of their inhabitants (Rappoport 1978; Turner 1976). The move to the new towns brought with it great social and cultural changes. Tents or other temporary structures for dwellings were replaced by stone and concrete houses in neighbourhoods organised on a tribal basis, in which residential density became much greater than was the case in the previous spontaneous settlements. These changes had a tremendous impact on Bedouin society at large, but have affected women even more dramatically. Great changes in the Bedouin economic lifestyle have also resulted. Most Bedouin have ceased to work in traditional agriculture and sheep herding (7 per cent) and have turned to modern forms of employment such as: construction (33 per cent), public services (15 per cent) and industry (15 per cent); about 70 per cent of those employed work outside the town they inhabit (Ministry of Housing 1995).

Spaces in Israel in general are strongly classified. A strict concern with separation and order (Sibley 1992) means that control is sometimes an important priority in the planning of space. This is most noticeable in development policies and planning schemes for non-Jewish ethnic groups, i.e. Palestinian Arabs and Bedouin. It is clearly expressed in the long-drawn-out disputes over ownership of land on which the Bedouin live. Both the state and Bedouins stake their claims to this land, each invoking relevant traditions of laws and amendments to prove ownership, and in the meantime Bedouin are evacuated from the land they live on. Then, a second means of control of space is expressed in the lack of choice of lifestyle for Bedouin. The only alternatives they have are to live in the towns built by the state or risk remaining in spontaneous settlements defined as illegal. Lack of choice has proved to be one of the fundamental flaws of modernised planning.

The effects of the move to towns on the Bedouin way of life has been discussed elsewhere (e.g. Fenster 1993, 1997; Meir 1986a, 1986b; Ben David 1993, 1995). This chapter focuses on how the move to towns negatively affected the gendered reconstruction of space and the reformulation of boundaries between private and public, forbidden and permitted spaces.

Gender and culture within the context of modernist planning

The state modernity project for the resettling of Bedouin exemplifies the use of planning schemes as a means of control over an ethnic group. Here planning is acting as a regressive agent of change (Yiftacheal 1994). This typically occurs in segregated societies with non-assimilated ethnic groups, where one of the fundamental issues of planning is the use of land. It has undoubtedly occurred in Western pluralistic democratic societies, although usually transpiring in relatively subtle ways, mainly influenced by market mechanisms (Harvey 1973) or male dominance (Fincher 1990; Sandercock and Forsyth 1996).

Modernist planning derives out of the procedural planning theory. This theory represents a modernist outlook on society, emphasising a rational comprehensive approach to planning, a formal, top-down process that ignores the 'others' – the marginalised – and therefore pays less attention to social relations and their expressions in space. It views society as one homogeneous entity rather than looking more deeply into its social and cultural structures. The planning procedure is an end in itself, dictated by planners' perceptions and ideas. In this type of Western modernist theory, the process and direction of change are seen as predetermined, while notions of empowerment and forms of social and environmental relations are ignored. Furthermore modernised planning thus involves an autonomous process of change rather than being a product of the integration of pre-modernised cultural codes, norms, values, social relations and environmental attitudes. This type of planning is insensitive to the complexities of processes of change.

Such a planning approach of control was employed when the Bedouin were forced to move to concentrated, densely populated towns rather than being allowed to choose small rural villages similar to spontaneous settlements for their new homes. The modernised approach was expressed in the basic assumption that Bedouin cultural norms, such as housing density, neighbourhood proximity, distance between tribes and women's modesty, would change and therefore did not need to be taken into consideration. This ignorance of cultural constructions of space within planning frameworks only created a double control over women. They were controlled as part of Bedouin society and they became more restricted by men who, themselves ambivalent about the transition, formed 'guards of honour' to further shield their women in the new realities of the modernised towns.

Progressive planning, in contrast, approaches the planning process not merely as a formal top-down exercise, but rather as an ongoing dialogue between institutions and beneficiary groups. This process serves as a means to achieve the social and political goals of people involved in the planning process, building beneficiary capacity and empowerment, and allowing equal access to resources. This approach includes: advocacy planning, negotiated planning, critical planning and radical planning (Alterman 1994). It derives from a postmodernist view of society, which challenges the 'grand theory' of modernism, emphasising the particular and the local (Ley 1989). Because of its pluralistic nature, this planning approach takes into consideration meanings of space in planning procedures.

Planning theory which perceives modernisation as a goal is criticised by feminists, who see such theory as a male bastion (Sandercock and Forsyth 1996). Modernistic components such as residential zoning which emphasise the division of home from work, or the distinction between down-town and neighbourhood, are seen as reiterating and reinforcing the

72 Tovi Fenster

familiar distinctions between the male and female spheres (Fainstein 1996). Still, there are diverse opinions as to where the analysis of gender is relevant, especially regarding the economic status of women; how women are located and move through space; the connection between capitalist production and patriarchal relationships and between 'public' and 'private' life; how women know about the world and how much they learn to define their needs; and what forms of communication women are most comfortable with (Sandercock and Forsyth 1996).

What is the significance of feminist contributions to planning theory? It is perhaps in highlighting the control over women in particular ethnic groups in planning policy, and the negative effects this has had on women. This is the reason why Friedman (1996) suggests radical planning as an appropriate planning approach, with the aim of achieving equality and emancipation. Another point of interaction between gender and progressive planning is the necessity to highlight the relevance of 'difference' in planning theories, how differences among people should be taken into account in practice (Moore Millroy 1996). This means taking the plural nature of a society into consideration in planning. Sandercock and Forsyth (1996) call it 'planning for multiple publics', at the centre of which is the 'acknowledgment and celebration of difference'. They consider this new planning theory the most significant theme in the rethinking of planning in the 1990s and on. This chapter attempts to make a modest contribution to the process of rethinking planning approaches by analysing the impact of private/public boundary remaking on the spatial movement of Bedouin women in the process of modernised planning.

'Private' and 'public' spaces as cultural constructions of the 'forbidden' and the 'permitted' spaces among Muslim societies

The purpose of this section is to discuss the contested dichotomies of 'private' and 'public' spaces and to show how these Westernised terms are culturally constructed into 'forbidden' and 'permitted' spaces in the Muslim culture.

There has been much debate over the categories which define boundaries between a household and a market economy as 'private', and boundaries between a citizen's political participation and the state as 'public' (Pratt 1994). Habermas provides the most influential distinctions between the two spheres in early and welfare state capitalist societies, emphasising the changes in importance given to each component (Habermas 1975). Feminists are critical of theoretical accounts which rigidify conceptual separations between public and private spheres without tracing gender components, since such theories only perpetuate gender inequalities (Pratt 1994).

Definitions of 'public' and 'private' spaces are extremely varied. From simplistic definitions, such as 'private' equalling 'home' and 'public' signifying 'outside the home', to more complex definitions, they all relate to the cultural context of the society in question. Boundaries between 'public' and 'private' change from one society to another, and from one group in a society to another group in the same society (Ardener 1993). What determine the boundary-making between the two spheres are generally cultural codes which create spaces containing specific meanings subjective to that society's members.

A definition of culture is complex, since it is both an abstract and a global concept. In the literature, a variety of definitions exist, according to the field of research and to different theoretical approaches. Culture is defined by Cosgrove and Jackson (1987, in Mitchell 1995: 99) as: 'the medium through which people transform the mundane phenomenon of the material world into a world of significant symbols to which they give meaning and attach values'. In 1989, Jackson suggested a 'working definition' of culture: 'the level at which social groups develop distinct patterns of life'. Cultures, says Jackson, are 'maps of meanings' through which the world is made intelligible (Jackson 1989: 2). Mitchell (1995) presents some twenty definitions of culture, saying that in most cases culture is symbolic, active, constantly subject to change and riven through with relations of power. Culture is represented in terms of spheres, maps, levels or domains. It becomes a medium of meaning and action. Culture is everything!

In many Moslem societies, the cultural constraints that are applied to women are stricter and the boundaries between private and public spheres are sharper than for men. In Iran, for example, many public areas are now sex-segregated, including schools and universities (Tohidi 1991). These restrictions are intensifying in Islamic fundamentalist countries (Beller-Hann 1995), not because the roots of the religion entail women's oppression, as commonly thought in the West, but because political ideals in Muslim countries use religion to restrict women's lives (Afshar 1996).

The practice of the veil is one of the explicit symbols of Islamic fundamentalism which serves as a means to define boundaries between 'private' and 'public'. How the actual imposition of the veil came about is disputed (Mernissi 1991). In several countries, such as contemporary Iran, all women, including non-Muslims and foreigners, are obliged by law to wear the veil and observe traditional Islamic *hejab* (complete covering of women). But in countries where this practice is not compulsory, such as Egypt or Turkey, women also dress traditionally for various reasons and the specific meaning attached to this practice varies according to its cultural and ideological context (Mohanty 1991). It is not possible, therefore, to assume that the mere practice of veiling women in Muslim countries indicates the universal oppression of women. In Iran, women veiled themselves during the 1979 revolution as an act of opposition to the Shah and Western culture colonisation (Tohidi 1991), while today Islamic laws dictate that all Iranian women wear a veil (Afshar 1996). For many Muslim women, the veil is a symbol of Islamification and of their revivalist ideals. For them the veil is liberating, and not an oppressive force (Afshar 1996). For others, the practice of veiling solves the problem of their desire to move freely, on the one hand, in 'public' and still acknowledge the cultural, religious restrictions imposed on them, on the other.

In Cairo, Macleod (1990) observed that young educated middle-class women choose to dress traditionally when they leave the house to go to work, in spite of the fact that this code is not demanded by the 'guards of honour' in their society (husbands, fathers-in-law, parents). The paradoxical situation that Macleod identifies is that these women, on the edge of modernity, use the symbol of their inferiority (as approached by Western feminism) in order to broaden the space of their activities outside the home. The function of the veil expands the 'boundaries of public space' for Moslem women living in severe restriction. As such, Muslim women have succeeded in adapting to fundamentalist laws by creating laws of their own regarding 'private' within 'public' by wearing the veil and the *hejab*. Veiled women feel less exposed to verbal or physical male abuse when using public transportation or when moving anywhere in a public space (Abu Odeh 1993). Both Afshar (1996) and Abu Odeh (1993) see the veil in the context of Third World feminism, as a mechanism that permits both spatial mobility for women and a sense of social and psychological safety. The veil enables women to become the observers and not the observed (Afshar 1996), and it provides a short-term and immediate practical solution which, though not replacing the long-term feminist struggle for equality and liberation, is not merely a sign of oppression but allows for women's modesty and gives them a means to navigate in the public arena.

This explanation is not new. Already in the eighteenth and nineteenth centuries, writings of Western women travelling in Mediterranean countries used the same explanation. The veil is related to as a mechanism of freedom. The covering of the face does not separate women from the world but rather mediates between the woman and the public space, and eases her movement outside the home. Some Western women writers perceived the Near and Middle Eastern woman as a symbol of liberation. According to their writings, the veil increased safety and spatial mobility. These Western women travellers compared their safety in Middle Eastern cities with their sense of insecurity in the West (Melman 1995).

Boundaries between private and public may be determined not only by cultural codes but also by codes of safety or fear. Feminist geographers such as Valentine (1989) and Pain (1991) have examined the effects of women's fears of attack on their mobility, and the relationship between women's fear of male violence and their perception and use of public space. Areas of safety are perceived to be 'private space' while unsafe areas are perceived to be 'public' (Ardener 1993). The meaning of spaces changes at different times of the day. Pred and Palm (1978) note that while women move freely in central areas of big cities during the day, the message is that they should not move in these areas at night if they want to avoid exposure to violence (also in Valentine 1989; Pain 1991). The control by men of public space in the evenings means that despite the career success and independence gained by some women in the past decades, fear of male violence deters the majority of women from being independent. Women's inhibited use and occupation of public space is seen as a spatial expression of patriarchy (Valentine 1989).

The Bedouin way of life in the Middle East in general is expressed in issues of territory and space. Some researchers presume that the fact that the Bedouin are nomadic reflects an aterritorial approach to land (Rappoport 1978). Others claim that this mechanism of spatial mobility resolves social conflicts by reducing the chances of unwanted meetings between rival tribes. The transition from a nomadic to a settled lifestyle has redesigned the relationship to territoriality by increasing interaction. This has caused many difficulties as the different tribes have been forced into proximity, and the Bedouin have in many cases been unable to deal appropriately with resulting conflicts (Bar 1989). Forced settlement has often proved destructive, even causing psychotic disturbances (Rappoport 1978). It has resulted in a need for immediate remedies on the part of the Bedouin for dealing with traumatic transition, such as becoming more religious or creating additional, stricter social rules. These changes, and particularly the increase in housing density, have made authority constraints stricter and, therefore, the whole process of forced settlement more destructive for women. This crisis will be further examined in the next section.

Studies dealing with gender in nomadic societies in the Middle East have distinguished between private space – the tent, which is considered women's space – and public space – the *ma'ahal* (a collection of tents), which is considered men's space – and have determined that because women have no role in the public space they are in an inferior position to men. However, other studies have opposed this distinction, suggesting that women have political power and influence in spite of their spatial limitations. All agree, however, that women have a passive role in the determination of their lives (Lewando-Hundt 1984).

Bedouin constructions of 'private' and 'public' spaces illustrate the relationships between these dichotomies and the 'forbidden' and the 'permitted'. The Bedouin define 'private' as the tent or home. But when a stranger enters the 'private' area, this area becomes 'public', and thus 'forbidden' to the women who live there, according to Bedouin codes. Even inside her home the Bedouin woman has to 'escape' to a modest space, so that she will not be visible. Waltzer's definition expresses very well the Bedouin definition of 'public' space as: the space we share with strangers, people who aren't our relatives, friends or work associates (1986, cited in Valentine 1989). Sibley (1995) suggests that boundary-making depends on how the outsider is perceived in relation to the host's conception of privacy in a particular culture. These subtle ambiguities, present in questions of gender and space as a cultural expression, serve as an example of the way in which planners need to familiarise themselves with cultural mores in order to accommodate the needs of ethnic groups.

The role of the veil for many Bedouin women living in planned settlements in the Middle East, in general, is similar to that for women in many Muslim countries. Bedouin women must cover their heads in order to go outside their home. But, unlike in these other Muslim societies, while the head-covering is part of a basic traditional cultural code, it does not facilitate spatial mobility. The need to safeguard the honour of women generally dictates the boundaries between private and public space. But for Bedouin women living in the new towns in the Negev, high residential density has created an increased likelihood of unwanted random meetings in the public space, which would not have occurred in the more spacious environment of the old spontaneous settlements. Traditional cultural constraints limit their movement in towns planned according to modern planning approaches which do not consider the ethnic and cultural needs of such societies.

A comparable reduction in women's freedom of movement has occurred among Bedouin in the new settlements built in Jordan, Egypt, Saudi Arabia and Iran (Rappoport 1978). The closer the proximity of other neighbourhoods, the greater becomes the severity of cultural constraints applied to women. The study of Lila Abu Lughod (1986) of a group of Bedouin in Egypt demonstrates this trend. The planned Bedouin settlements in Egypt are not as isolated as in the past, and they receive more visitors because of trade and commerce among men. Because of cultural codes that forbid women any contact, even eye contact, with men, more Bedouin women in planned settlements in Egypt wear the veil than was the case when they lived in traditional settlements, and their mobility is limited to the domestic arena. In other words, 'permitted' space has been reduced with the transition to permanent settlements, such that Bedouin women have undergone a most difficult transition. Restrictions in movement mean that they feel unable even to use social and welfare services located outside their neighbourhoods to overcome these difficulties. The transition to permanent settlements has worsened women's status and self-image because traditional roles no longer obtain, leading to a sense of worthlessness (Abu Lughod 1986, 1993). Patriarchal thinking determines the women's freedom of lifestyle.

Bedouin men's mobility in Egypt is limited neither within the planned settlements nor beyond. Codes of morality and modesty are not as strict for Bedouin men as they are for women. Nevertheless, there are other cultural constraints that limit Bedouin men's mobility. In the Negev, the Bedouin live in neighbourhoods within towns according to tribal affilia-

Space for gender in modernist planning 77

tion, and men avoid moving in other neighbourhoods, not because of modesty but rather because of accepted traditional rules of territoriality. Accordingly, one does not move in the territory of another tribe uninvited. But, unlike for women, men's limitations do not affect their ability to perform their double role (productive and community roles, see Moser 1993) whereas the limitation on women's mobility harms their ability to fulfil their 'triple' roles (reproductive, productive and community management, see Moser 1993) because they lack access to services.

Redefining the boundaries of 'private' and 'public' space in modernised towns has drastically affected Bedouin cultural norms. Such boundaries are evident in most cultures (Sibley 1995). Among societies where cultural codes are more strict, in a *gemeinschaft*, using Sibley's phrase, i.e. in a group with a closed, tightly knit community, the boundaries between public and private space will be more strict, especially when the community's identity is threatened by changing them. The 'modernity project' in the Negev has threatened Bedouin culture by producing high residential density where the new boundaries increase the likelihood of unwanted meetings, supplanting deeply engrained cultural codes concerning women's modesty. Accordingly, to compensate for this, the boundaries of private and public have become stricter in the new towns: larger areas are designated now as 'public' areas, forbidden to Bedouin women, though they are very close to a 'private' area, and women are subject to new cultural restrictions that were previously unnecessary.

The reconstruction of 'forbidden' and 'permitted' spaces among Bedouin in the Negev – results of fieldwork

Perceptions of the shortcomings of modernised planning in the new Bedouin towns have led to an increasing realisation of the benefits of progressive planning, which would take into account the need to include Bedouin participation in the planning stages to address their ethnic needs with greater sensitivity. The following analysis of the reconstruction of private and public spaces among Bedouin in the Negev is based on fieldwork carried out among Bedouin towns in 1994. This fieldwork was part of a study undertaken to prepare a 'Development Plan for the Bedouin Settlements in the Negev' for the Ministry of Housing. As the fieldwork progressed, it became increasingly obvious that participation should not only encompass ethnic needs, but gender issues also. The approach adopted for the plan was a marketing approach, along the lines of thinking of progressive planning. The Bedouin town was perceived as a product which should meet the needs of its consumers – the town residents.

The research method made use of questionnaires filled out by a statistical sample of the town's male residents. Access to women was limited by the fact that they could not be interviewed alone by people outside their own tribe. Therefore, the study among Bedouin women was achieved using a technique of focus groups in which the researcher met with ten to fifteen women together, from similar socio-economic backgrounds, and they discussed various issues in an open-ended fashion. Four such focus group meetings were carried out with Bedouin women in the towns. Generally, women from the same extended family or tribe took part in each meeting. They were mostly young (not older than 35), educated, and some were married. None of the women worked and all came from financially well-off families. About half the women (mainly from Rahat) were educated (most had completed high school). These women were married to educated men. The issues raised in these meetings concerned the adequacy of the 'modernity project' in relating to the lives and needs of women. Most issues and problems were raised by the women themselves.

As an Askenazi (European) Jewish woman, carrying out research among Bedouin for the government of Israel raises many questions regarding my positionality and ability to represent the community. To what extent would my position and power allow for open dialogue? I take Kobayashi's position (1994) that the question is not whether our position of power and authority denies us the right to conduct research but, rather, how we use our privilege to social ends. For me, the fight to include the voice of Bedouin women in this work has not been easy in a country where official planning systems, using a modernised planning approach, ignore issues of 'otherness' and representation, especially when a non-Jewish ethnic minority is involved. I chose to address this particular dilemma by focusing not on difference but on communality (Kobayashi 1994), taking the view that as women in a male-dominated Israeli society we all face various types of oppression, either social, cultural, religious or spatial. The four focus groups in fact expressed great relief to be working with, and more freedom to speak to, a woman outsider.

The following analysis is a summary of the main issues raised in the focus groups, regarding the construction of 'forbidden' and 'permitted' spaces and the adequacy of the 'modernity project' to meet Bedouin women's needs. The material is analysed first by relating to all Bedouin women at four levels: home, neighbourhood, town and region. An analysis of the comparative spatial mobility of different Bedouin women is then presented.

Gender mobility between the 'forbidden' and the 'permitted' at different levels of space

The domestic level

The domestic area (usually the tent) was traditionally considered 'private space', the security of which was guarded carefully by the Bedouin (Bar 1989). The area of the tent or home provided protection. If a man passed over the boundary into the domestic area, he would receive the protection of the head of the household and be considered a guest who would be sheltered by the owner. But this meant that the 'private' area would become 'public' when a guest entered the tent or home. The area where the guest sits is forbidden to women. Within the domestic space, some say that ten steps from the tent is the boundary of the 'private'; others define the boundary as the point at which the voice of a man requesting shelter can be heard, or measure the boundary in a fifteen-metre radius from the tent (Havakuk 1986).

With the transition to towns, boundaries of private space were reduced significantly. In the new towns most housing plots are located near to each other and are not greater than one dunam in size (0.1 hectare). Increasing residential density in towns, relative to the dispersed way of life in spontaneous settlements, drastically changed the boundaries between 'private' and 'public', both because of the greater fear that codes of honour would be violated, and because neighbourhood conflicts could not be reduced by distance between extended families. The effects of increased density were frequently alluded to by the Bedouin men. More than 80 per cent of the questionnaire respondents claimed that both plot size and distance between plots were too small.

The fact that residential density reaches two to three housing units per dunam means that Bedouin women usually live with parents-in-law or with the husband's family, and such living arrangements increase the feeling of confinement. Housing density also influences the degree of mobility in the public space because women are not free to move where men from outside their family congregate. The women in the focus groups said that this density was suffocating, and there were a number of young families in Rahat who were planning to move to a smaller plot in another area of the neighbourhood, just to get away from family supervision and control. While extended families could comfortably live in physical proximity in spontaneous settlements, high housing density makes it more difficult to tolerate in towns. Not only do families live in close proximity to one another, but extended families very often live in the same house (on different floors), whereas in spontaneous settlements each nuclear family would have a separate domestic unit. Lewando-Hundt (1984) points out that the move to towns increases the possibility for conflicts between wives and mothers-in-law concerning the organisation of the extended family life because they live in such close proximity to each other.

A second issue raised was that in spontaneous settlements the 'public' area does not threaten codes of honour and modesty as it does in the towns, because the chances of unwanted meetings are less than in the more densely built-up areas of the towns. Third, the increasing demand for public services such as education and health has resulted in a greater movement in the public space.

The neighbourhood level

Neighbourhoods are divided according to tribal affiliation, with extended families receiving a block of plots from the authorities. A typical Bedouin neighbourhood is planned around cul-de-sacs to avoid unwanted interactions. Such a confined area may be the only 'public' space open to Bedouin women in the towns. Most women in the focus groups can move freely within their neighbourhood; they do most of their daily shopping for bread and dairy products in the neighbourhood, while clothing and shoes are purchased in the nearby cities. The move to the new towns has changed the division of labour between couples. In spontaneous settlements men shopped for all goods, because the distance to service centres was large and the means of transportation few. By contrast, in the towns women are responsible for shopping because services are closer and public transportation from towns to nearby centres is more frequent (Lewando-Hundt 1984). But the women spend most hours of the day within the neighbourhood boundaries, and the sense of suffocation is therefore more serious for them than for men, who for reasons of employment spend much of the day outside the neighbourhood.

Density in the neighbourhoods and increased strictness of authority constraints have limited women's ability to enjoy the use of newly introduced services. Women do not feel comfortable in the public areas. Using Davis and Anderson's terminology (in Sibley 1995) the high-density network created in the new towns is strong, and gossip can strongly affect a family's standing in the community. So it can happen that parents do not always send their daughters to co-educational high schools for fear of unwanted meetings with males from other tribes and the rapid spread of rumours about such meetings. The result is that one of the requests of the women in the focus groups was that single-sex high schools be built for girls.

The town level

The high residential density in towns, and the fact that the Bedouin live very close to groups of other origins, increases the risks that codes of modesty will be violated because of the greater possibility of unwanted encounters. Such cultural constraints have reconstructed the boundaries of 'private' space. The town as a whole is a forbidden space for most women. Most women in the focus groups did not know any other neighbourhoods aside from their own. Bedouin women do not know or use services in other neighbourhoods, and most, aside from a few women in Rahat, the largest of the new towns, have no social relationships in other neighbourhoods.

An indication of the ineptitude of the modernised planners in creating appropriate public spaces for the resettled Bedouin is clearly seen in the

Space for gender in modernist planning 81

fact that a large modern park-like area was built in Rahat, away from the residential areas, and nobody visits it. Assize's story illustrates the fact that the complexity of culturally constructed space in Bedouin society creates forbidden spaces for women. She is 32, with four children, university-educated and works in a profession:

> One afternoon, my kids were bored and being naughty, as there is no playground in the neighbourhood, so I thought why not take them to the park that we have at the entrance to the town. You know, it is so beautiful, full of grass and flowers ... very pleasant. After all, why do we need this if we can't use it? So I went for the first time with my kids and after maybe ten or fifteen minutes my husband came hurrying to take me back to the neighbourhood. He was angry, and told me: 'Don't you know it is forbidden?' Apparently, his brother drove along the road and saw me, and went straight to my husband to tell him.

Public spaces such as parks in Bedouin towns have other functions than in Western-style towns. They cannot be used for recreation, because of the increased risk of unwanted meetings. So women's private space has shrunk, and their spatial mobility ends in their neighbourhood, with the next step in their spatial hierarchy only being other cities in the region – Be'er Sheva, Hebron and Daharia, which they visit occasionally.

The regional level

Almost all the women in the focus groups travel to Be'er Sheva, Hebron and Daharia once every two to four weeks to shop, always with other women or with their husbands. Women of Rahat go more often than do women of other towns. The explanation is that, while the proximity to other groups in the towns is what increases the fear of violation of traditional codes, the anonymity in other towns is greater. While the use of public spaces within towns is more restricted, travelling to public areas of cities nearby does not demand the same rules of modesty. It creates a fascinating spatial mobility pattern in the time–space model, in which Bedouin women's mobility is very limited within the town, but other cities, which are large and anonymous, are considered less 'public' in terms of codes of modesty than neighbourhoods in the town itself. As mentioned earlier, the wearing of a head-covering among Bedouin women is a prerequisite and, unlike for women in other Moslem countries, is not a means of expanding their public space.

The curious 'gap' in the hierarchy of spatial mobility demonstrates that for Bedouin women there is no direct relationship between distance and boundary formulations of public spaces. A more distant place may be considered more 'private', and therefore allowing women more mobility, than a place close by. The case of Bedouin women demonstrates that direct relationships do not necessarily exist between the distance between spaces and the cultural openness of their society.

Differences among Bedouin women – expressions in spatial mobility

Bedouin women, of course, cannot be looked at as one homogeneous group. There are many differences to be examined which involve age, tribal origin, socio-economic status and the length of time they have lived in urbanised settings. The gender construction of space may be different for older women than for young educated women married to educated men: they are more free to move around. Different tribes have different customs and laws, and women who have lived in the new towns for longer tend to have adapted variously to more open lifestyles.

Middle-aged traditional Bedouin women

A small number of the women who took part in the focus groups were older women who had married at a very young age (usually when they began to menstruate) and who now have ten to twelve children. These women never received education. Most rarely left their domestic area, and some still live in houses that do not have electricity or running water. Their days generally begin in the early hours of the morning when they heat water for their husband and children and bake bread. Some of them are the first wives of men who have subsequently married additional women and they accept this situation with submission. These women live according to very strict cultural roles, and for them public space beyond their neighbourhood does not exist. Most of them rarely visited nearby towns or any big cities in Israel.

Urbanised Bedouin women – women living in Rahat

Women living in Rahat, the largest and second oldest Bedouin new town, have a level of services which is higher and therefore are afforded greater mobility than women in smaller towns. Having also lived in a town environment for a longer period, their movement in urbanised space has become less restricted than that of women in smaller and newer towns. The women from Rahat who were interviewed in the study were not older than 35, most were married mothers, almost all had elementary and high school education, and none worked outside the home. Most mentioned that they go to shops and the bank in the town centre. The size of Rahat (27,000 inhabitants in 1996) somewhat reduces the chance of unwanted meetings compared to smaller towns, and some women can go to visit friends in nearby neighbourhoods. This group does not represent all the

Bedouin women in the towns. In discussions with other women (not as part of focus groups) it was clear that there are differing cultural constraints among tribes, with resultant variety in spatial mobility. Some tribes are more restricted by cultural codes than others and allow women less freedom to move in spaces outside their neighbourhoods.

What characterised the women interviewed from Rahat was a strong desire to go out to work (this issue will be discussed in the section dealing with employment), and their ambitions to have more 'permitted' public places: that is, access to playgrounds for children, parks and more education facilities. A commercial centre is being developed on ex-territorial land (state land which doesn't belong to any tribe) which allows women access, since it is considered common land. Some women from Rahat visit the bank in the centre and the few shops that have recently opened there. It means that boundaries of 'public' for the women of Rahat are broader than for Bedouin women in other smaller towns who do not have ex-territorial commercial centres.

Israeli Palestinian women married to Bedouin men

A substantial number of women living in Bedouin settlements today are Israeli Arab women from Arab towns and villages who married Bedouin men. Prior to marriage, these women lived in large towns like Lod and Nazareth, or large villages like Abu Ghosh near Jerusalem. Of all the categories, perhaps these women suffer most from restricted spatial mobility, because the majority had freedom of movement in their parents' home where they lived a modern way of life in terms of dress, level of education and daily behaviour.

The move to life in a Bedouin town, with all the resultant limitations, produces culture shock. Women used words like 'suffocating' and 'prison' to describe their situation. Fatma is 30 years old with seven children, was born in Lod and now lives with her Bedouin husband and his family in Kessifa. She describes her situation:

> In the town, everybody knows everybody and sees everything. My parents bought me a baby carriage to help me to take the kids to the health clinic, but my brother-in-law doesn't allow me to use it. My husband is a good man but my brother-in-law is bad. He is frustrated, and that is why he behaves like that. He is afraid that his wife will demand a baby carriage too, and in this way he will lose control over her. So I cannot use the pram, and have to carry my kids in my arms for long distances.

Another interesting example which emphasises their situation is the role of the head cover and traditional dress. Most Arab women are not accustomed to dressing traditionally, and therefore approach it as a burdensome obligation. When leaving the boundaries of the 'private' they stop the car and change into Western-style clothes, in a space that is culturally neutral for them and their husbands.

Employment among Bedouin women – between 'forbidden' and 'permitted'

Only 5 per cent of Bedouin women are employed (Ministry of Housing 1995). This rate is low when compared to 44 per cent of Israeli Jewish women and 15 per cent of Israeli Arab women. The reason for this low rate of employment among the Bedouin women is primarily cultural. Although there are no exact data regarding the distribution of employed women before and after marriage, field observations and discussions with women suggest that most employed women are single. When a woman marries and has her first child, she stops working because of social and cultural constructions of gender roles. This is a difficult situation, especially for educated women, and it leads to a very unique image of the ideal husband. Aisha, who is 21, single and Rahat's first kindergarten teacher, says: 'If you ask me what type of a husband I want, I tell you: he doesn't have to be handsome or rich. My only wish is that he lets me carry on working after marriage.'

Only a small percentage of women, with high school education and beyond, work outside the home. The few who work tend to be married to men who have twelve years of education themselves and are more open to modern lifestyles. The mobility of these women is much greater. Many women in this group have travelled to other towns in Israel. But the great majority of Bedouin women feel trapped by being unable to seek outside employment, particularly those who are educated and have matriculated. On the one hand they have acquired modern ideas and skills that make them different from their mothers, while on the other cultural codes preserve their inferior status, so they continue to live like their mothers but feel stifled.

Halima is 26 years old with three children. She lives in Rahat. She finished high school and successfully did the matriculation. Her story expresses the frustration of Bedouin women:

> When I studied in high school I was so unique, not many girls studied at high school in my times. I dreamt that I would go to university to study mathematics, but my husband's parents did not allow me. Even to work at the high school laboratory they don't allow me. I was once unique and educated and now I am exactly like other uneducated women.

This frustration highlights the gap between the modern education provided by the state to the Bedouin, and the lack of openness among the society's members themselves to accept modernisation among their women. This situation is becoming more and more extreme as statistics show that the education of Bedouin women is rising. In 1982, girls accounted for 35 per cent of Bedouin students, while by 1994 this number had risen to 44 per cent. (These statistics relate to students in elementary school, middle school and high school; Ministry of Education 1995.) The number of employed Bedouin women is growing at a much slower rate, and the number of girls in high school classes remains relatively low because of a high drop-out rate. Bedouin women recognise the complexities of going out to work: on the one hand, they can make a financial contribution to growing family expenses, and on the other, the constraints and social circumstances make employment so difficult (Tal 1993). To overcome cultural limitations, most women in the focus groups requested that employment opportunities be developed in the towns themselves, preferably in their own neighbourhoods. They believe that places of work within their 'domestic sphere' will make it easier for them to work.

Men's views of their wives going out to work have in fact become more flexible with the move to towns, as is shown by the findings of the field survey carried out for the Development Plan. Most Bedouin men in towns (75 per cent) support the idea of developing employment opportunities for women in the settlement, as opposed to only 30 per cent of men in spontaneous settlements who supported such a proposal.

'Space for women' – women's clubs

To overcome constraints on mobility and enrich the private space, women requested the establishment of a range of services that would make life easier in the town. They talked about clubs for women, where they could learn how to function better with modern electric equipment for cooking and cleaning, and also wanted sports and exercise facilities and make-up training programmes.

In 1996, women's clubs, organised by Israeli women's organisations, existed in only three of the towns. These groups are 'spaces for women': they serve as a women's equivalent of the *sheig*, a hospitality tent where gatherings take place to serve men. They are places where women can meet, share problems and enjoy themselves. The atmosphere is one of intimacy and sisterhood, and constitutes an emotional support system for women. It is something that is particularly necessary for women in Bedouin towns, especially in view of the dramatic changes taking place in their lives and the fact that the move to the towns releases them from many of their traditional roles, leaving them with much free time. Women from neighbourhoods without such women's clubs complained that men spent all day sitting in the sheig, talking with one another, when women had no such place where they could talk freely.

The process of establishing such social groups in the towns was long and hard, because Bedouin men felt ambivalent about them, fearing that traditional codes would be broken and that rules of modesty would be violated. It is also possible that they were afraid of losing control over their wives. With time, the men were persuaded that it would not threaten men's dominant status, and that their wives were learning how to be housewives in modern Western kitchens. The same cultural roles of forbidden spaces apply to these clubs: they serve only women living in the neighbourhood and belonging to the same tribe.

Gendered planning and the modernity project: practical implications

Cultural and social implications

This chapter has begun to examine changes in the cultural construction of private and public spaces for Bedouin men and women experiencing the 'modernity project'. The analysis has shown that, unlike women in other Moslem societies, traditional dress does not enlarge the public space in which women are permitted to move. Traditional dress is compulsory but does not increase freedom of movement. The situation in the Bedouin towns in the Negev is similar to the situation of the Egyptian Bedouin as described by Abu Lughod (1986). It is apparent that women experience the most difficulties during transition. Their living space shrinks and they do not find replacements for traditional activities, as men do. 'Permitted' spaces are limited because of the extreme density in the towns relative to the large space for mobility that existed in spontaneous settlements. These findings strengthen the claim that planning frameworks should provide solutions to delicate situations such as these. They expose the failures of modernised planning oblivious to cultural codes and the implications of changes in boundaries, and the fact that such changes have had a different influence for men and women.

Planning implications

The differences in spatial mobility and needs for men and women were defined. The data presented in this chapter demonstrate the need for a progressive planning theory which is more pluralistic in nature and sensitive to 'otherness'. Otherness, in this chapter, refers to a cultural construction of space unique to Bedouin society. An understanding of the nuances of Bedouin mores is crucial to the future planning of towns that will be more suited to their Bedouin inhabitants.

In planning for the Bedouin it must be emphasised that change takes place in stages, and that it has a pace of its own that is determined by the tribal origin, educational level, age and gender of its residents. This rate of change demands the use of various planning techniques which will ensure flexibility in planning in order to produce 'plans for multiple publics', with particular emphasis on gender differences. Different planning scales must be adopted in accordance with the needs of the different groups in the population. Planning analyses must begin to relate to the following components:

Housing density

The strong sense of density, felt particularly by Bedouin women, forces young couples to move to smaller separate housing plots to ease the effect of cultural constraints imposed on them by their families, and allow for more independence for new generations.

Planning of services

The construction of private/public spaces necessitates a flexible planning approach for certain services. The planning of services must suit the cultural constraints of the society. Perhaps during the first stages of settlement the services should be built on a neighbourhood basis or in the form of mobile services, particularly in the case of medical services. Today there is one clinic in each Bedouin settlement (except for Rahat, which has two) and Bedouin women, who are responsible for health matters in the family, have to walk long distances with their children to get to a clinic. (As we have seen, the use of baby carriages is still rare among the Bedouin.) Women never go alone to a clinic, partly because of lack of knowledge of Hebrew (unfortunately not all medical doctors speak Arabic) but mostly because of cultural constraints. Banking and commercial services could be mobile, as could informal educational services like libraries. It is also possible to make the services provided by women's organisations mobile, too. As mentioned earlier, women's clubs serve only neighbourhood residents and if the courses provided by them were set up on a more mobile basis, they could become available to more women. An example of this kind of activity exists in the youth centre for culture and sport in Tel Sheva, where some activities take place in women's homes. Any plan should take advantage of the infrastructure and services that urban life offers to become more sensitive to women's needs. Limitations today make it very difficult for women to fulfil their roles and responsibilities as mothers and homemakers, especially in terms of health and educational services.

Employment opportunities

In order to respect cultural constraints, a 'planning in stages' approach to employment opportunities for Bedouin women should be considered. This would challenge the current approach of zoning land use, which separates industrial and commercial areas from habitation areas and has produced a crisis of modernism. A 'planning in stages' approach towards the Bedouin would combine land uses, and encourage the establishment within the neighbourhoods of small, modern businesses, as well as non-polluting industries like sewing, weaving and craft workshops, in the primary stages of settlement planning. This recommendation does not negate the need for the development of specific industrial areas in all Bedouin settlements, and the hope is that, with time, public space available to women will grow, allowing them to work in more distant places.

Different voices: different opinions towards the 'modernity project'

It is largely accepted today that the category 'women' is not unifying: factors such as class, race, ethnicity and sexual preferences dictate different perceptions of space and different socio-economic and political needs. As suggested by Sandercock and Forsyth (1996), difference should not be lost in planning procedures, and 'planning for multiple publics' should always be taken into consideration.

In this light, I wish to emphasise the different voices that are echoing among Bedouin and Arab women regarding suggested frameworks of flexible planning. The framework used in our fieldwork followed the needs expressed by the women in the focus groups. As such it has come in for criticism from some feminists who suggest that such a flexible planning approach perpetuates the subordination of Bedouin women and legitimises the restricted movement of women in certain spaces. There is no clear-cut answer to this dispute. It illustrates the discourse between Western 'white' feminism and Third World feminism which may need to address more subtle cultural issues. It also introduces the notion of cultural relativism in planning, which needs further discussion. It is certainly important to acknowledge the range of opinions involved when implementing such planning practices.

Conclusion

This chapter has analysed how the modernity project for Bedouin has brought to light the need for awareness of cultural construction and reconstruction of space. By studying the patterns of mobility of the Bedouin in the Negev, it highlights the shortcomings of planning as control in a 'modernity project'. Perceptions of space as modest or permitted, or immodest and forbidden, were presented in terms of the cultural constraints that limit and reduce the boundaries of private space. This kind of analysis has particular meaning in discussing gender in the cultural construction of space among Moslem societies in general and among the Bedouin in particular. According to the findings of the focus groups,

Bedouin women in towns have very limited mobility, depending on the size of the settlement, its age, and factors relating to the status, age and origin of its residents. Their confinement to the domestic space and the neighbourhood is relaxed only with a spatial leap to anonymity at the regional level. This restricted mobility has important implications for the development and planning of services and industry in the settlements, in terms of both their scope and their location. Clearly, progressive flexible planning is required to meet the needs of distinct ethnic populations undergoing change.

While Israeli Palestinian women's groups in general have begun to define their needs in recent years, Bedouin women's aspirations have not yet been addressed on the international stage. It is hoped that we can learn to be sensitive to women's issues in a multi-ethnic context, both in order to encourage new freedoms and to preserve the cultures of fragile minorities as they evolve.

Acknowledgements

A different version of this chapter appears as 'Space for gender: cultural roles of the forbidden and the permitted' in *Society and Space* (forthcoming). This chapter is based on data collected for the Development Plan of Bedouin Settlements in the Negev for the Ministry of Housing. The author thanks the Department of Town Planning in the Ministry of Housing for permission to use the data for the purposes of this chapter.

References

Abu Odeh, L. (1993) 'Post colonial feminism and the veil: thinking the difference', *Feminist Review* 43: 26–37.
Abu Lughod, L. (1986) *Veiled Sentiments*, Berkeley: University of California Press.
Abu Lughod, L. (1993) *Writing Women's World*, Berkeley: University of California Press.
Afshar, H. (1996) 'Women and politics of fundamentalism in Iran', in H. Afshar (ed.) *Women and Politics in the Third World*, London: Routledge.
Alterman, R. (1994) 'The theoretical bases for planning and its implications in defining plans, objectives and goals', *The Master Plan for Israel – 2020*, Haifa: Technion, 99–113.
Ardener, S. (1993) 'Ground rules and social maps for women; an introduction', in S. Ardener (ed.) *Women and Space*, Oxford: Berg Publishers.
Bar, A. (1989) 'The design of the physical environment in Rahat – Bedouin perception as opposed to the state perception', MA dissertation, Ben Gurion University in the Negev (in Hebrew).
Beller-Hann, I. (1995) 'Women and fundamentalism in Northeast Turkey', *Women: A Cultural Review* 6 (1): 35–45.
Ben David, J. (1993) *The Settlement of the Bedouin in the Negev 1967–1992*, Jerusalem: Ministry of Housing.

Ben David, J. (1995) 'The land ownership conflict between the Bedouin and the State of Israel – historical, legal aspects', *Karka*, 61–91 (in Hebrew).
Cosgrove, D. and Jackson, P. (1987) 'New directions in cultural geography', *Area* 19: 95–101.
Fainstein, S. (1996) 'Planning in a different voice', in S. Campbell and S Fainstein (eds) *Readings in Planning Theory*, Oxford: Blackwell.
Fenster, T. (1993) 'Settlement planning under principles of pluralism', *Progress in Planning* 39 (2): 167–242.
Fenster, T. (1997) 'Spaces of citizenship: the Bedouin in the frontier development of the Negev – Israel', *Progress in Planning* 47 (4): 291–306.
Fincher, R. (1990) 'Women in the city', *Australian Geographical Studies* 28: 29–37.
Friedman, J. (1996) 'Feminist and planning theories: the epistemological connection', in S. Campbell and S. Fainstein (eds) *Readings in Planning Theory*, Oxford: Blackwell.
Habermas J. (1975) *Legitimation Crisis*, Boston: Beacon Press.
Harvey, D. (1973) *Social Justice and the City*, London: Edward Arnold.
Havakuk, J. (1986) *From As-Sahar to Stoned House*, Tel Aviv: Ministry of Defence (in Hebrew).
Kobayashi, A. (1994) 'Coloring the field: gender, "race", and the politics of fieldwork', *Professional Geographer* 46 (1): 73–80.
Lewando-Hundt, G. (1984) 'The exercise of power by Bedouin women in the Negev', in E. Marx and A. Shmueli (eds) *The Changing Bedouin*, London: Transaction Books.
Ley, D. (1989) 'Fragmentation, coherence and limits to theory in human geography', in A. Kobayashi and S. Mackenzie (eds) *Remaking Human Geography*, London: Unwin Hyman.
Macleod, A. (1990) *Accommodating Protest*, New York: Columbia University Press.
Meir, A. (1986a) 'Pastoral nomads and the dialectics of development and modernization: delivering public educational services to the Negev Bedouin', *Society and Space*, 4: 85–95.
Meir, A. (1986b) 'Demographic transition theory: a neglected aspect of the nomadism–sedentization continuum', *Transactions* 11: 199–211.
Melman, B. (1995) 'Freedom behind the veil; viewing the "other" in the 18th and 19th centuries: Western women look at Mediterranean women', in Y. Atzmon (ed.) *A View into the Lives of Women in Jewish Societies*, Jerusalem: The Shazar Center for Jewish History (in Hebrew).
Mernissi, F. (1991) *Women and Islam: An Historical and Theological Enquiry*, Oxford: Blackwell.
Ministry of Education (1995) *The Changes in the Bedouin Education System 1990–1995*, Jerusalem: Ministry of Education (in Hebrew).
Ministry of Housing (1995) *Development Plan for the Bedouin Settlements in the Negev*, Jerusalem: Ministry of Housing (in Hebrew).
Mitchell, D. (1995) 'There is no such thing as culture: towards a reconceptualization of the idea of culture in geography', *Transactions* 20 (1): 102–116.
Mohanty, C.T. (1991) 'Under Western eyes: feminist scholarship and colonial discourses', in C.T. Mohanty, A. Russo and L. Torres (eds) *Third World Women and the Politics of Feminism*, Bloomington: Indiana University Press.

Moore Milroy, B. (1996) 'Some thoughts about difference and pluralism', in S. Campbell and S. Fainstein (eds) *Readings in Planning Theory*, Cambridge: Blackwell.
Moser, C. (1993) *Gender, Planning and Development: Theory, Practice and Training*, London: Routledge.
Pain, R. (1991) 'Space, sexual violence and social control: integrating geographical and feminist analyses of women's fear of crime', *Progress in Human Geography* 15 (4): 415–31.
Pratt, G. (1994) 'Private and public spheres', in R.J. Johnston, D. Gregory and D. Smith (eds) *The Dictionary of Human Geography*, London: Blackwell.
Pred, A. and Palm, R. (1978) 'The status of American women: a time geographic view', in D.A. Sregran and R. Palm (eds) *An Invitation to Geography*, New York: New York University Press.
Rappoport, A. (1978) 'Nomadism as a man-environment system', *Environment and Behavior* 10 (2): 214–47.
Sandercock, L. and Forsyth, A. (1996) 'Feminist theory and planning theory: the epistemological linkages', in S. Campbell and S. Fainstein (eds) *Readings in Planning Theory*, Oxford: Blackwell.
Sibley, D. (1992) 'Outsiders in society and space', in K. Anderson and F. Gale (eds) *Studies in Cultural Geography*, Melbourne: Longman Cheshire.
Sibley, D. (1995) *Geographies of Exclusion – Society and Difference in the West*, London: Routledge.
Tal, S. (1993) *The Bedouin Women on the Path between Nomadism and Urbanization*, The Negev: Jo Alon Museum (in Hebrew).
Tohidi, N. (1991) 'Gender and Islamic fundamentalism: feminist politics in Iran', in C.T. Mohanty, A. Russo and L. Torres (eds) *Third World Women and the Politics of Feminism*, Bloomington: Indiana University Press.
Turner, J.F.C. (1976) *Housing by People*, London: Marion Boyars Publishers.
Valentine, G. (1989) 'The geography of women's fear', *Area* 21 (4): 385–90.
Yiftacheal, O. (1994) 'The dark side of modernism: planning as control of an ethnic minority', in S. Watson and K. Gibson (eds) *Postmodern Spaces*, Sydney: Basil Blackwell.

6 The feminisation of catastrophe
Narrating women's silences

Ronit Lentin

The station is not a station. It is the end of the track. They look and are distressed by the desolation around them.

In the morning, the mist hides the marshes.

In the evening floodlights reveal the white barbed wire as distinctly as astrophotography. They believe that this is where they are being taken, and they are afraid.

At night they wait for the day with the children heavy in their mothers' arms. They wait and wonder.

With daylight there is no more waiting. The columns start out at once. Women and children first, they are the most exhausted. After that the men. They are also weary but relieved that their women and children should go first.

For women and children go first.

(Delbo 1993: 60–1)

Introduction

Feminist works on personal narratives (see, for example, Personal Narratives Group 1989) argue for the centrality of women's experiences and women's autobiographies in the construction of gendered subjectivities. PNG argues that the feminist enterprise attempts to dismantle the traditional concepts of 'knowledge' and 'truth', which, though presented as 'objective', are primarily dominant white male concepts, and proposes replacing them with a 'more fully human conception of social reality' (PNG 1989: 3). The call to reflexively listen to women's voices, learn from women's experiences and use women's personal narratives as essential primary documents in reconstructing the social world (PNG 1989: 4) is particularly crucial in analyses, from the location of women's lives, of major catastrophes, where women's experiences have been, at best, subsumed into male perspectives and, at worst, ignored on the pretext that catastrophic events are 'too big' to 'do feminism', or to attempt a gender analysis (see, for instance, Ringelheim 1990: 144). Quite apart from the impossibility of understanding fully the nature of genocidal projects without locating the experiences, but also the images, of women at the heart of the analysis, this chapter posits the centrality of women's personal narratives in order to come to terms with and close the 'memory gap' in relation to catastrophic experiences.

Let me first stress, however, that gender, not simply an additive component in analyses of political projects such as genocides in the sense of 'adding women and stirring', must be seen as part of an intersection of subordinations (cf. Yuval-Davis 1997). An additive analysis posits sexist oppression as experienced by all women, regardless of class, race, ethnicity, nationality, sexuality, age. It masks the fact that white middle-class women often take part in perpetuating imperialism, classism and racism (cf. Amos and Parmar 1984). 'Hierarchies of domination are constructed and experienced simultaneously, their dynamics permeating one another ... they are not experienced the same way by all women' (Young and Dickerson 1994: 5).

It is also important that we analyse the ways women are targeted by major political projects and catastrophes, beyond women's victimhood, and address victimhood and agency in tandem, charting the routes of resistance available to women even when they are most deeply jeopardised. This chapter does not assume power as neatly locked into a binary structure of possessing power versus being powerless, with women viewed almost always as a powerless, unified group. This view of women as a universally oppressed group is, Chandra Mohanty argues, a Western feminism colonialist move, whereby Third World women never rise above the debilitating generality of their 'object status' (Mohanty 1991: 71). 'Women' cannot be considered a category of analysis across contexts, because the world is not neatly divided into the binary opposition of the powerful (men) versus powerless (women). But in spite of gender being part of an 'intersection of subordinations', patriarchal social relations are endemic and integral to social formations with regards to the distribution of material resources and power (Anthias and Yuval-Davis 1992: 109). Focusing exclusively on women as universal victims does not help the survivors of genocides and other catastrophes. Nor does it allow us to address women's participation as benefactors or perpetrators of genocidal processes, as has been the case, for instance, in the 1994 Rwandan genocide (African Rights 1995: 4), or the Shoah[1] (Rittner and Roth 1993: 320–3; Milton 1993: 224–5).

Elsewhere, I and contributors to *Gender and Catastrophe* (Lentin 1997) argue for the gendering of catastrophes such as genocides, wars, 'ethnic cleansing', the Shoah, black slavery, sex slavery, famines, nuclear experimentation, 'natural' disasters, mass rapes. In this chapter I would like to argue that catastrophes are not only gendered but also 'feminised', both via images of women used to symbolise atrocities and in their consequences in women's lives, and that by feminising catastrophe, its impact is often belittled in popular accounts.

There are several reasons to privileging women's experiences as an authoritative location from which to begin inquiry. Women oppressed or marginalised in catastrophic political projects are better able to see the 'line of fault' between their experiences and the dominant world view (Smith 1987, cited by Young and Dickerson, 1994: 2). As party to knowledge, due to oppression, which men or other women not thus targeted are not party to, they can, if we know how to listen, offer insights to embodied knowledge linked to particular historical processes. The standpoint approach, posited, for example, by Harding (1991), argues that starting inquiry from women's lived experiences not only decentres hegemonic knowledges, it also adds to the complexity of knowledge based on the multiplicity of women's experiences. De Lauretis (1990: 260) defines feminist theory as 'theory of the relationship between experiences, social power and resistance'. Telling catastrophe from the site of women's experiences not only reclaims its depth: it is also, I would argue, the only way of closing the 'memory gap' (cf. Grunfeld 1995; Ringelheim 1997) between the catastrophic event and the discourses available to us to make sense of catastrophe.

Since I position women's experiences at the centre of feminist theory and scholarship, I wish to locate myself. I am a Jewish woman, many of whose family are Shoah survivors and some of whom were Shoah victims, and an Israeli woman, whose state, in occupying Palestinian lands and dispossessing the indigenous Palestinian population in the process of establishing a 'national home' for the Jewish people, brought about calamities to many Palestinian women, children and men. I am also a migrant, albeit a voluntary one: for the past twenty-eight years I have been living in Ireland, where I have had experiences of displacement and resettlement. My interest in the ways women are targeted by genocides and catastrophes arose out of my doctoral research, an auto/biographical feminist exploration of the gendered relations between Israel and the Shoah, between a fighting, active, 'masculinised' Israel and a passive, 'feminised' Jewish diaspora who had allegedly gone passively to its death during the Shoah (Lentin 1996).

I begin this chapter with an attempt to define catastrophe and argue that in order to understand the full impact of catastrophic projects, definitions of catastrophe, and of genocide itself, must be gendered well beyond the discursive level. Despite the tendency in the social sciences to express 'things', or social processes, as 'words', or 'discourses', women know full well the meaning of 'things' in their lives. 'Things' such as genocide, hunger, displacement, sexual exploitation, war and migration cannot be dismissed as mere 'discourses', as certain postmodernisms would have us believe (cf. Barrett 1992; Linden 1996). I then look at the link between the gendering of catastrophe and its feminisation. This derives from the use of images and discourses of suffering 'woman' and 'mother' (cf. Kelleher 1997a, 1997b) and the converse 'masculinisation' of ethnic conflicts (cf. Lentin 1996; Hague 1997), and from strategies used by genocidal regimes to target women as the biological reproducers of the next generation of collectivities. In positing the feminisation of catastrophe, I argue for reclaiming women's experiences of catastrophe as historiographic and analytical resources, in order to understand the targeting of women, but also the overall nature of those very catastrophic projects. The chapter concludes by positing the feminist research strategy of personal narratives as the only means of reclaiming the full enormity of catastrophic events and making the experiences of women visible, thus allowing the silences to speak, closing the gap between the memory of the catastrophic experience and women's narratives of catastrophe.

From (en)gendering catastrophes to the feminisation of catastrophe

> Algeria-woman is Algeria which does not want to fall into the hands of the enemies so as not to be reduced to slavery and subjugation, which does not want to be possessed by others ... [and] would rather be dead than be possessed by others. Finished are beautiful words and love songs; if you are men, the women cry to their own, show it on the land, in battle. If you have red blood in your veins, prove it, don't recoil.
> (Dejeux 1987, cited by Cherifati-Merbatine 1994: 51)

Trying to determine what constitutes a 'catastrophe', particularly when a catastrophe is gendered, is not only definitionally complex, it is also a political minefield, particularly for women. Helen Fein's definition of genocide (Fein 1993) includes 'the sustained purposeful action by a perpetrator to physically destroy a collectivity directly or indirectly, through interdiction of the biological and social reproduction of group members'. As the bearers of the next generation of a collectivity, women are put uniquely at risk as members of a group targeted as 'racially inferior'. The definition of genocide must be gendered, to include political projects involving: slavery; sexual slavery; mass rape; mass sterilisation, aimed, through women, at 'ethnic cleansing'; and the elimination or alteration of a future ethnic group. Catastrophes, genocidal or otherwise, target women in very specific ways due to their social, ethnic and national construction.

In the last hundred years many millions of people have been the casualties of genocides and catastrophes. Additionally, in the twenty-five years from 1970 to 1995, some 134 million people were killed, injured or made homeless by catastrophes with a natural trigger (earthquakes, droughts and famines, high winds, landslides, volcanoes) or a non-natural trigger (accidents and fires). In 1995 alone, some 14.4 million people were refugees and asylum seekers, and 21.6 million people were internally displaced, having fled their homes for the same reasons as refugees, but without crossing international borders (International Federation of Red

Cross and Red Crescent Societies 1996: 124–37). According to the Red Cross, women, together with children, are particularly vulnerable to food deprivation, particularly when, in warfare, they stay behind while men migrate in search of food or are conscripted into armies. Women suffer disproportionately from disease, as a combination of malnutrition and the lack of sanitation and water puts them more at risk. Women are often the victims of violence and hunger, especially in refugee situations (ibid.: 27–8).

It is universally assumed that black slavery, the Shoah and other genocidal projects, colonisation, the sexual slavery of thousands of East Asian women by Japan, the African, Bengali and Irish famines, Asian floods, nuclear testing in the Pacific and 'ethnic cleansing' in the former Yugoslavia were major catastrophes with disastrous consequences, not only for women. It is less clear-cut whether wars, liberation struggles, population movements and Islamisation projects can be considered catastrophic. Considering such political processes a catastrophe may be politically dangerous for the women targeted and for the women researching these processes, because we cannot be sure whether fundamentalist regimes which target women as repositories of national and familial shame and honour do not imagine themselves as so unquestionably dominant as not to tolerate critiques that tar them with a 'catastrophic' brush.

Genocidal projects, wars and other political processes which result, among other things, in mass population movements are, I argue along the social constructionist position (cf. Sharoni 1992), the consequence of the construction of masculinity and femininity in society (cf. Connell 1987). Gender must be the explanation of the way the military reproduces the ideological structure of patriarchy 'because the notion of "combat" plays such a central role in the construction of "manhood" and justification of the superiority of maleness in the social order' (Enloe 1983: 12). While neither masculinity nor femininity are universal propositions, nor is power-positioning common to all masculinities. Euan Hague (1997) argues, for instance, that the Serb and Bosnian Serb military policy of genocidal rape constructed a specific type of 'hetero-national masculinity' and a converse inferior, powerless 'femininity'. During the Nazi period, 'predicated on authority in the form of brutality, the concentration camp was an ultimate expression of the extreme masculinity and misogyny that undergirded Nazi ideology' (Goldenberg 1990: 163), in that both Aryan and non-Aryan women were targeted on the basis of their 'biological destiny'. Similarly, Lorraine Dowler (1997) argues that the war in Northern Ireland constructed gender roles in oppositional terms: men were perceived as violent and action-oriented and women as compassionate and supportive to the male warriors.

Population movements and mass migration are often generated by 'political manoeuvres' such as the 1947 division of India (Butalia 1997), the break-up of the former Soviet Union (Kosmarskaya 1997) and of the former Yugoslavia (Boric 1997), the Zionist expropriation of the Palestinians, to cite but a few examples. But they are also generated by political projects such as colonisation, with the attendant ideological and political domination of the colonised and the resultant enslavement, exploitation, expropriation and expulsion of indigenous populations. In the course of mass population movements, women are targeted by state and ethnic violence, and their needs are not being adequately catered for in resettlement projects.

The distinction some writers (for example, Davis 1993) make between 'natural' and 'man-made' disasters can be used as a guiding yardstick in answering the definitional dilemma posited above in relation to the gendering of catastrophes. I am not proposing to essentialise 'women' either as a unitary victim group or as more peace-oriented than 'men', nor to accord 'men' the exclusive universal power to inflict catastrophes upon a civilian population of 'women and children'. However, the gendered nature of political processes such as war, religious and political fundamentalism or population movements may elucidate the catastrophic consequences, for women, of such processes, which women usually do not generate. Furthermore, resulting from the fact that, 'aside from natural disasters, humanitarian emergencies in the contemporary world frequently emerge from military engagements' (Gordenker and Weiss 1991: 1), international institutions tend to turn to armed forces for assistance in humanitarian emergencies. This means that not only catastrophes, but also their resolution, are gendered; they are both inflicted and assuaged by the military, based on a 'hegemonic masculinity' and a military apparatus as a classic dominance-oriented masculine structure (Connell 1994: 158). If the perpetrators are 'masculinised', the victims of catastrophe, though not all are women and not all women are victims, are feminised.

I would therefore argue that catastrophe is not only gendered, it is also feminised, via the symbolic representation of 'woman' as the victim of catastrophe, and via targeting women as mothers, chattels, sexual objects, repositories of family and national honour and the symbolic representational trope of the nation: nation as beloved mother, 'the defeated nation being reborn as a triumphant woman' to be protected, fought for and liberated 'for the sake of the women and children back home' (Boland 1989: 13).

The figure of woman is the chosen representative image of catastrophe, as was demonstrated by the picture of the Algerian 'Madonna in Hell' published in October 1997 in the world's press.[2] A beautiful tearful Algerian woman whose eight children had been massacred, her mouth open and eyes hollow, being comforted by another woman, both veiled, was chosen to represent Algeria's grieving response to its current catastrophe. Woman as universal victim, motherhood as the epitome of suffering, shattered female beauty as symbol of 'man's inhumanity to man', catastrophe's feminised images served for media consumption as part of a lexicon of victimhood.

As victims, but also as repositories of national and family honour, it is women, not men, who are required to fulfil codes of moral behaviour in times of catastrophe, when familial, class, communal, religious and national politics affect the construction of women's familial roles, as argued by Santi Rozario (1997) in relation to Bangladeshi society.

An example of the feminisation of catastrophe is the choice of the figure of woman to represent crisis or breakdown, as argued by Kelleher (1997a, 1997b) in relation to the Irish and Bangladeshi famines. Individual experiences of victimisation continue to yield female images: emaciated and suffering female figures denoting passivity and despair, a dry-breasted woman unable to feed her child, a child suckling at the breast of its dead mother, a woman snatching food from her child, or her 'heroic' opposite, a mother sacrificing her last food for her child. 'The spectacle of famine finds its most graphic form through the female body, objectified and exposed by the controlling gaze of the powerful spectator' (Kelleher 1997b: 246). Famine, through its contemporary representations of helplessness and passivity, is feminised and, Kelleher argues, the figure of woman in relation to famine representations stands out not only as a horrific image of famine's effects, but as a key indicator of the inequalities which cause individual hunger and large-scale starvation.

Another example of the feminisation of catastrophe is the ways genocidal projects target women due to their 'biological destiny', as is evidenced in Nazi ideology, which, resting on the eugenic conviction of German 'racial superiority', inevitably discriminated against women as child-bearers. The Nazis had already legalised race-hygiene sterilisation in the 1930s when 400,000 people with mental illness were sterilised because they were judged 'unworthy to reproduce' (Burleigh 1995). At the same time, the Nazis encouraged German women to become mothers and to bear illegitimate children, fathered by SS men and other 'racially valuable' Germans. Elderly Jewish women (and men), useless to the Nazis, were sentenced to death; women of child-bearing age, although useful as workers, posed a menace because they could bear Jewish children and ensure the continuity of Jewish life (Rittner and Roth 1993). As surgical sterilisation was slow and expensive, German doctors, serving genocidal interests, experimented with X-rays, injections and drugs as faster and more easily applicable procedures to control the reproduction of 'racially inferior' women. Roma and Gypsy women married to Germans were sterilised, as were their children after the age of twelve. Jewish and Gypsy women were forced to become guinea pigs in Nazi medical experiments (Laska 1983).

The feminisation process was revisited upon Shoah survivors upon their arrival in the state of Israel. The social construction of manhood in Israel has its roots in a particular historical context, especially in relation to the

Shoah and the creation of the Jewish state. Sharoni (1992: 457) argues that the state of Israel can be seen as a reassertion of masculinity, justified by the need to end a history of Jewish weakness and suffering by creating an image of an Israeli man who is exceedingly masculine, protective and emotionally tough. As a result, Shoah survivors were not only silenced and stigmatised in the new Israeli state, which negated diasporic Jewry and derided the passivity of Jewish victims who allegedly had 'gone to their death like sheep to the slaughter': they were also feminised, in opposition to the newly constructed masculine Israeli discourses (Lentin 1996).

Women Shoah survivors speak of sexual humiliation, rape, sexual exchange, pregnancy, abortion and vulnerability through their children – concerns male survivors tend not to describe. Female concentration camp survivors speak of the humiliation surrounding the entrance to the camp, being nude, being shaved all over in a sexual stance straddling two stools, being observed by men. Women often survived the Shoah through sex, used as a commodity in some ghettos and camps. In some concentration camps there were brothels reserved for the SS and other selected privileged male inmates (Tillion 1975). The Japanese military used a complex system of military sex slavery during World War II, when Philippine, Korean, northeast Chinese, Indonesian and Malaysian women served as 'comfort women', according to Nelia Sancho of *Lila Filipina* (1997). Fewer than a third of these comfort women survived: some were summarily executed or forced to commit suicide together with defeated Japanese soldiers.

The use of mass rape as a political instrument provides an additional illustration of the feminisation of catastrophic projects. During the 1970–1 West Pakistani occupation of Bangladesh, between 200,000 and 400,000 Bangladeshi women were raped by the Pakistani army (Rozario 1997). The claims that it was military policy, consciously planned by West Pakistan in order to create a new ethnicity and dilute the Bangladeshi nation, resonates with the genetic warfare arguably employed by the Serb and Bosnian Serb policy of genocidal rape, particularly the version that uses forced pregnancy as a kind of biological warfare (Allen 1996).

All this means that catastrophes, no matter what their origins, are always gendered in moulding historically specific social constructions of masculinities and femininities in the light of these very catastrophes. But, via the usage of feminine images to represent the collectivity's catastrophic events and via targeting women as the (re)producers of collectivities, they are also feminised, casting women as universal victims, despite the active role they often play in resisting victimisation (and, sometimes, perpetrating catastrophes). That this feminisation belittles the depth of the catastrophe is demonstrated by describing women and girls as the principal victims of the Rwandan genocide, despite the fact that throughout the genocide it was Tutsi men who were the main target. This also tends to obscure, according to African Rights (1995), women's roles as aggressors. The involvement of women in the genocide and murder of Hutu opponents failed to attract national and international attention, precisely because of the construction of women as the universal victims of the Rwandan genocide. According to African Rights (1995: 4–5), many women perpetrators enjoy impunity, live in comfort in exile or are employed by international organisations in the refugee camps in Zaire, Tanzania and Burundi.

Narrativising catastrophic experiences as a feminist research strategy

> The women pass by near us. They are shouting. They shout and we do not hear anything. This cold, dry air should be conducive in an ordinary human environment. They shout in our direction without a sound reaching us. Their mouths shout, their arms stretched out towards us shout, everything about them is shouting. Each body is a shout. All of them torches flaming with cries of terror, cries that have assumed female bodies. Each one is a materialized cry, a howl – unheard.
>
> (Delbo 1995: 33)

Privileging women's lived experiences as primary resources militates against universalising 'womanhood' across contexts, and deepens our understanding of catastrophic events by reclaiming experiences of women, 'hidden' in 'malestream' historiography and scholarship, shaped, among other things, by the gendered construction of knowledge itself. Women's accounts of catastrophe, particularly the accounts of women without access to the centres of power or to literacy, are often clouded in silence because, as the Delbo quote illustrates, catastrophic events are rarely expressible at the time they happen. Later, as the implications of women's victimhood during catastrophes may be unacceptable because women are seen as the tropes of the collectivity's honour or shame, their narratives are all too often officially, or unofficially, silenced. Feminist projects of recording oral histories of catastrophic events are therefore an important strategy of making women's silences speak, and of de-feminising images of ethnic and national traumas.

In inscribing experience into feminist scholarship, simply speaking 'as a' may run the risk of speaking 'for', as Liz Stanley cautions (1995). My commitment to situated experience stems from the deconstruction of the supremacy of 'theory' in academic feminist writing, which, as Stanley and Wise (1990) argue, 'is theory with a capital T, one produced by theorists who are supposed experts on the relationships between categories and thus on the "real meaning" of social experience and behaviour'. Academic feminism, they stress, becomes 'the legitimation for a new form of expertise, that of feminist theoreticians over "mere women"' (Stanley and Wise 1990: 24). It is important to stress that beyond 'words' and 'discourse', 'a real world and real lives do exist, howsoever we interpret, construct and recycle accounts of these by a variety of symbolic means' (Stanley 1993: 214). Gender cannot be universalised nor can gendered experiences be presented without context; but neither can the demand that 'we must learn to theorise without categories' (Traweek 1995: 29, cited by Linden 1996) be sustained if we acknowledge the importance of 'things' in women's lives and deaths.

There is no one precise definition of narrative, but it is agreed that a life story is not an unconnected chain of experiences whose meaning is created at the moment of telling. Rather, it is a process which must be backgrounded against a multi-layered context, involving the historical moment of the telling, and the political, race, class and gender systems that narrators manipulate to survive and within which their narratives are interpreted (Personal Narratives Group 1989).

Personal narratives as a social construct raise questions about the interrelationship between auto/biographical texts and life itself (Rosenthal 1993: 60). Do narrators, in recreating accounts of catastrophe, tell or 'construct' the 'truth'? One theoretical answer to this dilemma is to view life and story as part of the same fabric, in that life informs and is formed by stories. Widdershoven (1993: 2–20) argues that the meaning of life cannot be determined outside the stories told about it; neither can the meaning of a story be determined without reference to human life as it is lived. Stories are important for our identity: they tell us who we are; a story interprets experiences and makes their meanings explicit.

Traumatic experiences are often dealt with by banishing them from consciousness: survivors of catastrophe often silence themselves or are silenced by society. Funkenstein (1993: 22) argues, for instance, that the memory of Shoah survivors is fragmented; although many survivors wanted to remember, they had been robbed of their identity by the Nazis, a claim reiterated by Charlotte Delbo, who links 'memory' and 'self': 'since Auschwitz, I always feared losing my memory. To lose one's memory is to lose oneself' (Delbo 1995: 188).

Liz Stanley (1993) provides a clue to the relation between self (auto), life (bio) and text or account (graphy) in arguing that accounts of the past which constitute the major elements of our lives are structured by means of referential assumptions, but they do so because the tellers are well aware that these are historiographical accounts, not history itself. The process of 'accounting' that personal narratives, or auto/biographies, constitute is an important means of making real and present what we all know is memory and past. Since women's lives have been outside of or subordinated to what Smith (1987: 105–6) calls 'the apparatus of ruling', women's personal narratives are especially suitable documents to illuminate women's multiple realities.

The feminist research strategy of women's personal narratives can be employed as a means of making sense of catastrophic events. Urvashi Butalia (1997) has been recording women's oral histories in relation to the partition of India, during which some 75,000 women are thought to have been raped or abducted by men of religions different to their own, and around which memories are constructed and communal strife is measured. She argues that women's personal narratives not only explain the catastrophic experiences of the past, but also aid us in acting in the present and looking to the future. Beyond official accounts of partition, and beyond women's silences, Butalia attempts to disentangle the web of women's experiences of catastrophic incidents to ask how they impacted on women, how women themselves are implicated in them, and how their experiences are represented and who represents them.

Judith Zur (1997) compares the personal narratives of Guatemalan Mayan Indian war widows' accounts of *La Violencia*, the period of army occupation during the early 1980s, with official accounts. While official accounts, fabricated by the military state, vilified the women's dead husbands and sons as Communists, the women use their narratives to rework, relive and make sense of the traumatic events which changed their lives. Giving voice to these narratives, Zur assists the women in constructing the past in a way which makes sense to them. The official discourses of memory of *La Violencia* exclude the unofficial secret memories of the women who have turned the private memories of victimisation into articulated political acts of resistance.

Conclusion: closing the 'memory gap'

Taking herself to task for merely recording the differences between the experiences of women and of men during the Shoah in her earlier research, Joan Ringelheim (1985, 1993) argues against a 'cultural feminism' (Alcoff 1988) stance, which shares with liberalism a belief in individual solutions and in humanism and addresses a universal 'woman' while privileging some women over others. A cultural feminism stance, which tends to valorise women's oppression, damages not only our politics, but also our research. Excavating an 'archaeology of silence' (Foucault 1967: xi), that is reclaiming women's experiences, hidden from history as they may be, is not sufficient without contextualising these experiences within the gendered analysis of catastrophic events.

One aim of genocidal projects is to erase not only the physical presence of a collectivity but also its memory. Traumatic and catastrophic experiences, too horrific to remember and too difficult to find words to articulate, often result in the temptation to succumb to silence. Because genocides often have no witnesses, they do not 'exist' in the conventional form and thus signify their own death and reduction to silence. Their survival in memory inevitably implies the presence of informal discourses, a degree of unconscious witnessing that could not find its voice during the catastrophe itself.

The search for a discourse for telling catastrophe requires establishing a delicate balance between silence and the duty to tell: remembering catastrophic events must always include the temptation to succumb to silence, or avoidance. Grunfeld (1995) posits a 'memory gap' which separates between the material, bodily immediate knowledge of catastrophe and the discursive, mediated memories that follow. More specifically, Joan Ringelheim (1997) writes of the split memory between genocide and gender, split between traditional versions of history and women's own experiences. Split memory is a metaphor that represents the barriers against the inclusion of gender in analyses of catastrophe.

The feminisation of catastrophe often belittles the depth of catastrophe and belies male anxieties about the assumed infringement of a collectivity's honour, which is invariably seen as invested in women's, not men's, bodies. The feminist strategy of employing women's personal narratives as primary sources is one way of making visible women's experiences of victimisation and resistance in our scholarship and writing. It is also a way of delinking the feminised images of catastrophe and the larger political contexts of catastrophic events, restoring women's agency and reclaiming the depth of catastrophe, not from a site of a collectivity's honour, but from women's own human experiences. Beyond victimhood and universal subordination, theorising the construction of gender and perceptions of 'masculinity' and 'femininity' offers a forum for feminist scholars and activists to break the silences and close the memory gap between catastrophic events and the discourses available to represent them, and thus embody experience, which is at the heart of feminist epistemological processes (cf. Stanley 1995). By (en)gendering catastrophe, we not only enhance and deepen our knowledge, we also put women's claims to be heard, and be compensated for past injustices, firmly on the feminist political agenda.

Acknowledgements

This paper is a revision of my presentation at the Women's Studies Network (UK) tenth annual conference 'Women, Policy and Politics', London, July 1997. Some themes developed here have first appeared in the introduction to *Gender and Catastrophe* (Lentin 1997).

Notes

1 I prefer using the Hebrew term 'Shoah' meaning catastrophe or cataclysm, to the English term 'Holocaust', which derives from the Greek *holocauston* and literally means 'whole burnt', and which many Jews, conscious of the implicit Christian notion of a Jewish sacrifice or calvary, reject (Young 1990: 87).
2 The photograph was taken by an Algerian photographer who wishes to be identified only by his first name, Hocine, and was wired by AFP .

References

African Rights (1995) *Rwanda. Not So Innocent: When Women Become Killers*, London: African Rights.
Alcoff, L. (1988) 'Cultural feminism versus post-structuralism: the identity crisis in feminist theory', *Signs* 13 (3): 405–36.
Allen, B. (1996) *Rape Warfare: The Hidden Genocide in Bosnia-Herzegovina and Croatia*, Minneapolis: University of Minnesota Press.
Amos, V. and Parmar, P. (1984) 'Challenging imperial feminism', *Feminist Review* 17: 3–19.
Anthias, F. and Yuval-Davis, N. (1992) *Racialized Boundaries: Race, Nation, Gender, Colour and Class and the Anti-Racist Struggle*, London: Routledge.
Barrett, M. (1992) 'Words and things: materialism and method in contemporary feminist analysis', in M. Barrett and A. Phillips (eds) *Destabilizing Theory: Contemporary Feminist Debates*, Cambridge: Polity Press.
Boland, E. (1989) *A Kind of Scar: The Woman Poet in a National Tradition*, Dublin: Attic Press.
Boric, R. (1997) 'Against the war: women organizing themselves in the countries of the former Yugoslavia', in R. Lentin (ed.)*Gender and Catastrophe*, London: Zed Books.
Burleigh, M. (1995) *Death and Deliverance: 'Euthanasia' in Germany 1900–1945*, Cambridge: Cambridge University Press.
Butalia, U. (1997) 'A question of silence: partition, women and the state', in R. Lentin (ed.) *Gender and Catastrophe*, London: Zed Books.
Cherifati-Merbatine, D. (1994) 'Algeria at a crossroads: national liberation, Islamization and women', in V.M. Moghadam (ed.) *Gender and National Identity: Women and Politics in Muslim Societies*, London: Zed Books.
Connell, R.W. (1987) *Gender and Power*, Cambridge: Polity Press.
Connell, R.W. (1994) 'The state, gender and sexual politics: theory and appraisal', in L.H. Radtke and H.J. Stam (eds) *Power/Gender: Social Relations in Theory and Practice*, London: Sage.
Davis, L. (1993) *Man-Made Catastrophes: From the Burning of Rome to the Lockerbie Crash*, New York: Facts on File.
de Lauretis, T. (1990) 'Upping and anti [sic] in feminist theory', in M. Hirsch and E. Fox Keller (eds) *Conflicts in Feminism*, New York and London: Routledge.
Delbo, C. (1993) 'Arrivals, departures', in C. Rittner and J.K. Roth (eds) *Different Voices: Women and the Holocaust*, New York: Paragon Books.
Delbo, C. (1995) *Auschwitz and After*, New Haven: Yale University Press.
Dowler, L. (1997) 'The mother of all warriors: women in West Belfast, Northern Ireland', in R. Lentin (ed.) *Gender and Catastrophe*, London: Zed Books.
Enloe, C. (1983) *Does Khaki Become You? The Militarization of Women's Lives*, London: Pluto Press.
Fein, H. (1993) *Genocide: A Sociological Perspective*, London: Sage.
Foucault, M. (1967) *Madness and Civilization*, London: Tavistock.
Funkenstein, A. (1993) 'The incomprehensible catastrophe: memory and narrative', in R. Josselson and A. Lieblich (eds) *The Narrative Study of Lives, Vol. I*, Newbury Park: Sage.

Goldenberg, M. (1990) 'Different horrors, same hell: women remembering the Holocaust', in R. S. Gottlieb (ed.) *Thinking the Unthinkable: Meanings of the Holocaust*, New York: Paulist Press.
Gordenker, L. and Weiss, T.G. (1991) 'Introduction: the use of soldiers and peacekeepers in coping with disasters', in L. Gordenker and T.G. Weiss (eds) *Soldiers, Peacekeepers and Disasters*, London: Macmillan.
Grunfeld, U. (1995) 'Holocaust, movies and remembrance: the pedagogical challenge', unpublished paper, Pennsylvania State University.
Hague, E. (1997) 'Rape, power and masculinity: the construction of gender and national identities in the war in Bosnia-Herzegovina', in R. Lentin (ed.) *Gender and Catastrophe*, London: Zed Books.
Harding, S. (1991) 'Who knows: identities and feminist epistemology', in J.E. Hartman and E. Masser-Davidow (eds) *(En)gendering Knowledge: Feminists in Academe*, Knoxville: University of Tennessee Press.
International Federation of Red Cross and Red Crescent Societies (1996) *World Disasters Report 1996*, Oxford: Oxford University Press.
Kelleher, M. (1997a) *The Feminization of Famine*, Cork: Cork University Press.
Kelleher, M. (1997b) 'The figure of woman in Irish famine narratives', in R. Lentin (ed.) *Gender and Catastrophe*, London: Zed Books.
Kosmarskaya, N. (1997) ' "I have a feeling of being exiled here": adaptation experience of Russian women migrating from the "near abroad" ', in R. Lentin (ed.) *Gender and Catastrophe*, London: Zed Books.
Laska, V. (1983) *Women in the Resistance and in the Holocaust*, Westport, Connecticut: Greenwood Press.
Lentin, R. (1996) 'Reoccupying the territories of silence: a feminist auto/biographical exploration of the gendered relationship between Israel and the Shoah', unpublished PhD thesis, Trinity College Dublin.
Lentin, R. (ed.) (1997) *Gender and Catastrophe*, London: Zed Books.
Linden, R.R. (1996) 'Troubling categories I can't think without: reflections on women in the Holocaust', *Contemporary Jewry*, 11: 18–33.
Milton, S. (1993) 'Women and the Holocaust: the case of German and German-Jewish women', in C. Rittner and J.K. Roth (eds) *Different Voices: Women and the Holocaust*, New York: Paragon House.
Mohanty, C. T. (1991) 'Introduction: cartographies of struggle: Third World women and the politics of feminism', in C.T. Mohanty, A. Russo and L. Torres (eds) *Third World Women and the Politics of Feminism*, Bloomington: Indiana University Press.
Personal Narratives Group (1989) *Interpreting Women's Lives: Feminist Theory and Personal Narratives*, Bloomington: Indiana University Press.
Ringelheim, J.M. (1985) 'Women and the Holocaust: a reconsideration of research', *Signs* 10 (4): 741–61.
Ringelheim, J.M. (1990) 'Thoughts about women and the Holocaust', in R.S. Gottlieb (ed.) *Thinking the Unthinkable: Meanings of the Holocaust*, New York: Paulist Press.
Ringelheim, J.M. (1992) 'The Holocaust: taking women into account', *Jewish Quarterly* 39 (3): 19–23.
Ringelheim, J.M. (1993) 'Women and the Holocaust: a reconsideration of research', in C. Rittner and J.K. Roth (eds) *Different Voices: Women and the Holocaust*, New York: Paragon House.

Ringelheim, J.M. (1997) 'Genocide and gender: a split memory', in R. Lentin (ed.) *Gender and Catastrophe*, London: Zed Books.
Rittner, C. and Roth, J.K. (eds) (1993) *Different Voices: Women and the Holocaust*, New York: Paragon House.
Rosenthal, G. (1993) 'Reconstruction of life stories: principles of selection in generating stories for narrative biographical interviews', in R. Josselson and A. Lieblich (eds) *The Narrative Study of Lives, Vol. I*, Newbury Park: Sage.
Rozario, S. (1997) ' "Disasters" and Bangladeshi women', in R. Lentin (ed.) *Gender and Catastrophe*, London: Zed Books.
Sancho, N. (1997) 'The comfort women system during World War II: Asian women as targets of mass rape and sexual slavery in Japan', in R. Lentin (ed.) *Gender and Catastrophe*, London: Zed Books.
Sharoni, S. (1992) 'Every woman is an occupied territory: the politics of militarism and sexism and the Israeli–Palestinian conflict', *Journal of Gender Studies* 1 (4): 447–62.
Smith, D. (1987) *The Everyday as Problematic: A Feminist Sociology*, Milton Keynes: Open University Press.
Stanley, L. (1993) 'The knowing because experiencing subject: narratives, lives and autobiography', *Women's Studies International Forum* 16 (3): 205–15.
Stanley, L. (1995) 'Speaking "as a …", speaking "for the …": on the mis/uses of the category "experience" in recent feminist thought', *University College Galway Women's Studies Centre Review* 3: 19–28.
Stanley, L. and Wise, S. (1990) 'Method, methodology and epistemology in feminist research processes', in L. Stanley (ed.) *Feminist Praxis: Research, Theory and Epistemology in Feminist Sociology*, London: Routledge.
Tillion, G. (1975) *Ravensbrück*, New York: Doubleday.
Traweek, S. (1995) 'Acting on images: patiently exploring Ob/Gyn in Japan, England and the US', paper presented to the conference on 'Revisioning Women, Health and Healing: Feminist, Cultural and Technoscience Perspectives', San Francisco, October 1995.
Widdershoven, G.A.M. (1993) 'The story of life: hermeneutic perspectives on the relationship between narrative and life history', in R. Josselson and A. Lieblich (eds) *The Narrative Study of Lives, Vol. I*, Newbury Park: Sage.
Young, G. and Dickerson, B.J. (1994) 'Introduction', in G. Young and B.J. Dickerson (eds) *Color, Class and Country: Experiences of Gender*, London: Zed Books.
Young, J.E. (1990) *Writing and Re-writing the Holocaust: Narrative and the Consequence of Interpretation*, Bloomington: Indiana University Press.
Yuval-Davis, N. (1997) *Gender and Nation*, London: Sage.
Yuval-Davis, N. and Anthias, F. (eds) (1989) *Woman – Nation – State*, London: Macmillan.
Zur, J. (1997) 'Reconstructing the self through memories of violence among Mayan Indian women war widows', in R. Lentin (ed.) *Gender and Catastrophe*, London: Zed Books.

7 Gendered diaspora identities
South African women, exile and migration (c. 1960–95)

Elaine Unterhalter

In 1995 I worked on a tracer study designed to locate one hundred randomly selected South Africans who had received scholarships to study in the UK over approximately thirty years. A surprising and unexpected finding of this study was the existence of a powerful socially constructed map of collectivity among exiles, men and women, who were living, or had lived, in very different parts of the world (Europe, North America, South America, South Asia, Australia and Africa). This collectivity encompassed people who had been defined by apartheid in terms of different racial categories, who spoke different languages, practised different religions (or were militant atheists) and were members of different political organisations (Unterhalter and Maxey 1996). This chapter is an attempt to explore to what extent this group was a loose assemblage of migrants and exiles, who happened to know a great deal about each other's whereabouts, and to what extent it was a diaspora. It is also an attempt to consider whether diasporas are gendered and the particular gendered forms of diaspora identities in the South African exile community, particularly in the period up to, and just beyond, the first democratic elections in South Africa in 1994.

The chapter first looks at ways in which diasporas have been theorised and the extent to which these analyses do or do not acknowledge gendered differences. Second, drawing on the interviews conducted for the tracer study and other published material by South African women, whose lives have been disrupted and disjointed by migration and exile, I consider the meanings these women give to exile and home in an attempt to reflect on the theoretical literature.

In summary, the argument is that the majority of women portray going into exile and living in exile in terms of constructions of family, strongly inflected with perceptions of themselves as daughters (chiefly of fathers) or wives. Exiles view their collectivity in ways that echo writing on diaspora. In this constructed family a space is created where boundaries of race are to some extent minimised. Exile brought for many women a journey beyond their view of themselves, bounded by South Africa and its racialised and highly patriarchal categorisations, but it also conferred strong obligations of service to the liberation struggle and to going home. The meaning of the diaspora experience, as portrayed by a majority of exiled South African women, was to return home, reunite themselves with the landscape and give service to the new nation. Much of this duty is strongly expressed in terms of patriarchal relations. Women who for various reasons have not conformed to these diasporic identities feel they have failed.

Diasporas, migrants and the concept of home

There are three very different ways in which diasporas have come to be theorised, coming from contrasting traditions, and each theoretical approach has been further developed by feminist writers.

First, in analyses from what could be loosely termed an ethnic studies approach, diasporas are seen as defining any collectivity that has experienced migration and dispersal for reasons based on economic choice or compulsion, political or cultural persecution, educational aspiration or an amalgam of these, and that maintains a notion of national, racial or ethnic identity under conditions of dispersal across numerous national boundaries and social divisions. Robin Cohen has developed a taxonomy of different types of diaspora using this largely descriptive approach (Cohen 1997). In his work, and in others using this approach, it is the evidence of linkage between members of transnational communities – through language, religion, food or dress – that identifies them as members of a particular diaspora and that singles them out from 'natives' or members of other diasporas in a particular context. Often in this form of analysis these signs of diaspora identity are not considered problematic, contested or in any difficult relation with notions of 'home' (see, e.g., Segal 1987), although Cohen considers how historical shifts might alter the meanings of the markers of diasporic identification (Cohen 1997). Feminist critiques of this position have highlighted the gendered dimensions of these diasporic signifiers, that it is women who are used and strongly controlled to delineate the ethnic or racial boundaries of these diasporas (Anthias and Yuval-Davis 1989; Anthias and Yuval-Davis 1992; Williams 1996). This critique poses questions about the sexual politics entailed in the construction of diasporas, and highlights gendered inequities, which most of the work from this perspective ignores. It advances the notion of diaspora from a notion of natural affiliations to one of structured power and inequity.

A second approach to theorising diaspora comes out of postmodernism, colonial discourse theory and post-colonial theory. Here diaspora communities are analysed not in terms of processes that maintain their unique and self-constructed identity, but rather in terms of the hybridity of their culture, the obviously fractured and constantly sliding and relational aspects of identities, both for individuals and communities. Diaspora communities are analysed not only in terms of their internal effects, but in the ways in which they shape and are shaped by dominant discourses (Hall 1992; Hall and Chen 1996; Bhabha 1990). For these writers, diasporas and their counter-hegemonic quality are set against unitary notions of the nation-state and essentialist notions of unitary cultural identity. Gilroy contrasts the notion of diaspora with that of nation, stressing that it is the latter with its essentialising linking of bio-politics and control over women's bodies that is androcentric, while the notion of diaspora for him is anti-essentialist (Gilroy 1993). Unlike the genealogical account of kin relations, given in accounts of the nation, diasporas, for Gilroy, suggest different modes of linking (Gilroy 1997: 334–5).

> Their plurality and regionality valorize something more than a protracted condition of social mourning over the ruptures of exile, loss, brutality, stress and forced separation. They highlight a more indeterminate and, some would say, modernist mode in which a degree of alienation from one's place of birth and types of cultural estrangement are capable of conferring insight and creating pleasure, as well as precipitating anxiety about the coherence of the nation and the stability of its imaginary ethnic or cultural core.
>
> (Gilroy 1997: 335)

The implication, not pursued or developed in this text, is that diaspora identities allow destabilising and transgressive versions of masculinity and femininity to flourish. It is evident that much of the focus of these writers is on the creation and recreation of cultures in different political and economic settings. Diaspora peoples' alternative narratives of nations, perceptions of time and space, and evident multiple identities clearly articulate what Ali Rattansi has called the postmodern frame (Rattansi 1994). In a much-used play on words, while for the first group of writers diaspora peoples are defined in terms of roots, for this second group of theorists they are to be understood in cultural constructions and reconstructions that take place along the routes of their journeying.

Feminist writers within this framework have pointed to the forming and reforming of feminised identities in the process of diasporic counter-narration and shifting identities (Spivak 1987; Mohanty 1988). Gendered identity for these writers is just one of other shifting sets of relationships and their achievement has been to note the implications of shifting gendered identities. For example, Avtar Brah sees diasporas as conceptual frameworks for thinking about relationality; they are not to be confused with specific historic diasporas – of Jews, blacks or South Africans. In addition, she develops a notion of diaspora space which marks the simultaneous conditions of dispersal and staying put, and attempts to theorise dimensions of cultural, political, economic, psychic and social intersectionality (Brah 1996: 241–8). By implication, the gendering of diaspora space entails theorising a gendered modality of all these intersections, but the theorisation refuses any privileging of gender or any other 'grand' relation. Thus, while feminist critics of the first ethnic studies position challenged some of its analytic assumptions, feminist writers in the second postmodern position discussed above have enlarged the scope of mainstream writers without critiquing their theorisation.

Set against the ethnic studies and the cultural studies perspectives on diasporas there appears to be a third position, which I will tentatively term the interpretative sociological position. Unlike the first position, where the diaspora is largely delineated in terms of a set of constant cultural markers, and the second position, where the diaspora is contingent, constantly created and re-created in relation to other formations, in this third position the diaspora provides its own meanings which interact with those of the analyst and of diaspora peoples.

An example of this approach is Ronald Segal's book about African enslavement and resistance (Segal 1995). The book ends with the affirmation:

> Yet surely, five centuries of distinctive experience cannot be without some underlying meaning, some redeeming force, a very principle of identity that may be called the soul. The soul is freedom. It was in slavery that the Diaspora was born, together with the longing and struggle for freedom.
>
> (Segal 1995: 439)

Central to Segal's notion of the black diaspora is a notion of enslavement and longing for freedom. The diaspora for him is not simply a community of migrants, but a community that is held together by particular experiences of horrific loss, and aspirations for universal freedom. In his preface he links his birth into a diaspora community of Jewish South Africans to his commitment and obligation to chronicle the aspirations of diaspora communities:

> I believe ... that a people with a past infused by oppression and suffering is charged with a special responsibility to remember and remind; to redeem the past with a creative meaning; to recognise and insist that we must treat one another as equally human, beyond differences of race or nationality, religion or culture, if we are not to become mere beasts that talk.
>
> (Segal 1995: xii)

Interestingly, feminist writers in this tradition tend, like feminist postmodernists, not to privilege gendered meanings of redemption in the diaspora or to single out special feminised interpretations of diasporic meanings because of their own gendered identity. Thus, for example,

Elizabeth Grosz, exploring the relationship between 'the lived experience of Jewishness' and the way in which this contributes to understanding the position of social marginality or exile which the Jew shares with other groups, does not privilege feminised marginality (Grosz 1993: 57). Grosz considers different meanings of diaspora for Jews and the ways they might form agency 'uniquely privileged in terms of social transgression and renewal' (Grosz 1993: 70), but interestingly for an important feminist writer she presents this as an ungendered form of agency carrying ungendered meanings.

In the three ways of analysing diaspora I have identified, there is a slightly different inflection of migration. For the first approach, the diaspora is linked because of its construction of common features of 'home' from which the migrants have come. In the second approach, the diaspora is held together because of its common construction of hybridity and transnationality, that is by the experience of journeying and transition, a collective process of border crossings. For writers in the third approach, the diaspora is linked because of its common construction of a different notion of 'home', in this case conceived in terms of more abstract principles (like freedom or social renewal), to which diaspora peoples aspire to go.

None of the approaches to theorising diaspora I have outlined, with the exception of the feminist critics of the ethnic studies approach, gives gender (or any other social division) any special explanatory force. In all the mainstream approaches, gendered differences are either ignored or treated equivalently to other shifting (or fixed) boundaries of identity. I now want to look at the ways in which South African women who have experienced migration and exile portray their experiences in what they delineate as a diaspora, to explore further the question of whether gender is insignificant in thinking about diaspora or not.

South African women, exile and migration

As yet there is no published history of South African exile and migration. This gap makes it difficult to situate fully an analysis of South African diaspora identities. We do not know how large the exiled population was, when it began, nor what proportion of people returned after 1990. Nor do we know whether there was more migration from some regions of South Africa than others and from which collectivities. While the largest waves of migration were probably linked to key events in the history of apartheid and of the opposition struggles, like the Sharpeville massacre of 1960, the Soweto uprising of 1976 and the State of Emergency between 1985 and 1990, it became clear from the 1995 tracer study that there had been a migration of South Africans to the UK and other parts of Africa before 1960 (Unterhalter and Maxey 1996).

This study also revealed how different racialised and ethnicised groups in South Africa were forced to leave the country in very different ways and had markedly different access to material, educational and cultural resources (ibid.). The ways in which gender marked routes into exile and access to resources in countries of refuge was evident in this work. Women comprised a significantly smaller proportion of candidates put forward by all liberation movements for scholarships. The women who received scholarships often did so because of the connections of male relatives to the resources of the liberation movements. The South African exile communities thus appear strongly marked by male authority. For significant numbers of women access to education had to be negotiated through relationships, that generally invoked kin ties, with men.

Although the lack of any more detailed history makes it difficult to assess the significance of the findings from the tracer study, I now want to turn to some of the themes that have emerged from my still preliminary analysis of South African women's experience of exile, drawing on the interviews conducted for that study and other published writings by South African women exiles. A full list of sources from which this analysis is drawn is set out in Appendix 1. I have considered life histories, published interviews and autobiographies and the unpublished interviews collected for the tracer study and have made my analysis drawing on the views of ninety women appearing in various places and forms. All left South Africa because of a more or less explicit opposition to the apartheid regime. I do not draw on material of women who left for other reasons to do with work or family. While the data sources are uneven, eclectic and not systematic, I believe they are wide enough in scope to draw some preliminary conclusions.

Diaspora identities – an elusive South African collectivity

One of the first points that emerges from the data is that not all of the women who consider themselves, and were considered by their interviewers, as part of a South African migrant collectivity are South African by birth. Two women aged around 40 interviewed for the tracer study had married South African political exiles, and experienced a further exile with their husbands that removed them from their countries of birth. One of these returned to South Africa after the unbanning of all formerly illegal political parties in 1990 and spoke of this as 'returning home because of my involvement with the South African struggle' (AET interview files 1995). The second, although now divorced from the South African father of her children, contemplated a future for herself and her children in South Africa 'if the right opportunity' came up (AET interview files 1995).

Two younger women interviewed by Hilda Bernstein were the children of South African exiles whose partners were not South African; Tanya Hodgson was born in Leipzig and thought of herself as 'largely South African, but I think a little bit will always be German and a little bit will always be British' (Bernstein 1994: 490). Nandi Vileika, who was born in London, had spent time in southern Africa but had spent most of her life in Sweden, said of herself: 'I don't know if I'm South African, I don't know if I'm a Brit. But I'll never be a Swede' (Bernstein 1994: 495).

These examples illustrate how malleable a construct national identity can be. Younger and older women, who had not been born in South Africa, considered it part of their identity. This was articulated as an aspiration or the reality of 'home'. Clearly some powerful process of diaspora identification was at work here. But what did it comprise? Before examining that question directly I want to discuss women at the other end of the continuum, who were born in South Africa but believed they had lost some or all of that identity.

For the AET study there were a number of women interviewed, who for various reasons (to be discussed below) did not consider returning to South Africa, and who felt their South African identity intermixed with other identifications. One, who had lived in many parts of the world, considered herself shaped by the different experiences she had had in other countries; layer upon layer of ideas and attitudes had been heaped on what she portrayed as her 'narrow South African self' (AET interview files 1995). Several felt themselves linked to South Africa by strong bonds of identification, but equally strongly held in the UK by the benefits of the health system (for themselves) and the education system (for their children).

Pam Dos Santos, interviewed by Hilda Bernstein in 1990, was the wife of the president of Mozambique; she was born in South Africa but had been forced into exile because, classified white at the age of 19, she had been found guilty of having a sexual relationship with a man classified as coloured. Her parents wanted to have her locked up until she was 21 in a home for juvenile offenders, but she left South Africa for Tanzania. She lived with ANC and FRELIMO exiles in a shared community in Dar es Salaam, eventually marrying a Mozambican and returning to live in Mozambique in 1975 after the defeat of Portuguese colonial rule. In her view she slips between nationally inflected identities:

> At this point, really I must say that I'm Mozambican. I carry Mozambique nationality. I live Mozambican privileges. And I have represented Mozambique at different levels at different times – through the Women's Organisation, as the wife of my husband, etc. But, you know, I come from South Africa. That's where I was born. That's what made me what I am – although perhaps I learned much more in terms of political development and understanding of people through participating in the struggle for the Mozambican people's liberation. What I've contributed to Mozambique in the long run is a contribution also to South Africa, because free Mozambique obviously

means a free South Africa comes nearer. I think the two things are perfectly combined.

(Bernstein 1994: 391)

In this section of the interview she presents her experience of dual identity quite seamlessly; the two appear to complement each other.

My own experience has been far more disjointed and difficult. Although I am almost at the point where I have lived more years in Britain than in South Africa, and although I made and have owned the decision to stay in London after 1990 and not return, I do not feel easy or comfortable. I feel fragmented: neither fully British nor South African, despite what my official documentation says. One particularly difficult moment for me was during the visit of Mandela and a large South African delegation to Britain in 1996. I was invited to a meeting at the CBI to represent my employer, a British university. I found myself sitting with the British delegation at one end of the room, while my friends, the people I felt close to, sat at the other. I found it almost impossible to speak; my voice was a hoarse croak, and I had no inkling how to pitch any comment because it was not clear what position I spoke from. Was this the essence of fragmented diaspora identity?

Gillian Slovo, at the end of her moving book about trying to search out the truth about her family's lives in South Africa, their transition through exile and return, concludes that migration brings not only fragmented identity, but also unstable versions of that:

I'd realised that memory, experience, interpretation could never be fixed or frozen into one unchanging truth. They kept on moving, relentlessly metamorphosing into something other so that the jagged edges of each fragment would never, ever slot together. I thought of the images of my parents that I had collected; each one different from the one before. The dead stay still but the rest of us keep going. When we finally looked back distance distorted what we saw.

(Slovo 1997: 281)

In contrast with some of the women, who have an assurance of their South Africanness, she highlights how the memories and stories on which that notion is built might be unstable, changeable and altered by the very process of attempting to preserve it.

It therefore appears that a range of different forces are at work in the construction of a South African diasporic identity for exiled women. There are forces of inclusion, drawing women into an exiled community through ties of marriage and kinship. There are also forces that unravel that identity, attaching women to new nationalities, as in the case of Pam Dos Santos, or confused fragmented identities, like my own. But these forces, as Gillian Slovo indicates, are themselves shifting and constructed. Are they constructed around any of the versions of diaspora I identified earlier?

To explore this fully I now want to look at the perceptions that emerge from the main body of writing I have examined to draw out the ways in which women from a range of backgrounds who have experienced migration, exile and thus diaspora articulate their South African identity.

Women's diaspora identities

It seems to me there are three main ways, each itself quite complex and inflected by gender relations, that South African women have formulated diaspora identities. First, these identities have been expressed in terms of constructed families, and women have been positioned, or have located themselves within these families as daughters or wives or mothers. Each positioning, in my view, is one of subservience. There are only a handful of accounts of exile and the imaging of family where different locations are articulated. Second, these identities are expressed in terms of a self journeying to wider horizons. Often the journey is undertaken not in terms of self-exploration, but as part of an enactment of 'family' aspirations. Lastly, exile is discussed in terms of a long journey home, with home conceptualised in strikingly similar ways in terms of either a longing for 'place', often defined in terms of patriarchal relations, or a commitment to a particularly feminised notion of submission and service.

The exile community as family

It is striking, in reading the reflections of the women I have selected, how the South African exile community is described in terms of family relations. Metaphors of kinship are frequently used to describe the liberation movements. For example, Meisie Martins told Hilda Bernstein: 'the ANC, I took it as my mother and my father; they brought up my kids and they also brought up myself, because when I came I was still young' (Bernstein 1994: 117). Even living outside official structures of a liberation movement, Linda Mvusi described South African exiles living in other African countries as 'family' (Bernstein 1994: 36).

Many women invoke kin relationships in explaining their actions either in going into exile or in choosing a particular course while in exile. For some, who were children, there were no choices (see Bernstein 1994: 434–89; Slovo 1997). Similarly, a number of wives linked themselves without questioning with their husband's exile (Matthews 1995; Podbrey 1993). But for those who did make choices, it is striking how younger and older women often invoked their fathers in their decisions to go into exile. Zoleka Dilimini, interviewed by Hilda Bernstein, participated in the student uprisings of 1976–7. Her father had been on Robben Island for his ANC activities. She was arrested repeatedly, beaten and attacked by the authorities. Her decision to go into exile was shaped in response to her father's death:

> Whilst I was arrested my father used to come and see me in jail. Who's going to look after me? All such things. So I said I should leave South Africa. I was taken out of the place by these other fathers who were also from Robben Island. My mother didn't know that I was going.
>
> (Bernstein 1994: 76)

Mary Benson was much older than Zoleka when she went into exile, and describes in much greater depth than most of the other participants the difficulties she experienced in reaching the decision to go. But she partly explains her deciding moments in terms of the views of her father (Benson 1989: 214). Gloria Nkadimeng, also interviewed by Hilda Bernstein, outlines her ambivalent feelings for her father, a senior member of the ANC. On the one hand she went into exile to be near him; on the other she constantly felt rejected by his treating all the children in an ANC residence as equivalent to her, showing her no special attention as his daughter. But despite this she sums up her experiences:

> You know, every little step I used to take I used to think of my dad. I think he's gone through a very difficult time, and I just thought I always had to do my best to help him, to make his life so much easier for him; I shouldn't be a trouble. So I used to feel I should put up with anything that came about. And the only gift I could give them was finishing up my education.
>
> (Bernstein 1994: 136)

Similar feelings of ambivalence, pride in a father mixed with sadness at his rejection, are explored by Gillian Slovo in her autobiographical book (Slovo 1997). Ten young women interviewed for the tracer study mentioned their relationship with their fathers as part of their depiction of their lives in exile. For one he was a source of inspiration, for the others a constant reminder of obligations (AET 1995).

It therefore appears that positioning in the diaspora is linked, for many women, not to self-affirmation, even if living in the diaspora entails journeys and educational activities, but much more often to an enactment of daughterly affiliation, however hard and painful that might be. For all the women I have quoted, the father who is linked to their actions in exile is generally linked by absence, rather than presence.

Another strand in many of the interviews and writings I studied was of women feeling that exile, entry into the diaspora, positioned them as mothers either in an endless and painful longing for children who have been lost or left behind, heartbreakingly articulated for example by Ruth Mompati (Bernstein 1994: 20; Russell 1990: 112–13), or as mothers of multiple children, either blood relatives or the figurative children 'of the movement'. Jane Dumasi describes part of her commitment to the ANC in these terms: 'So in my mind I said, "My own children and the children of the ANC, as long as I live they should not live the life I experienced"' (Bernstein 1994: 106).

An articulation of self in relation to motherhood is a feature of many of the other interviews conducted by Hilda Bernstein, interviews with women who both did and did not have their own children (see, for example, interviews with Eleanor Kasrils, Beatty Du Toit, MaMercy Mntabo, Phyllis Naidoo, Bunie Sexwale). It is also a theme in the writing of a number of women who experienced exile (Wolpe 1994; Podbrey 1993; Slovo 1997). While motherhood is not the only location these women take, it is nonetheless an important, for some a pivotal, one.

The invocation of kin in describing the exile community entailed an assumed intimacy. The erected boundaries of family echo in the words of the ANC cabinet minister Mac Maharaj, who told Gillian Slovo that her sister Shawn needed 'a good slap' for writing a film that depicted her parents as ambiguous in their heroism, because this heroism entailed neglecting the needs of their children (Slovo 1997). Similar assumptions of intimacy and the obligation to dutiful daughterhood was part of the initial outcry at the publication of her autobiographical work *Every Secret Thing* in South Africa, where cabinet ministers wondered in diary columns in the newspapers 'How could Gillian do it?' The phrasing assumes obligations of secrecy to a family's honour. Some of the women interviewed for the tracer study spoke about the policing of their sexuality, a screening and vetting of their lovers, by members of the exile community, often older women, acting in this respect as 'family'. In a number of ANC regions, ANC members had to request the permission of the Chief Representative before they could marry (see, for example, Bernstein 1994: 115).

It is striking that this constructed family of exiles sought to obliterate the apartheid lines of racial exclusivity which characterised the majority of South African families. Thus ANC chief representatives, generally men but sometimes women, who might have been classified in South Africa as coloured or African, assumed responsibilities of parenthood for ANC members coming from a range of different racialised groups. The policing of sexuality condoned certain relationships across racialised boundaries, but class and finegrained nuances of race and ethnicity also appear to have been part of what was deemed appropriate in terms of cross-racial sexual relationships in this apparently non-racial exile family (AET interview files 1995).

This portrayal of the exile community – the diaspora – in terms of family, both real and imagined, has much in common with the first theorisation of diaspora I outlined at the beginning of this chapter. The ethnic studies approach stresses the construction of a community. The writing of South African women exiles portrays the community as the exile 'family'.

But, while for the first group of theorists gender divisions were not visible in the community, in the experience of South African women they are markedly evident and striking in the ways in which they invoke patriarchal relations. These govern both entry into the diaspora, even under conditions of 'choice', and many of the delineations of diaspora identity. However, this dimension of subordination within a real or imagined family intertwines for some women, but not all, with a more fluid version of shifting identities.

Diaspora journeyings

Intertwined with this view of women enmeshed through exile in an imagined family is another view of them finding widened horizons, a form of liberation, that entails overcoming the degradation and difficulty of home. In this view the diaspora loosens the chains of South Africanness, particularly tradition, often perceived as difficulty. This version of diaspora identities has similarities with the second position on shifting diaspora identities I outlined above. But in the accounts of these South African women, the acquisition of a wider perspective is often achieved and facilitated through the mediations of kin – either literally through fathers in leadership positions securing scholarships, or through imagined fathers assisting with the publication of books, or through access to new and enriching knowledge (Unterhalter and Maxey 1996; see also Magona 1992). Thus the first version of diaspora is a stepping stone to the second; and the second does not negate the first, but is held in a dialectical relationship with it.

Ironically, however, the assumed non-racialism of the exile family disappears in relation to exile journeys undertaken by women who wished to loosen South African identifications of race or subordinated femininity. The freedom to travel, and the prizes of high status education or artistic achievement in, for example, the UK or Canada, were achieved much more easily by women who had been classified white, and to a lesser extent Indian and coloured, than for women classified as African. For this latter group, unless they had a male relative of high standing in one of the exile movements, the scope of their exile journeyings was considerably circumscribed.

Nearly all the women interviewed for the tracer study spoke of having been enriched by experiences of a 'wider world' beyond South Africa. A number spoke of their experiences of UK higher education in terms of overcoming a stigma they carried from South Africa that they were 'not good enough'. Others outlined how they had become aware of complexity in the UK, while in South Africa things had appeared simple. 'In South Africa,' said one informant, 'you only saw people as black or white; now I see people differently' (AET interview files 1995). 'I had been narrowly stuck in struggle mode in South Africa,' said another. 'In the UK I was jettisoned from this and forced to take a broader international vantage point' (AET interview files 1995).

Acquiring this global view was rarely portrayed as easy. Frene Ginwala, currently the Speaker of the South African parliament, told Hilda Bernstein in 1990 that exile for her had been a long period of 'battling along' (Bernstein 1994: 13). Jane Dumasi saw exile as bringing opportunities of education for her children not dreamed of in South Africa, but also enormous difficulties of dislocation and loss (Bernstein 1994: 107). A woman, interviewed for the tracer study, saw her opportunity to leave an ANC training camp and come to study in London as 'a dream come true', but also spoke of her loneliness and the difficulty of learning to take decisions. 'I missed my father. Alone in a strange country I had to take decisions. I did not ask anyone's permission. I had to be responsible because I was alone' (AET interview files 1995).

This comment indicates a strong link between her relationship with her father and her acquiring independence through studying and taking responsibility. The diaspora provides a taste of being away from 'family' and ordered society.

It is striking that exile and migration has been a major spur to South African women's creativity. A considerable number of books by South African women have emerged out of their stay in exile and the experience of exile and migration is a major theme in this writing, unlike that of many men in exile (see Appendix 2 for a preliminary list of this work). Exile has also led to an expression of visual artistic creativity in the work of Linda Mvusi and Hilda Bernstein, for example. However, exile did not give a voice or an audience equally to all women. Women categorised as white predominate in the list of those whose creative works gained recognition.

This portrayal of exile in terms of journeying towards new identities, a different vision of the world, echoes the second, post-structuralist approach to theorising diaspora identities as a journey of shifting selves. But while, for writers in this framework like Gilroy and Brah, gender is not privileged in construction of the hybrid identities of the diaspora, South African women's gendered relations, primarily the dependence of women on male sponsors, often their fathers (real or imagined), shape the extent to which this journeying can be given a formal direction – towards a degree, for example, or the publication of a book. Neither gender nor race is just one of a multiplicity of identities, but both frame very strongly the extent to which diaspora journeyings are or are not sliding and in a non-sequenced flux.

The image of home

The two versions of diaspora I have outlined above are both held in tension with a third idea. That is the idea of the absent home. It is the home that has been lost that binds the family closer, and often legitimates the patriarchal relations of the imagined family. Similarly it is the home that is desired that gives meaning to the diaspora journeyings. They are frequently interpreted not in their creative intersectionality but in a normative intertextuality. These journeys entail a destiny, given by what has been lost, a destiny of national liberation or service to a new South Africa.

In the interviews and other writings, home is very frequently condensed to a single location, its multiplicity refined down to a few images, often of landscape. Mary Benson, wandering around London, immersed herself in a nineteenth-century journal of life in South Africa written by her great-grandfather, and in recording and recounting the history of the liberation struggle of the twentieth century. It is the family journal that stirs her longings to return home:

> I wished I could return to search out the far-off patch of scrubland where he and the family struggled to survive. I longed to go 'home'. A longing I've deliberately repressed. But at times I am taken unawares; the cooing of an African dove suddenly heard in some wild-life programme on television never fails to arouse a pang of nostalgia – a primitive essence of sun, heat, summer-dry grass, everywhere buzzing insects hovering above bright flowers, while doves call from a eucalyptus tree.
>
> (Benson 1989: 221)

The passage carries an intensity of feeling, side by side with a hint that maybe such feelings are inappropriate 'nostalgia', or 'primitive'.

And yet other women express similar longings. Ruth Weiss told Hilda Bernstein of her emotional responses to South Africa, not even the country she had been born in, but nonetheless the one for which she felt the most intense longing (Bernstein 1994: 46). Betty Du Toit, suffering a grave illness throughout virtually all her time in exile, longed for South Africa as the home where she wanted to die (Bernstein 1994: 63). The notion of home as a place where one could settle and be still is a strong theme. Gloria Nkadimeng said: 'The only time my home can settle is in South Africa' (Bernstein 1994: 137), and a number of women interviewed for the tracer study spoke of buying a house for the first time or marking their place on the South African landscape by similar acts affirming belonging; one spoke of making sure she did not lose her *roots*. Another spoke of returning to the place of her birth and enjoying the *fruits* of freedom (AET interview files 1995).These metaphors locate home as a place of natural belonging.

The link between home and place on the land is interestingly expressed without any reference to the way race marked the landscape of South Africa in the apartheid years. There is no place in South Africa that does not have a history of racialised identification, and despite constitutional commitments to overcome this, it will not be an easy matter. But diaspora women, from a range of different racialised backgrounds, in seeking to go home obliterate the racialised connotations of any particular home.

The notion of home as a naturalised deracialised place, however, is not the only way women exiles portray it. For many it is delineated in terms of a range of relationships with society. Interestingly, in contrast with the way the exile community is portrayed in terms of family, home is portrayed in terms of non-kin links. For some it is a place of strangeness, of new work to be done (see, for example, interviews with Frene Ginwala, Meisie Martins, Bunie Sexwale in Bernstein 1994; see also Wolpe 1994). For others it is a place of friendship (Linda Mvusi in Bernstein 1994). For a large number in the tracer study it was a place of service, to carry out the work for which they had received training (Unterhalter and Maxey 1996). For many, it is a place to enact political commitment and obligations to the liberation movement. One respondent in the tracer study suggested she had no option in this: 'I had to come home. I had a political obligation to come home' (AET interview files).

This is in contrast with another respondent in the same study who said, 'This is my life. It is also my choice.' For some, service appears compelled by strong obligations; for others, it is chosen. It is interesting how these obligations are expressed in non-personalised terms. The journey from exile to home is a journey, it seems, of growth to adulthood, leaving the imaginary family for an imaginary society where largely abstractly formulated goals can be put into practice. One respondent in the tracer study did personalise the act of coming home. She said: 'I love my country. I have fought so hard for it. But there is so much to be changed' (AET interview files 1995).

Home here is not a place and not a neutral space for service: it is beloved. This is expressed not as the obedient or dutiful love of exiled daughters and wives, but as a very passionate adult love about notions of self. There is a similar strand in Mary Benson's book where she recounts a conversation with Athol Fugard about their relationship forged in opposition to the dominance and cruelty of apartheid. She recounts Fugard saying to her:

> We recognize something in each other. I think we love, respond in the same way and that is a powerful and mysterious bond. I can look to you to see if I have, in a new piece of work, affirmed what exists as a common denominator between us. It's to do with complexity, the awesome nature of being a true lover of South Africa.
>
> (Benson 1989: 233)

I am certain the ideas expressed by Fugard are also Benson's, for she calls her book *The Making of a South African*. Maybe she puts the words into the voice of a male friend because it is difficult for women to own this kind of love that is not conventional. These extracts raise difficult questions for analysts, because so much of the feminist writing of women and nationalism has stressed how much women are manipulated into a false consciousness, against their more universalistic interests (Anthias and Yuval-Davis 1989; Williams 1996).

These conceptualisations of home resonate with the third view of diaspora I outlined. This approach sees exile and diaspora in terms of the redemption of the journey home. Home and the meaning of exile and the diaspora are realised in a physical connection to the land, or a relational service to the society, or through some particular fulfilment of self. Interestingly similar themes were all expressed by male respondents in the tracer study, although a full reading of a wider sample of writings by male exiles is still to be done. Here, gender and race does not appear to mark the diaspora in the striking ways it did in relation to notions of community or journey.

However, what was striking from the tracer study was how, in contrast to men, women exiles, who had remained outside South Africa, felt themselves failures. Their reasons for not returning home varied. Some felt they could not return home, because they had not achieved enough in terms of education or training. As one woman who had not completed her studies said: 'At home everybody is progressing. I have failed. Where can I hide?' (AET interview files 1995). Others were compelled to remain outside South Africa, generally because of strong commitments to husbands or children who were not able to settle in South Africa. Those who had work that allowed them to visit South Africa frequently were not as desolate as those who felt they could never return. This was strikingly different to the men who had not returned and who appeared much more comfortable with their decisions, possibly because they were generally better off materially and in higher status occupations than the women. It therefore appears that home might give equivalent meanings to men and women who fulfil diaspora destinies, but that for women who do not carry out diasporic obligations the psychic and material costs are heavier than for men. Diaspora, for women who do not fulfil its demands, is not an enabling space, as both Avtar Brah and Elizabeth Grosz suggest. For women who do not live as they should in the diaspora, it becomes an area of constant difficulty.

Conclusion

In this paper I have looked at a particular diaspora and attempted to reflect on a range of theorisations of diaspora in the light of this. The diaspora identities of South African women appear strongly marked by gendered obligations to family and by duty to home. This diaspora and the relationships it has formed have not transformed the sexism of South African society, although many diaspora journeyings have given some women access to networks and ideas that have helped them build on feminist achievements inside the country. But the hardship of persistent sexism is not expelled simply through journeying or redeemed in the mere fact of service and return.

Appendix 1

The data for this paper comes from diverse sources (see Table 1). Twenty-six women were interviewed for the Africa Educational Trust tracer study conducted in 1995 (AET interview files 1995; Unterhalter and Maxey 1996). Hilda Bernstein's book on the exile experience of South Africans contains interviews conducted mainly in 1989 and 1990 with fifty-three women (Bernstein 1994). Three women in exile (two of whom are also the subjects of lengthy interviews in the Bernstein book) are interviewed in Diana Russell's collection of lives of South African women, and Diana Russell herself meditates in her introduction on her relation with the land of her birth (Russell 1990).

In addition, I draw on the published writings of ten South African women who have experienced migration or exile (two of whom were separately interviewed by Hilda Bernstein). These are Benson (1989), Levitan (1993), Magona (1991; 1992), Makhoere (1988), Matthews (1995), Ntantala (1991), Podbrey (1993), Slovo (1997), Wicomb (1987), Wolpe (1994). Lastly, I have used some of my own memories and perceptions of identity as a South African exile. I have not systematised these personal reflections but developed them as counterpoints to some of the themes that emerge from thinking about the perceptions of other South African women.

Table 1 Sources of data on South African women's experiences of exile

Source of information	Numbers of women
AET tracer study	26
Bernstein collection	10
Russell collection	4
Published autobiographies	10
Personal reflection	1
Total	93 *

* Four women's accounts of their lives were published in two different sources

Appendix 2

Table 2 A preliminary bibliography of South African women empowered to write creatively in exile

Name	Form of work
Mary Benson	history; political analysis; autobiography
Hilda Bernstein	political analysis; novel; autobiography
Betty du Toit	history
Ruth First	autobiography; biography; political analysis
Frene Ginwala	political analysis; history
Esther Levitan	autobiography
Norma Kitson	autobiography
Sindiwe Magona	autobiography
Caesarina Makhoere	autobiography
Tessa Marcus	history; political analysis
Freda Matthews	autobiography
Ilva McKay	poetry
Loretta Ngcobo	novel
Phyllis Ntantala	autobiography
Bunie Sexwale	political analysis
Gillian Slovo	novels; autobiography
Shawn Slovo	screenplays
Robyn Slovo	short stories
Elaine Unterhalter	sociological analysis; history
Zoe Wicomb	autobiographical stories
Ruth Weiss	political analysis
AnnMarie Wolpe	sociological analysis; autobiography

References

AET interview files (1995) Material collected through interviews by researchers working on the Africa Educational Trust commissioned tracer study of South Africans studying in the UK and Ireland, 1960–95.

Anthias, F. and Yuval-Davis, N. (eds) (1989) *Woman – Nation – State*, London: Macmillan.

Anthias, F. and Yuval-Davis, N. (1992) *Racialized Boundaries: Race, Nation, Gender, Colour and Class and the Anti-Racist Struggle*, London: Routledge.

Baard, F. (1986) *My Spirit is not Banned*, Harare: Zimbabwe Publishing House.

Benson, M. (1989) *A Far Cry. The Making of a South African*, London: Penguin.

Bernstein, H. (1994) *The Rift. The Exile Experiences of South Africans*, London: Jonathan Cape.
Bhabha, H. (1990) *Nation and Narration*, London: Routledge.
Brah, A. (1996) *Cartographies of Diaspora. Contesting Identities*, London: Routledge.
Cohen, R. (1997) *Global Diasporas. An Introduction*, London: UCL Press.
Gilroy, P. (1993) *The Black Atlantic: Modernity and Double Consciousness*, London: Hutchinson.
Gilroy, P. (1997) 'Diaspora and the detours of identity', in K. Woodward (ed.) *Identity and Difference*, London: Sage.
Grosz, E. (1993) 'Judaism and exile: The ethics of otherness', in E. Carter, J. Donald and J. Squires (eds) *Space and Place: Theories of Identity and Location*, London: Lawrence and Wishart.
Hall, S. (1992) 'The question of cultural identity', in S. Hall *et al.* (eds) *Modernity and its Futures*, Cambridge: Polity Press.
Hall, S. and Chen, K.-I. (1996) 'The formation of a diasporic intellectual', in D. Morley and K.-H. Chen (eds) *Stuart Hall. Critical Dialogues in Cultural Studies*, London: Routledge.
Levitan, E. (1993) *The Book of Esther*, Tel-Aviv: Holan Wordshop.
Magona, S. (1991) *To My Children's Children: An Autobiography*, London: The Women's Press.
Magona, S. (1992) *Forced to Grow*, Cape Town: David Philip.
Makhoere, C. (1988) 'No child's play', in *Prison under Apartheid*, London: The Women's Press.
Matthews, F. (1995) *Remembrances*, Bellville: Mayibuye Books.
Mohanty, C. (1988) 'Under western eyes: feminist scholarship and colonial discourses', *Feminist Review* 30.
Ntantala, P. (1991) *A Life's Mosaic*, Cape Town: David Philip.
Podbrey, P. (1993) *White Girl in Search of the Party*, Pietermaritzburg: Hadeda Books.
Rattansi, A. (1994) '"Western" racisms, ethnicities and identities in a "postmodern" frame', in A. Rattansi and S. Westwood (eds) *Racism, Modernity and Identity on the Western Front*, Cambridge: Polity Press.
Russell, D. (1990) *Lives of Courage. Women for a New South Africa*, London: Virago.
Segal, A. (1987) 'The Caribbean Exodus in a global context: comparative migration experiences', in B. Levine (ed.) *The Caribbean Exodus*, New York: Praeger.
Segal, R. (1995) *The Black Diaspora*, London: Faber and Faber.
Slovo, G. (1997) *Every Secret Thing. My Family, My Country*, London: Little Brown.
Spivak, G. (1987) *In Other Worlds. Essays in Cultural Politics*, London: Methuen.
Unterhalter, E. and Kees Maxey (1996) *Educating South Africans in Britain and Ireland: A Review of Thirty-Three Years of Sponsorship by the Africa Educational Trust*, London: Africa Educational Trust.
Wicomb, Z. (1987) *You Can't Get Lost in Cape Town*, London: Virago.
Williams, B. (ed.) (1996) *Women Out Of Place. The Gender of Agency and the Race of Nationality*, London: Routledge.
Wolpe, A. (1994) *The Long Way Home*, London: Virago.
Yuval-Davis, N. and Anthias, F. (1992) *Racialized Boundaries*, London: Routledge.

8 No fixed abode
Feminism in the 1990s

*Debbie Epstein and
Deborah Lynn Steinberg*

In its original incarnation, this paper was a response to an invitation to answer the question 'What is the state of feminism?' (in a thousand or fewer 'well-chosen words' – inevitably later increased!).[1] Each of us found this a somewhat amusing request. Two further questions immediately suggested themselves: which feminism? and which state? And yet it gives one pause for thought to consider why, indeed, it is so difficult to summarise 'where feminism's at', not only generally, but for ourselves personally.

It can be argued that feminism has never had a fixed abode. That even during that era, which both of us remember, in which feminism seemed to be housed everywhere (and even had its own houses), it was never an 'it'. However reified it seemed to become in some narratives, feminism has always been a journey with divergent as well as coalescent paths, a process of contestation and a politics of motion: in a word, a 'movement'.

In our discussions about this, we found ourselves preoccupied with our own personal histories as feminists and with the ways in which our pasts on the one hand encompass quite significantly different routes (and roots) to and through feminism and yet, on the other hand, have resulted in us travelling what seems to be, in many respects, the same road now. For example, we have moved through organised (often adversarial) socialist and 'radical' feminisms respectively to our present shared commitment to the development of more complex versions of feminism: feminisms which encompass an analysis not only of gender but also of the ways in which gender relations shape and are shaped by a range of other inequalities and differences. For both of us, dissatisfaction with the interpersonal and political agendas with which we had been working became, at some crucial point, untenable. At the same time, both of our histories are marked by a relatively recent but dramatic and painful dislocation from activist feminist politics (which are linked to the dissatisfactions we experienced in the groups with which we had been involved). While we still retain membership in some of the few remaining feminist organisations, this is largely a paper and financial membership.[2] Insofar as our experiences are emblematic of the 'state of feminism' and of those of us more or less stateless (and homeless) within it, it would seem imperative to examine the conditions under which feminism seems no longer to be found at many previous addresses, while being accommodated more or less contingently in the academy and incorporated more or less comfortably within popular culture. In this short chapter, then, we are talking about three states of feminism: our state(s) as feminists; the state of feminisms in our own immediate (British) contexts; and the state of feminisms beyond ourselves.

Accommodation un/wanted: feminisms in the 1990s

It is treacherously easy, in bemoaning the loss of our feminist activism, to entrap ourselves in self-blame, to refuse responsibility for our own actions or to become enwrapped in a romantic nostalgia for some mythical golden age of feminism and the women's movement. It is also ironic to be writing about this loss of activism from the vantage point of being pretty comfortably (or not, as the case may be) installed in the academy. It has often been claimed that the carving out of spaces for feminism within universities *is* activism. Universities, after all, are as 'real' as any other part of the 'real world'. And yet. And yet ... it's just not the same. This is not only because the academy, as it is currently organised, largely remains an elitist institution in racialised, classed and gendered (among other) terms. It is also because there is a specific institutionalisation of inequalities within universities – inequalities between teachers and taught, hierarchies among teachers and between managers and teachers for a start. Our times together are zoned, our speech is circumscribed within the protocols of university teaching/learning practice.[3]

It is true that there can be and often is a joy and an incipient, or even sometimes explicit, radicalism in teaching and studying. Indeed, in our own areas of Cultural/Women's Studies there is often a sharing of a political project, but it is a delimited sharing. To paraphrase bell hooks (1994), we may be teaching and studying to transgress, but at the end of the day we subject that process to the normalising gaze of discipline (or punishment) that constitutes the penal economies of education. If the academy becomes our only viable outlet for feminist activism then, however valuable the academic work we do may be in political terms and no matter how marginal we and our work may remain within the academy, that politics is manifestly invested in a range of institutional practices which, as feminists, we seek to oppose.

Indeed, one of the things we have lost, in the loss of abode(s), fixed or otherwise, for feminism is the myriad opportunities to organise (in)formally around joint political projects. And, over the last decade, feminism has lost addresses right and left.

Compulsory purchase – order?

In understanding the shrinking spaces which feminisms are able to occupy, it is important to consider the shifting contexts (geo-political and academic) within which so many feminists have found themselves, dispossessed or displaced, more or less comfortably accommodated (or accommodating), selling up (or even selling out).

It is a cliché of our time that the political ground in international and local terms has shifted so far to the right that the left, notwithstanding 1997 elections in the UK and France, has become almost unrecognisable. Or, where it does seem to hold fast, often seems quaintly anachronistic. There is a sense in which, at least in Britain, the choreography of radical activism through mass demonstration, through telling slogans, through teach-ins, consciousness-raising and strike action has come to be dismissed as passé. Certainly it is true that, over the past two decades, these actions have been regularly passed over, as if their speech was of no consequence, as if they made no history and no real comment on anything of any significance. How many tens of thousands of people demonstrated against the Asylum Bill[4] or the Alton Bill,[5] to name but two repressive initiatives of those years, without achieving even 15 seconds of acknowledgement (let alone 15 minutes of fame)? The erosion of feminist activism of all kinds has been part of the erosion of left activism combined with the Rightward-Ho movement of the political scene more generally exacerbated by recession, compromised spending in the public sector, job insecurity, trends towards monopoly in the private sector (including in the market of popular and academic media); the autonomous margins of political protest and dissent seem to have been repossessed. Indeed, it seems that we have come to a pretty pass when hopes for progressive social change have to be pinned on recuperated 'left' (right-left) politicians like Bill Clinton and Tony Blair!

Repossessions

There are some paradoxical elements in the erosion of the autonomous margins previously inhabited by feminism. For example, even as there seems to be an arguable 'backlash' (Faludi 1992) against feminism there are ways in which it seems to have become simultaneously accommodated as popular common sense in a number of respects. From the *Oprah Winfrey Show*[6] to *Roseanne*, from *Prime Suspect*[7] to *Brookside*[8] to *Dispatches*,[9] from *Cosmo*[10] to *RiotGirrls*[11] and even, some might say, the Spice Girls, feminism has certainly shifted the ground, albeit ambiguously, of popular representation. These and other less obviously feminist-influenced media seem to share assumptions that, for example, women are entitled to be free from domestic and sexual violence, that women have a right to education, to work and even to equal pay, and furthermore, that male power and men are legitimate objects of critique and that men should change. We can see the centralisation of feminism in other spaces, too, where certain forms of sexism have become unpopular, if not unspeakable. As we saw in the 1997 British general election, crass sexism and homophobia from politicians was not a vote-winner. Even the clichéd statement, 'I'm not a feminist but ...' can be read as a euphemism which creates a permissive space within which to claim some of the aspirations of feminism while disclaiming the negative connotations of the label.

So, in some ways, it could be argued that the extent to which feminism seems now to occupy the 'centre' obviates the need for marginal space. However, it should not come as a surprise (to paraphrase Dr Benton's brother-in-law in *ER*!) that the world doesn't change just because we move up in it. Rather than feminism having purchase of the centre, what we have here is feminism repossessed. We would argue that it is a good, even exciting, phenomenon that feminism has entered the mainstream in these ways, but it has been at the expense of what bell hooks (1984) identified as sites of radical possibility.

What happens when we lose the marginal space? One consequence of the centralisation of feminism is clearly the loss of the means of its production. Who makes movies? Who makes television? Notwithstanding the success of individual feminist film makers like Pratibha Parmar or Mandy Merck,[12] there are few of them around and they bear an increasingly disproportionate burden of representation for 'the state of feminism'. There have, of course, never been more than a few at the 'centre', but the margins, at one point, seemed chock-a-block with vastly diverse groups of women defining feminism in vastly diverse and everyday kinds of ways. Being a feminist (or lefty) by watching 'alternative television' on Channel 4 is not the same as making it happen in your neighbourhood and your life. There is a way in which the diminishment of the myriad possibilities for activist feminisms and the emergence of televisual feminism have given a much more voyeuristic character to what it means to be a feminist and a much more voyeuristic character to the 'state of feminism'.

A second consequence of the centralisation of the political economy of feminism in a range of contexts is that the least dangerous, the least threatening version of feminism is what invariably gets taken up as common sense (even as tired old clichés of man-hating lesbians continue to be recycled). This is a version which is primarily invested in liberal reform and white middle-class institutions. Indeed, it could be argued that the extent to which feminism has been made palatable within popular culture is in direct proportion to the ways in which it has been made compatible with capitalism and the reproduction of heterosexuality – indeed, the freedom of the *Cosmo* woman, *Cosmo* feminism or 'girl power' is precisely grounded in these aspirations.

A third consequence of the centralisation of feminism in this way is the loss of a sense of debates within feminism and of feminism *as* a process of debate. Feminism reduced to spectacle and object of consumption displaces and redefines feminism as method (notwithstanding our sometimes 'voyeuristic intentions').[13] The homogenisation of feminism (and its recuperation for at best a marginally altered status quo) in this context is perhaps inevitable given the ontological positions and institutional infrastructures involved.

Subsidence – i/ensuring the future?

It is interesting, if not ironic, that at the very same time that simplistic and universalising constructions of feminism seem to be reaching their apotheosis (though not a terribly dramatic one) in popular culture, academic feminisms have become increasingly complex and invested in discussion of difference. In this context, liberal feminism, far from being celebrated or central, has much more often been substantively criticised. Similarly, the tendency to universalise both white middle-class experience and white middle-class feminism has become increasingly problematised.

Feminism is curiously marginal-yet-central/central-yet-marginal within higher education. There are in Britain, for example, some (if not many) professors of Women's Studies, degrees in Gender and Women's Studies have become widely available and most courses in arts, humanities and social sciences incorporate at least some attention to gender (if not feminism) in the curriculum. The sense of feminism as a process of debate flourishes here. And, proportionally speaking, the means of production of feminisms (or feminist knowledge) are within reach of those who are neither 'stars' nor even that much out of the ordinary within the academic community. And universities (even in their 'post-Fordist' configuration) are, relatively speaking, more hospitable to radical thought than most other places. 'Academic freedom', after all, must allow for radical critique and the existence of radical critics (of different persuasions) is generally taken as 'proof' of academic freedom.

This is, of course, one of the ways in which higher education constitutes a marginal site of radical possibilities in itself. At the same time, the elitism of universities is at the core of the reproduction of both social conservatism and social inequality. At their best, contemporary universities constitute Platonic democracies in which citizenship confers the privileges of democracy, but that citizenship is selective. Feminist scholars rarely achieve full citizenship; most of us hover at the edges of an uncomfortable, yet at the same time exclusive, residency.

Renovations (restorations?)

We find ourselves and the state of feminism enmeshed in a paradox. Theoretically and politically we no longer believe in the value of attempting to fix a notional unity for feminism or to fix an address in

terms of its location or mode. But this leaves us stranded, in some crucial way homeless
and in need of an address.

Notes

1 D. Epstein and D.L. Steinberg (1996) 'No fixed abode: feminism in the 1990s', *Parallax* 3: 1–6.
2 We have remained activists; however this has been largely confined to limited opportunities for more or less temporary accommodation within lesbian and gay politics, often in single issue campaigns (for example, the Stop the Clause campaign against Section 28 of the Local Government 1988 Act which has prohibited the 'promotion' of a homosexual lifestyle in schools in receipt of local government funding – and which the Labour government has not yet repealed).
3 See Steinberg (1997) for an extended discussion of the zoning of speech in the disciplinary economy of penalty which constitutes higher education.
4 The Asylum Bill 1996 (now an Act) further restricted entry to the UK by: (a) setting up a category of 'bogus asylum seekers', which constitutes the majority of those seeking asylum; (b) removing the rights of asylum seekers (even 'genuine' ones) to claim social security support while their cases are heard (subsequently ruled unlawful by the courts, with the result that the financial obligations of support were devolved to local authorities, mainly in hard-pressed inner-city areas); and (c) setting up a 'whitelist' of countries from which it is assumed that petitions for asylum are, prima facie, not genuine (including many war-torn areas and countries with military dictatorships).
5 The 'Alton Bill' (Abortion (Amendment) Bill) in 1987 proposed to lower the upper time limit of legal abortion from 28 weeks to 18 weeks gestation on the basis that, at 18 weeks, a foetus had presumptive personhood and therefore fell under the protection of the Infant Life Preservation Act 1927. The Alton Bill ran out of time before it could become law, but the principle of criminalisation of 'late abortion' was partly incorporated in the subsequent Human Fertilisation and Embryology Act 1990 (which lowered the upper time limit for legal abortion from 28 weeks to 24 weeks, with the exception of cases of maternal endangerment or abortion of 'damaged' foetuses). For further discussion of the Alton Bill, see Steinberg (1991).
6 See Epstein and Steinberg (1995, 1997).
7 *Prime Suspect* (a British crime drama) featured a feminist detective inspector. The first in the series, *Prime Suspect 1*, had as a major focus sexism in the police force.
8 The storyline about domestic violence in the British soap opera *Brookside* was explicitly influenced by feminism. It featured women in organised activism and, indeed, became a key reference point in the campaign to release women in British prisons for killing their violent partners.
9 *Dispatches* is only one of the many documentary slots in British television which frequently features explicit engagement with issues raised by feminism.
10 For a discussion of *Cosmopolitan*'s own particular brand of capitalist, aspirational feminism, see Winship (1987).
11 RiotGirrls is a radical group of feminist young women in the USA which produces a publication by the same name (and was, in fact, featured on the *Oprah Winfrey Show*).

12 Both Parmar and Merck have made a name for themselves in the production of alternative/lesbian and gay television. Most notable, perhaps, was the *Out* series on Channel 4 in Britain.
13 As aptly sung by Magenta in 'Time Warp' from *The Rocky Horror Picture Show*.

References

Epstein, D. and Steinberg, D.L. (1995) 'Hetero-sensibilities on the *Oprah Winfrey Show*', in J. Purvis and M. Maynard (eds) *(Hetero)sexual Politics*, London: Taylor & Francis.

Epstein, D. and Steinberg, D.L. (1997) 'All het up! Rescuing heterosexuality on the *Oprah Winfrey Show*', *Feminist Review* 57: 1–6.

Faludi, S. (1992) *Backlash: The Undeclared War Against Women*, London: Chatto and Windus.

hooks, b. (1984) *Feminist Theory From Margin to Center*, Boston, MA: South End Press.

hooks, b. (1994) *Teaching to Transgress: Education and the Practice of Freedom*, New York: Routledge.

Steinberg, D.L. (1991) 'Adversarial politics: the legal construction of abortion', in S. Franklin, C. Lury and J. Stacey (eds) *Off-Centre: Feminism and Cultural Studies*, London: HarperCollins.

Steinberg, D.L. (1997) 'All roads lead to … problems with discipline', in J.E. Canaan and D. Epstein (eds) *A Question of Discipline: Pedagogy, Power and the Teaching of Cultural Studies*, Boulder: Westview.

Winship, J. (1987) *Inside Women's Magazines*, New York: Pandora.

9 Who knows best?
Politics and ethics in feminist research into 'race'

Suki Ali

Mary: When someone's angry with me and they're not my friend, they'll go behind my back and they'll go, um, 'oh, she's white!' and they'll like say 'oh the white b-i-t-c-h' something like that.

SA: And do you think you are Yoruba?
John: Yeah, but I like people calling me half-caste.

SA: If I asked you to describe yourself [in terms of 'colour'] what would you say?
T: I love yo-yos.
SA: You'd say that you loved yo-yos?
T: That's the only way I can describe myself.

The children quoted above all come from the same North London primary school and are aged 9 and 10. They are all talking about their sense of themselves and their 'racial identities'. They all define themselves, with different forms of language, as 'mixed-race', and eloquently express the ways in which 'race' is a partial, contradictory and unstable aspect of identity.

I became a student of Women's Studies in 1991, and at that time I would not have placed the word 'race' in speech marks. I would have characterised my concerns about feminism, rather than 'women's liberation', which I had subscribed to in the 1970s, as a need for equality and reclamation of women's power and influence in the world. Or something like that, all based on my own limited knowledge of life and the world as I had experienced it, directly or indirectly. Throughout my developing interest in feminist theory and practice, I have come to be slightly dismissive of those 'woolly liberal feminists' who want equality within an unjust world order, and impatient with feminism that tries to label itself in ways that become, inevitably, limiting and exclusive. I am now much more concerned about the concept of power – who has it, who wants it, and what forms it may take. The reason for the inclusion and exclusion of individuals or groups to positions of power is often based upon perceived 'difference'. Difference is determined in relation to our own self-defined positions, identities, beliefs, politics, economics, material constraints and so on. As some groups (of individuals) dissolve, so other groups form and align themselves, and it is this constant shifting that allows similarity to be found among previously unconnected groups.

As a woman with a white English mother and a Caribbean/South Asian father, I have been charting my own personal political journey through theoretical and emotional developments in meanings of 'race', ethnicity and culture and their implications for political transformations of the white supremacist society that is Britain today. My shifting identifications parallel the fact that not only are subjectivities 'becoming', but that theories, ontologies and epistemologies are dynamic and constantly evolving. In particular, I am interested in the way that those who come from 'mixed-race', 'dual-heritage', 'multi-racial' or 'mixed-parentage' backgrounds choose to identify, and how these positions often challenge the existing theories of 'race' and 'ethnicity'. This chapter will focus on the words of three of the children who took part in a research project which began in 1997 and continued for the following year. The first section looks at the ways in which I became interested in the research through readings of Women's Studies; the second will contextualise the research and introduce the children. The third section will consider the ways that feminist theories may be utilised in order to understand what the children are saying. Finally, the ethical problems of dealing with sensitive data and remaining politically focused in research will be explored using the existing interview data. I will draw out the way in which 'doing feminism', whether in academia or in the research process, raises tensions and leads to difficulties that are often insurmountable. In order to develop inclusive and non-discriminatory practices we need to continually check whether our discursive selections are perpetuating hierarchies of knowledge, and whether research processes are remaining true to our political intentions or in some way perpetuating the problems they are seeking to challenge. In this case the focus will be the meanings of 'race' and 'racism' in the lives of young children.

What is this thing called feminism?

I have been 'different' since childhood. Haven't we all, in some way or another? As a young woman, I looked to feminist theory as a way to understand this. In a sense I was looking for an explanation for my identity, and did not find it in what I read. I wanted to intellectualise the injustices of my life, both the privileges and the disadvantages. Reading the histories of the women's movement and the developments of Women's Studies helped. It appeared that within the women's movement itself, women did not feel equal. They did not have equal access to power and effect and resources, and felt that they had particular needs that were not being addressed. Some felt that they did not actually want the kind of 'equality' that was striven for.

Early second wave feminism was characterised by the slogan 'the personal is political'. The analysis of women's lives and experience at consciousness-raising groups was the basis for feminist theorising. The development of feminist activism into strands of feminist thinking has been well documented elsewhere (see Coate (forthcoming)). Access to material power and influence such as the ability to get published meant that certain voices were heard more loudly than others in the movement. Bitter debates ranged about the inclusion and exclusion of certain issues as 'feminist', and on the best ways of overthrowing 'patriarchy'. Most vociferous critiques of a somewhat complacent 'white middle-class' position came from women who saw issues of class, (hetero)sexuality and 'race' as having equal import to gender. Many will recognise the terms Marxist feminism, liberal feminism, socialist feminism, radical feminism, black feminism, and there was also the suggestion that the term 'womanism' was more appropriate for black women (Walker 1984). In the 1980s when Margaret Thatcher was in power in Britain and New Right politics were hegemonic (arguably they still are), these different strands of feminist thinking developed and metamorphosed into new forms of 'identity politics', which will be discussed in more depth below.

The 'popular' face of feminism in the 1980s was a form of liberal feminism that called for women to be given equal opportunities with men. To this end the Equal Opportunities Commission was set up to act as a monitoring and advisory body and to help enforce laws against 'sex discrimination'. The Commission for Racial Equality has a similar remit but works upon cases of 'racial discrimination'. The two bodies have developed their own distinct ways of working and quite separate political identities since their inception. Originally, the notions of 'equality' and fairness were central to the legislation. Most institutions and private organisations, whether business, leisure or educational, have some sort of equal opportunities policy, regardless of whether it is enforced or not. The whole notion of equality is based upon the idea that women should be given the same rights as men, and also that not all men are equal. Men who come from ethnic groups who are in the minority in the 'white supremacist' society in England also have the right to equality with their white counterparts – or rather, white middle-class male counterparts.

This is where my reading led me first, through the developments of feminist theory as categorised by standard 'readers' on Women's Studies courses (Humm 1993; Richardson and Robinson 1993; Tong 1993). However, Judith Evans has chosen to reposition these conventional ways of categorising. She has argued that it is more effective to look at whether feminists share a belief in 'sameness' either within or across gender divides, or differences within or across gender divides (Evans 1995). She charts the development of second wave feminism and takes the position that 'same/different' from men remains a binary way of thinking that may be more harmful than useful (ibid.: 25). She also suggests that equality is a concept that has not been fully theorised and that this is another failing which needs to be addressed in order to develop new ways of thinking about these issues (ibid.).

Where are we?

My own concerns with difference were more relevant than equality. I always wondered about who I was supposed to be equal with, but was sure that I was not being treated 'equally' or with respect in many situations, despite a comparatively privileged childhood. Much of this had to do with being a brown child in the 1960s in a small town on the south coast of England full of white people.

The writing by black women in Britain throughout the 1980s echoed that of black women and women of colour in the USA, although the history of 'race relations' in the two countries is extremely different. Hazel Carby wrote an impassioned piece called 'White women listen! Feminism and the boundaries of sisterhood' which shows forcibly the anger and frustration felt about the racism that marginalised and negated the experience of black women, thus actually worsening the problem (Carby 1982; see especially Bryan *et al.* 1985; Amos and Parmar 1984). For women who refused the institution of heterosexuality, the failure of feminism to critique this imperative was a central issue when theorising. In the 1980s women often asserted their 'difference' as a difference of identity, and with it came the need for 'authenticity' when stating one's position. The groups of women who had been silenced through the history of the women's movement effectively silenced those who claimed to speak 'for them'. Critics suggested that this identity politics seemed to be based on a form of essentialism similar to that which had been critiqued in certain forms of 'radical feminism' of the 1970s. Blackness became a category around which to organise, regardless of differences such as nationality, geography, history, class, language and culture within that category. Needless to say, such a position became untenable. Prathiba Parmar criticised women leading 'ghettoised lives ... unable to move beyond personal and individual experience' (1990: 107). As a woman with a white mother, my credentials were often challenged from all quarters. The pressure to be black was great, the impossibility of 'authenticity' painful.

At the time of my own increased interest in feminist theory, things were changing again. The late 1980s and early 1990s were characterised by the acknowledgement that 'space–time compression' and the ways in which cultural and economic globalisation and increased population movement and migration were influencing all 'identities' in some way. Stuart Hall wrote of the need to move beyond the idea of a unified black subject and to recognise that 'it must be the case that they are constructed historically, culturally, politically – the concept this refers to is ethnicity' (Hall 1992: 257). The concept of 'race' as a biological category was deemed untenable and the theories that worked with 'ethnicity' gained ground. Ethnic collectivities are formed by those both within and outside the groups, and their boundaries may be constantly drawn and redrawn 'to serve processes and interests that form part of a diverse set of political projects, including economic ones' (Anthias and Yuval-Davis 1992: 8). These new theories of ethnicity served to offer more fluid and subtle subject positions than did ideas of 'race'. However, Anthias and Yuval-Davis suggest that 'All ethnic groups are characterised by a notion of "community"' (ibid.) and 'although cultural commonality is one of the ingredients that characterises ethnic groups, ethnic and cultural groups are not coterminous' (ibid.). Into these complex ideas about meanings of 'race', ethnicity and culture we must feed the fact that physical markers such as skin colour and hair type remain highly significant in everyday social interactions and are often seen to signify 'race'.

It is the real need for more complex understandings of 'race', nationality, and ethnicity and culture that prompted the research detailed below. Often these terms are used interchangeably in academic discourse, and may not be used in the same ways in an everyday situation. The rise and rise of post-structuralist theories of identities has, of course, had a profound effect on research methods. One of the major impulses behind feminist research, as mentioned above, is the desire for the research to be non-hierarchical wherever possible and to have the potential for positive transformation. While racism remains endemic in Great Britain it is imperative that we continue to challenge the ways that 'race', ethnicity and culture are constituted and perpetuated in hierarchical order. Even as we try to transform and develop new language and understandings of social relations, it is necessary to ask in what ways such changes are meaningful at the level of everyday social interaction. The impact of global movements has increased the need to look at the ways in which ethnicities and nationalities are relocating and forming 'cultural hybrids'. Along with cultural hybridity in Great Britain we are seeing a huge increase in inter-national, -ethnic, and -racial partnerships with the possibilities for the children of these relationships to offer unique perspectives on what these terms mean to them. Considering such transboundaried locations will inevitably help with the process of dismantling the hierarchies of 'race' in theory and practice. 'The answers are not to be found in a new system of classification, but in deconstruction, synthesis and evolution' (Root 1992: 11).

There has been very little empirical research in this area to date. One of the most recent studies in Britain involved young teenagers (Tizard and Phoenix 1993), another the parents of 'children of mixed-parentage' (Katz 1996). The authors discussed the terms and their use at length. By setting the research within the framework of 'mixed-race', one may be seen to be perpetuating old ideas of blood mixing or miscegenation. Katz settled on the more recently evoked 'mixed-parentage' which, I believe, means something and nothing. The other term that is commonly used is 'dual-heritage' which limits the categorisation as much as 'mixed-race'. In the USA the terms 'bi-' and 'mono-' multi-racial also imply 'blood-mixing' (Root 1992). Jayne O. Ifekwunigwe's recent study of black African/white *metis/se* adults eloquently shows the importance of narratives of kinship to the formations of identities. (see Ifekwunigwe 1997 and forthcoming). She also believes that '[W]hat is needed is a term which does not glorify "race" yet acknowledges the existence of racism while also centring on the lived manifestations of the sociocultural markers of ethnicity, class, gender and generation' (Ifekwunigwe 1997: 130). Ultimately, none of the terms is satisfactory, but I chose to continue to use the term 'mixed-race' for some children as it was a term that they all understood and many used, as did teachers and families. I also acknowledged that I would work with children who were 'same race' but mixed-nationality, or multi-ethnic, or some combination thereof.

A major concern was that by asking questions about 'race', ethnicity and culture and their hybrid, partial or multi-faceted aspects we may simply be serving to reinforce the original finite categories. Can we research this area paying full regard to the ways in which gender, sexuality, ability and class serve to constitute identities concomitantly with 'race'? It has been suggested that if we wish to pay attention to the full complement within possible intersections of existing social classifications we could end up dealing with approximately 288 at any given time (Cealey-Harrison and Hood-Williams 1998). If we look at all contextual specificities the numbers grow endlessly. With this in mind, how might we attempt to gain meaningful data, especially from young children who were to be the subject of this study?

Who are you?

Feminist standpoint theory argues that the particular position one occupies gives rise to unique insights into the social world. Patricia Hill Collins argues that black women who are often 'outsiders within' hegemonic white cultures and societies offer unique perspectives on dominant paradigms and discourses, and that 'self-defined standpoints can stimulate resistances' (Hill Collins 1990: 28). Other developments about the difficulties with theorising from one position have been argued about at length elsewhere (see Harding 1991; Stanley and Wise 1993). It would seem to be appropriate to the lives of those of 'mixed-race' to try to access these positions by using autobiography or, to be more precise, the personal verbal narratives. The research considered how children chose to represent their lives through stories, conversations and domestic photography illustrating their interpretations about their homes, their school life and their relationships. Stories may not be the same at all times in all contexts but we can see 'narrations as social acts, points of public negotiation between self and others' which offer insights into the way we negotiate stories of self (Nayak 1993: 127). The children were contacted through schools, and the policies and practices for anti-racist and multi-cultural teaching provided a context for the interviews.

Working with children raises particular ethical dilemmas, as the power dynamics are more starkly drawn between adult and child and had to be kept to the fore at all times. The other major factor was a concern not to raise issues which children would find disturbing then leave them with no support. Needless to say, these are considerations in any kind of research but they are extremely pertinent to research with children, as will be discussed further below (see also Mayall 1994; Alderson 1995; Maybin 1993; Mauthner 1997; Epstein 1998).

In 1997 I began to collect data from children in primary schools in London and in a small town in Kent. The three children selected for this chapter all came from the same school, but were in different classes. The school is situated in north London and is one of the larger primary schools in the area. It is multi-ethnic and multi-racial and has a large number of children from the many refugee families that pass through the borough. The school has been under the existing head since the junior and infant schools amalgamated four years ago. The head teacher was developing policies on anti-racism and anti-bullying at the time the research was taking place. Both she and the staff freely offered their time and support to the project, as did the children.

The data was collected using several methods, including videotaping children from target classes in groups and talking to them about their understanding of terms such as 'race' and 'racism', also ascertaining whether they knew what 'mixed-race' meant and whether they used those terms or others. They were also asked about school policy and anti-racist teaching, as were members of staff. Children who self-identified as 'mixed-race' were interviewed on a one-to-one basis, about who they lived with, about their day-to-day cultural processes, their ideas about 'home' and about the way they would choose to describe themselves and others, as well as how others have talked about them. In supplementary interviews alone and with friends they were asked about their aspirations, general likes and dislikes, friendship groups and so on. They were also shadowed in class and at playtime. In the second phase, where possible, I interviewed the parents (and siblings) of these children. There was a problem with accessing parents who were often suspicious of a researcher coming 'from the school', but if I presented myself as independent this appeared to be even less of a personal recommendation. There was a fine balance between school affiliations and independent status that was effective in arranging meetings, and in most cases where direct personal contact could be made the parents agreed to be interviewed. At this stage it should be noted that 'parents' in the overwhelming majority of cases turned out to be mothers. It was mothers who mostly came to the schools and therefore presented opportunities for contact (see also Reay 1998). Some of the mothers also arranged for fathers to be present for interviews, who then may not have been able to take part for one reason or another. If the fathers were absent from a great deal of the day-to-day interaction with the children they were also unlikely to present themselves as available to be interviewed. In the cases represented below, two mothers were interviewed, and no parents of the third child. They were interviewed in their own homes in a relaxed and informal style, and were fully briefed as to the nature of the project. Parents were asked about concepts of family and home, about family traditions and about the way they thought about and discussed, if at all, the terms 'race', ethnicity and culture.

Just as the language of racial and ethnic belonging has been shifting, so has that of identities. Again, Hall makes the observation that we now understand that

> identities are never unified and, in late modern times, increasingly fragmented and fractured; never singular but multiply constructed across different and often intersecting and antagonistic discourses, practices and positions. They are subject to radical historicization, and are constantly in the process of change and transformation.
>
> (Hall 1996: 4)

The way the children chose to represent themselves upheld the notion of multiple selves with one or more foregrounded at any one moment. In some cases the things the children said revealed already strongly held ideas about themselves, which have clearly come from a variety of sources but mainly their educational and familial contexts. The extracts below come from a wide variety of materials gathered over a year. They have been chosen not to be representative of all children of these ages but to illustrate some of the ways in which the relationships between intentions and results in research may be strained. They also focus on the particular parts of interviews that specifically address some of the discourses in question for this piece. These three children show some of the complicated ways 'racial identities' may be in process. They are necessarily partial and incomplete, both for the time at which they were recorded and in view of long-term developing identifications.

Meli

Meli lives with her sister and mother (who works as a teacher at the school) in a large flat within walking distance of the school. She is a bright and lively pupil who was always happy to help with the research. She was a popular member of a large group of girls who were friends across classes in Year Six. Meli had very strong 'racial' identifications.

SA: Do people ever say to you … 'Oh Meli, where do you come from?'

M: Well they don't … they aks me and but they mostly aks me what colour are you? … 'cos they say, like, 'cos I'm weird sort of … they think I'm, like … I don't, I'm not exactly, er, white, and I'm not exactly black so they aks me, 'What colour are you?' and I say that I'm mixed-race, and sometimes they aks me, 'What mixed-race are you?' and I have to tell them in the rude way sort of thing, like, 'I'm quarter-caste, yeah?'

She went on to say that she often just says she's 'mixed-race' because her mother has told her that 'quarter-caste' is 'rude'.

When asked if she could say something about 'racism' she responded:

M: Yeah, um sometimes when someone would ask me my colour and then they'll see my mum and they won't believe me, and they'll go, 'She doesn't look it though,' and sometimes when I say that I'm that colour, something like that and then, like, I'll go up to them and say something like 'Excuse me! You don't know my family and … you haven't seen my grandma, you haven't seen, like, my grandfather, you don't know nothing about my family, my background or nothing!'

Meli said again in a later interview how angry she got when she was called 'white', and that she thought of herself as, at least in part, black. Her anger is shown by her frustration at those who call her a 'white b-i-t-c-h', and this is clearly an insult to her as it is said when people are 'not [her] friend'. In this context 'whiteness' is a racial insult.

Meli showed a strong identification with black British and African American popular culture. She listened to black music, went to dance clubs and watched imported American teenage comedies featuring young African Americans. She has an older sister, and both of them attend an interdenominational church with their mother on a regular basis. She describes herself as a Christian and her religious beliefs are important to her. While one of her best friends, S, is white, she spends most of her time with groups of black girls.

She talked about being criticised by her father and his new partner (who is 'Indian') for not speaking 'nicely' and using 'slang' that is heavily influenced by some patois and 'black British' styles of speech.

Meli had strong emotional links to her family in the Cook Islands. For this reason she wanted to emigrate to New Zealand, as her family were more important to her than her friends, whom she saw as transient. She expected family to be loyal to her for the rest of her life. Meli came from a home where the politics of race were talked about openly, as she said her mother had talked to her about the terminology that she used, such as 'quarter-caste'. Her mother had also told her to be proud of who she was. Clearly a great deal of Meli's pride came from her familial identifications. She argues against her positioning as 'white' by using her genealogy and invoking ties of blood. Indeed, the term 'quarter-caste' resonates with the old-style 'miscegenation' fears.

Similarly, Meli's primary 'problems' come from crude ideas about race and skin colour. She resents being classed as white, and focuses on that rather than on whether she is called the gendered term, 'bitch'. She claims allegiance to blackness in terms of 'colour' even if her appearance would belie this, as it is in her blood, passed on from her family. Meli's mother also describes herself as 'mixed-race', and talked about her own positioning by others as problematic. Ambiguous appearance resonates with many accounts by other children and adolescents, but Meli is actively resisting 'passing' in the old sense of the word. Her racial identity transcends her skin colour, and is based on familial, national and cultural factors that may be combined under the term 'ethnicity'. She occupies a diasporic space that is heavily grounded in her passion for her family. Her parents are divorced, her father remarried and she believes she has a 'right' to see her brothers, sisters, half-siblings and cousins, and not to 'miss out' seeing them grow up.

Meli also has very complex cultural affiliations. At present she is most heavily influenced by the common cultural icons of her peers. Her mother has strong links with other Polynesians in Britain and has made sure that Meli and her sister acknowledge their cultural heritage. Yet this is while she remains in England, secondary to her 'social geography' and spatial geography (Frankenberg 1993) which are multi-ethnic British.

John

Another pupil, John, talked about himself as assuredly as Meli, but from a more surprising and complex perspective. John had taken part in some of the earlier general discussions and had not offered a great deal about himself, other than that he was from Nigeria and not long in England. A friend of his suggested he should be interviewed because he was 'half-caste' and had a white dad. John agreed to be interviewed and, after some reluctance based on shyness, began to talk more freely. At first it was hard to follow what John was saying, as I had made assumptions about his family and it took a great deal of discussion to understand the situation. John had a father in Nigeria whom he saw occasionally, and a man he also called his father who had been with his mother for several years and lived with them as a family.

SA:	Have people ever talked to you about racism and stuff like that?
J:	Yeah.
SA:	What have they said to you?
J:	They said, 'Oh no, look at that boy, his dad is white!'
SA:	Have they?
J:	Yeah … and … and some people cuss me because my dad is white.
SA:	Do they?
J:	Yeah.
SA:	That's nasty, isn't it.
J:	Yeah.
SA:	What kind of things do they say?
J:	Like … um … like 'Look at this half-caste boy, he doesn't look like a half-caste, he looks like a Yoruba,' and stuff like that, and they cuss me and say f-words to me.
SA:	Oh no, that's awful!
J:	And all those things.
SA:	Yeah. And how would you describe yourself, though?
J:	Ummm … I would describe myself like … I, I don't mind what they're saying, but … but it's quite nasty.
S:	Do you mind being called half-caste?
J:	Um, no.
SA:	You don't mind?
J:	No.
SA:	So you think that's right, would you call yourself that?
J:	Yes.
SA:	You would?
J:	Yeah.
SA:	Umm, do you know what it means?
J:	Yeah, like your dad is white and your mum is black and that would make you in the middle and that is what half-caste means.
SA:	And do you think that is what you are?
J:	Yeah, 'cos my dad is white and my mum is black.
SA:	Right.

Later, when asked about his family in Nigeria, he said:

J:	That would make me Yoruba.
SA:	Yoruba.
J:	'Cos my mum's boyfriend was Yoruba.
SA:	Uh huh, and do you think you are Yoruba?
J:	Yeah, but I like people calling me half-caste.

He explained that this was because his new dad treated his mum well.

SA: You want to be with this dad and you like being called half-caste, then?
J: Yeah, I would like to be called half-caste.
SA: Yeah.

Although John recognised and enjoyed similar types of popular culture to the majority of his peers, he was less influenced by them than the other two respondents. He talked about his mother, and about Nigeria as his home, and described his favourite foods as Nigerian. He clearly had strong familial and cultural links to Nigeria that affected his 'cultural' identity. John also had a strong sense of family, and although he missed his family in Nigeria, he simultaneously developed the tie to his step-father that led to him choosing to incorporate his father's whiteness into his own racial identity. The children rarely knew that the term 'half-caste' was considered, as Meli said, 'rude'. John used the term from preference with such frequency that his friend knew that he would not mind being interviewed for the research. With such a complicated history, it is no wonder that John chose to hold two clear 'racial' identities – that of Yoruba and implicitly black African, and of half-caste, that is 'mixed-race'. His logic was impeccable – his new father is indeed white. Discourses of family that are increasingly available to young children allow them to recognise variations on the old nuclear family theme. As his new father is family, then he is undoubtedly half-caste. Further, if race is untenable, and biology and skin colour erroneous choices for categorical positions, why should John not choose to be 'mixed-race'? One might argue that this would be a question of politics, the politics of identity, but maybe more importantly the politics of 'race' in a society which perceives 'white' as the norm and desirable.

John may provide us with the biggest challenge. His family were not available to be interviewed, but both his parents are living at home. His mother is a doctor and his father a teacher in a local secondary school. It would seem unlikely that they would be unaware of John's desire to reassess emphases on 'blood' in his family history and thus his identity. Perhaps they do not know the exact language being used, such as 'half-caste'. The way the family perceive the politics of race is hard to gauge, but the family structure and interrelations themselves, with the attendant movement and relocation, have obviously been the major factors for John. Is John attempting to 'pass' as 'mixed-race' or is his decision based on affiliations? I would suspect the latter.

Tito

Tito lived with his mother and his twin sister in a flat very close to the school. His (white) mother walked to and collected the children from school every day. Tito was perceived to be a 'difficult' boy who had a low boredom threshold, strong opinions and a quick temper.

Who knows best? 145

Tito had nothing to say on the subject of his racial identity, and repeatedly said, 'I don't know' when asked to talk about 'race'. During the course of the fieldwork within the school he developed a good relationship with me, yet always shied away from the subject when the tape recorder was switched on. The following is typical of our interactions on 'sensitive' subjects:

SA: If I asked you to describe yourself [in terms of skin colour] what would you say?
T: I love yo-yos!
SA: You'd say that you loved yo-yos?
T: That's the only way I can describe myself.

By contrast, his twin sister, who attends the same school, had a very sophisticated understanding of herself as a 'mixed-race' daughter of a white mother and black father. She told me that she understood the terms and the concept of racism.

Tito presented an interesting paradox in his use of language. He used black British styles of speech, as did many of the children. This is not surprising and has been well documented by Hewitt (1986), Back (1996, especially Chapter 6), and more recently confirmed in a small-scale study of youth language (Ali and Hillman with Davies 1998). In a school assembly about peace, Tito asked me what a 'racist attack' meant, yet he had clearly understood the concept in an earlier group discussion. In a different context he seemed to be unsure of the meaning. During interviews, Tito claims to have no language for racial identity; he can 'only' describe himself in terms of his character, likes and dislikes. When asked to describe the interviewer or his mother he did consider physicality, describing his mother's hair and that she was pretty. Tito's mother told me that he had once told her that she should attend the school's club for black mothers, like the other black mothers did. He said he looked more like his father than his mother and never mentioned colour of hair, eyes or skin in any description when asked directly. In a later interview with his sister, Talia, when describing a member of class he said:

Ti: And she always got these Hi Tec trainers.
Ta: She's got Hi Tec.

[both talking]

Ta: She sits, she sits, ah ... near uh ...
Ti: Talia, she's Talia's colour, black and white.

Again he talks around the subject, utilising the markers of status, the Hi Tec trainers, in order to position the girl he is trying to describe. He then clearly describes her as 'mixed-race' but by using crude 'colour' terminology, not in relation to himself, only in relation to his sister.

For Tito and his family there are particular social and political considerations to the fore which are also strongly influenced by a single mother running the home, but whereas Meli's mother is herself 'mixed-race', Tito's mother is white. Her analysis of her situation as a white woman in relation to her children is grounded in her own unique set of narratives, yet nonetheless shares commonalities with others in her position. Her political position *vis-à-vis* the racial identity of her children is clear. For her the children were to be 'mixed-race', and also to be 'proud of who they are', and proud of the fact that they are both black and white. Tito's mother was also keen on black British popular culture and had been described as a 'white black woman' by a black friend. She and her children mixed with the members of her Jamaican ex-partner's family even though the children saw their father on an irregular basis.

What do you mean?

During my time spent with these children I got to know something of them and their relationships in school and at home. I felt that we had developed mutual trust and I had come to genuinely like and respect them. I am not sure whether the children always positioned me as researcher. They may have originally intended to, but our sessions took on a form of their own that was a mixture of interview, informal chat or personal confessional, to name but a few. I believe that this fuzziness was in part due to my own failure to 'control' the context, and partly the young age of the children involved, as they showed a very high level of trust once they had understood that the research would be confidential. Despite this, I was never just 'one of the girls' (see Hey 1997). How can one take the words of these children, and in Meli and Tito's case their siblings, friends and parents, and transform them into data that remains true to their intended meanings? Further, what interpretation may we place upon the meanings they intend, and how will this act to 'empower' them and others?

The ways in which we choose to interpret their words are based upon political and ethical beliefs. Do we try to find a way to make what they have said 'all right' in some way? Have they been represented accurately? What would these children think about the way their words may be interpreted by others? Most importantly, should one choose to pull out certain areas for focus when they may not be of primary importance to the child themselves? Again, I should add that these are dilemmas not just associated with research with children, but they are still particularly acute.

The children construct 'racial' identities from available discourses which they then continue to manipulate and develop. The children were receiving their education on ' race' from school, home, peers and, significantly for many, through popular culture. For Anthias and Yuval-Davis, the development of new nation-states and geographical boundaries containing diverse languages and cultures means 'ethnicity is the active face of ethnic consciousness and always involves a political dimension' (Anthias and Yuval-Davis 1992: 8). They add, 'Ethnicity is more than merely a question of ethnic identity.' (ibid.: 9). With this in mind it becomes hard to see where the children's possible ethnicities 'fit'. Another factor of concern is that these children are not part of a 'community' of 'mixed-race' individuals as such, and it is the very uniqueness of each child's historical and socio-psychic development that leads to the challenges to 'race' and ethnicity theory.

Meli clearly embraces 'blackness' in an open way. For her this would seem to be a narrative that comes from the 'diasporic' and familial, yet for her mother it also engages explicitly with the politics of 'race'. Meli uses the term 'mixed-race' but prefers to focus on her blackness and black ancestry, and will defend that position when under attack about her appearance – most often her skin colour. She chooses to immerse herself within black British culture, as do all her friends.

Tito claims a singular position that he refused to name for me, despite our friendly relationship. He states clearly that loving yo-yos is the *only* way he can describe himself, a very firm rebuttal to enquiry. He was positioned as 'difficult' at school and was referred to as black by teachers, if not his peers, who would (re)position him according to the circumstances. It is hardly surprising that he came to talk of his ethnic or racial position reluctantly, and decided either to say that he did not know or to describe himself in terms of his character, his likes and his dislikes. He chose to describe himself using the narratives of the popular in clothes, style and hobbies which were generally available and not specifically gendered. He chose to be one of the naughty boys (see, e.g., Connolly 1998), but was a loner and spent most of his time apart from the main groups of children, searching out his favourite teacher at breaktime. Tito had a strong sense of independence, yet took on the role of protector to his sister. In this he was acting in the most 'masculine' way, at one point claiming he would beat up another child who had hit her.

John continues to be unconcerned at this stage of his life with 'traditional' politics of 'race'. Of all of the three, he would be most likely to be seen to be having 'false consciousness' about his blackness. Of all the children, he shows most acutely the problem with trying to impose meaning upon the narratives. He occupies a very strongly felt cultural partiality, which may be why the importance of his family happiness has had such a profound effect upon him. It has been noted that people who watch television soaps may choose to identify with those who are not obviously like them. When asked who he would be if he could be anyone in the world, John replied, 'Princess Diana', showing that he identified with characteristics, material circumstances and aspirations rather than the physical person. Despite his terminology, John is manipulating discourses of family to create his own complex multi-ethnic and 'multi-racial' position; he shows a great deal of creativity in the way he thinks through his position in relation to his new father, and expresses no inherent conflict about this.

All of the children are showing a clear ability to manipulate discourses of 'race', ethnicity and culture in order to negotiate daily positions which are both contingent and in some way fixed, perhaps 'fictional and "real"'(Katz 1996). In all their dealings with the research process, the children remained enthusiastic and engaged with talking about themselves and their lives. The children are not only creating meaning through the talk they have with their friends, but building upon that in their retelling within the research process. They often showed the way in which 'personhood is constructed ... through the reporting [of dialogue] and taking on of other people's voices' (Maybin 1993: 148).

The way they claim their narratives and histories in all their fullness shows that they are indeed both of and not of a time and place, and certainly *not* fragmented identities but coherent and cohesive. Just as Felly Nkweto Simmonds chooses to name herself according to her location, so the children 'rename' themselves for their own purposes, 'quarter-caste', 'half-caste', 'lover of yo-yos' (Simmonds 1996). It is a form of 'ethnic identification' which is 'operationally situational', therefore flexible and malleable even to children of this age (Okaura cited by Ifekwunigwe 1997: 129).

Where are the 'others'?

For those who are choosing to interrogate their own and others' positions in increasingly dis/ and trans/located nationalities and cultures, and the way in which we may access the political through our positions, the notion of 'identity' has been extremely fruitful. Identity has been an area of immense interest to those in academia for some time, and the development of Cultural Studies in particular has brought new ways of thinking that do not rely entirely upon the psychoanalytic or individual psychologies for understandings (although there continues to be a lot of very interesting work done in these areas), or upon using 'pure' anthropological or sociological terms of reference.

The fragmentation or destabilisation of selves, I believe, lends itself to the possibilities for multiple allegiances and alliances for political projects. Postmodern theories have been embraced by many, and with caution by some feminists. The changes in the position of feminists within the academy, such as the increase in Gender Studies, and the (re)location of feminist educators across disciplines, reflect the need for more dispersed approaches to the inclusion of feminist theory and praxis as tools for transformation in educational futures. If the terms 'woman' and 'gender' have been deconstructed to unsustainable limits, there may be the need to reassert some group categories for political action. The same can be said for labels attached to sexuality and sexual orientations. Queer theory would seem to be the most postmodern of the approaches to the work around sexuality, and there are still as many vigorous debates about the politics of sexuality today, in which the dissolving of traditional boundaries has given rise to charges of apolitical libertarianism from others (Vance 1989; Segal and MacIntosh 1992; Maynard and Purvis 1995; Steinberg *et al.* 1998). Discourses of dis/ability, although marginalised, are perhaps slightly more visible in the academy but generally located within pockets of specialism. It continues to be an issue that requires centrality in debates and more sophisticated understandings than are reflected in much 'mainstream' work. This is by no means to suggest that the debates about sex, class, 'race' and ability are equal or directly parallel, but with the general move to embrace more complex and particular subjective positionings it is inevitable that these terms that have been central to the understandings of identities and affiliations should all have been interrogated.

The literature on all these developments has been catalogued well elsewhere, as mentioned above, and some of the chapters in this volume also refer directly or indirectly to these issues. What is clear is that in order to theorise the conditions of those who live in hetero-patriarchal societies such as Britain, we now need to be more aware than ever of seeing the details that make the differences and similarities between groups and individuals, to recognise the many possibilities for identities and identifications, and to acknowledge that those may now be the best ways to form allegiances around which to organise for change. However, when talking to the children, some of these issues were at times obscured.

Patterns of conversation with the children inevitably radiated out from the central point of, first, their friendships and social groupings at school and, second, friends out of school. When asked about specifics outside the school environment they all talked openly about their lives, but their unprompted conversation was based in the immediate social environment. The transcripts above show the importance of the positions ascribed to the children by others in facilitating negotiation and response. This is not to say that their identities were totally reactionary, but that they are indeed contingent. In expressing agency the children often showed that they were aware of the gendered and sexualised nature of their racialised locations. In the above transcripts, Meli is a 'bitch', John is just a 'boy', and teachers see Tito as a naughty 'black boy'. Racial and gendered categorisations go hand in hand. The relationships between the children conform the kind of gendered and sexualised play that has been recorded by researchers elsewhere (Epstein 1998; Thorne 1993). While there is no space to go into detail about this aspect of the data, it was clear that the many variables were often visible, with one or more of the 'triumvirate' plus sexuality clearly visible to the researcher and often to the child themselves at any given time. The discourse of heterosexuality and the 'rehearsal' of dating were constant themes for discussion, and the children described these interactions with enthusiasm.

One discourse that was hardly ever mentioned was that of ability. In the school there were no severely physically challenged children; however, there were several with behavioural difficulties. The only public acknowledgements of either of these that were noted were couched in the somewhat patronising language of support for those who were 'special' rather than that of integration and respect. In the absence of such data, how is this to be written into the analysis in a meaningful way? It is clear that the sense of themselves as 'able' is so comfortable as to be invisible in most cases, just as 'whiteness' has been rendered invisible in analyses until recently. The centralisation of ability automatically renders disabled as 'other', the negative of the able-bodied, just as blackness or being 'of colour' is also being non-white.

The children interviewed all had very different ideas about what their 'mixed-race' identities meant to them. The term 'mixed-race' was not used by them all, and some of them had a greater political understanding of the importance of terminology than the others. It would be easy to dismiss the terms and identifications the children claim as underdeveloped, incomplete or just plain wrong. As a feminist researcher, one must try to understand the way the children choose to identify and respect that at all times. However, with an area as emotive as 'racial' identity it is a task fraught with dangers, particularly where children are concerned. Although the extracts are chosen to highlight 'race' and ethnicity, it is clear that the children see themselves as gendered, and are aware of the importance of heterosexuality as hegemonic and that they know the 'right answers' about 'racism' and '(hetero)sexism'.

If 'race' is merely the one factor in the formation of ethnic identity, and we must include equally the constructions of the variables mentioned above, we will inevitably run into conflict with the way some of these children chose to label and identify themselves. The gap between 'theory on stilts' and children in London primary schools is shown in stark relief against the rhetoric of 'anti-racism'. The school is acutely aware of racism and racist bullying tactics and was working on a new anti-racist policy at the time. Of the staff members interviewed, only one admitted to instigating a conversation with children about multi-ethnic positions (she herself was in a mixed-race marriage and had two children, one of whom was at the school). The liberal model of multi-culturalism through tolerance applied to the way 'ability' was (not) talked about. This model is in a sense uncritical of what who you are might be, or even unaware that who you are may be something complicated and unstable, as this may render you dangerous and undesirable.

Conclusions

How we choose to understand these children, of course, depends on our own positions. What we hope to learn from them will depend on our own histories. In taking their words out of context for this chapter, I have offered a very partial and directed view of some of the things they had to say about 'race'. Ultimately they and their families will be represented as sympathetically as possible, and despite this one may still choose to disagree with some of what they have said. The children themselves chose to foreground particular issues that were of importance to them. These were usually about gender and sexuality, sometimes about race and ethnicity, often about culture and almost never about dis/ability. Indirectly, they also said a great many things about the issues mentioned above, but trying to maintain those issues centrally to the work I am doing about identity and identifications is very difficult and results in the sense of reading into the texts things that the children may strongly disagree with, or at the very least hold different opinions about. The children seem to be unhindered by conventions in the way they try to place themselves in their social worlds. Should we try to see new possibilities in the ways in which they do this? Can the position of these children be seen to be new forms of personal identity politics, or are they simply apolitical or 'not-yet-political'? I would like to see the creativity of the children as offering us new ways of being political, that allow us to continue to struggle for change and transformation from quite unique positions. If I do this, I am guilty of removing whole sets of discourses from the centre of the text to the margins – again. There are no answers to these problems as yet, but as feminists we must continue to struggle with them as they are crucial to epistemological and ontological discursive development and, in the end, to our ethical praxis.

References

Alderson, P. (1995) *Listening to Children: Children Ethics and Social Research*, Ilford: Barnados.

Ali, S., Hillman, S. with Davies, H. (1998) 'Youth talk', unpublished research commissioned by BBC Television.

Amos, V. and Parmar, P. (1984) 'Challenging imperial feminism', *Feminist Review* 17 (July): 3–19.

Anthias, F. and Yuval-Davis, N. (1992) *Racialized Boundaries: Race, Nation, Gender, Colour and Class, and the Anti-Racist Struggle*, London: Routledge.

Back, L. (1996) *New Ethnicities and Urban Culture; Racism and Multiculture in Young Lives*, London: UCL Press.

Bryan, B., Dadzie, S. and Scafe, S. (1985) *The Heart of the Race: Black Women's Lives in Britain*, London: Virago Press.

Carby, H. (1982) 'White women listen! Feminism and the boundaries of sisterhood', in Centre for Contemporary Cultural Studies *The Empire Strikes Back: Race and Racism in '70s Britain*, London: Hutchinson.

Cealey-Harrison, W. and Hood-Williams, J. (1998) 'More varieties than Heinz: social categories and sociality in Humphries, Hammersley and beyond', *Sociological Research Online*, 3 (1) http://www.socresonline.org.uk/socresonline/3/1/8.html

Coate, K. (forthcoming, 1999) 'Feminist knowledge and the ivory tower: a case study', *Gender and Education*.

Connolly, P. (1998) *Racism, Gender Identity and Young Children: Social Relations in a Multi-Ethnic Inner-City Primary School*, London: Routledge.

Donald, J. and Rattansi, A. (eds) (1992) *'Race', Culture, Difference*, London: Sage/OU Press.

Epstein, D. (1998) 'Are you a teacher or are you a girl?', in G. Walford (ed.) *Doing Research About Education*, London: Falmer Press.

Epstein, D. and Johnson, R. (1998) *Schooling Sexualities*, Buckingham: Open University Press.

Evans, J. (1995) *Feminist Theory Today: An Introduction to Second Wave Feminism*, London: Sage.

Frankenberg, R. (1993) *The Social Construction of Whiteness: White Women, Race Matters*, London: Routledge.

Hall, S. (1992) 'New ethnicities', in J. Donald and A. Rattansi (eds) *'Race', Culture, Difference*, London: Routledge.

Hall, S. (1996) 'Introduction: who needs "identity"?', in S. Hall and P. Du Gay (eds) *Questions of Cultural Identity*, London: Sage.

Harding, S. (1991) *Whose Science? Whose Knowledge: Thinking From Women's Lives*, Milton Keynes: Open University Press.

Hewitt, R. (1986) *White Talk/Black Talk: Interracial Friendship and Communication Amongst Adolescents*, Cambridge: Cambridge University Press.

Hey, V. (1997) *The Company She Keeps: An Ethnography of Girls' Friendships*, Buckingham: Open University Press.

Hill Collins, P. (1990) *Black Feminist Thought: Knowledge, Consciousness and the Politics of Empowerment*, London: HarperCollins Academic.

Humm, M. (1993) *Feminisms: A Reader*, Hemel Hempstead: Harvester Wheatsheaf.

Ifekwunigwe, J.O. (1997) 'Diaspora's daughters: on lineage authenticity and "mixed-race" identity', in H.S. Mirza (ed.) *Black British Feminism: A Reader*, London: Routledge.

Ifekwunigwe, J.O. (forthcoming) *Scattered Be-longings: Cultural Paradoxes of 'Race', Nation and Generation in the English–African Diaspora*, London: Routledge.

Katz, I. (1996) *The Construction of Racial Identity in Children of Mixed-Parentage: Mixed Metaphors*, London: Jessica Kingsley.

Mauthner, M. (1997) 'Methodological aspects of collecting data from children: lessons from three research projects', *Children and Society* 11: 16–28.

Mayall, B. (ed.) (1994) *Children's Childhoods: Observed and Experienced*, London: Falmer Press.

Maybin, J. (1993) 'Children's voices: talk, knowledge, identity', in D. Graddol, J. Maybin and B. Stierer (eds) *Researching Language and Literacy in Social Context*, Milton Keynes: Open University Press.

Maynard, M. and Purvis, J. (1995) *(Hetero)Sexual Politics*, London: Taylor & Francis.

Nayak, A. (1993) 'Narratives of racism', *Cultural Studies from Birmingham* 2: 124–54.

Parmar, P. (1990) 'Black feminism: the politics of articulation', in J. Rutherford (ed.) *Community, Culture, Difference*, London: Lawrence and Wishart.

Reay, D. (1998) *Class Work: Mothers' Involvement in their Children's Schooling*, London: UCL Press.

Richardson, D. and Robinson, V. (1993) (eds) *Introducing Women's Studies*, London: Macmillan.

Root, M.P.P. (1992) (ed.) *Racially Mixed People in America*, New York: Sage.

Segal, L. and MacIntosh, M. (1992) *Sex Exposed: Sexuality and the Pornography Debate*, London: Virago.

Simmonds, F.N. (1996) 'Naming and identity', in D. Jarrett-Macauley (ed.) *Reconstructing Womanhood, Reconstructing Feminism: Writings on Black Women*, London: Routledge.

Stanley, L. (1992) *The Auto/biographical I: The Theory and Practice of Feminist Autobiography*, Manchester: Manchester University Press.

Stanley, L. and Wise, S. (1993) *Breaking Out Again: Feminist Ontology and Epistemology*, London: Routledge.

Steinberg, D.L., Epstein, D. and Johnson, R. (eds) (1997) *Border Patrols: Policing the Boundaries of Heterosexuality*, London: Cassell.

Thorne, B. (1993) *Gender Play: Boys and Girls in School*, Buckingham: Open University Press.

Tizard, B. and Phoenix, A. (1993) *Black, White or Mixed Race: Race and Racism in the Lives of Young People*, London: Routledge.

Tong, R. (1993) *Feminist Thought*, London: Routledge.

Vance, C.S. (1989) (ed.) *Pleasure and Danger: Exploring Female Sexuality*, London: Pandora.

Walker, A. (1984) *In Search of Our Mother's Gardens*, London: The Women's Press.

Wilson, A. (1987) *Mixed Race Children: A Study of Identity*, London: Allen and Unwin.

10 Fast capitalism, fast feminism and some fast food for thought

Jane Kenway with Diana Langmead

Introduction

This chapter will identify the dominant forces that are shaping university life in Australia and elsewhere, now and in the predictable future. Its main purpose, however, is to consider what they might mean for feminist work and workers in universities, and thus for the future of feminism in the academy. In the paper we will avoid the postmodernist feminist preoccupation with mini-narratives and talk of meta-narratives, dominant discourses and driving forces, conscious, though, of the problems of such accounts. Our plan is to bring together several bodies of literature that tend neither to speak with each other nor to discuss the contemporary university. In combination, these are helpful in understanding some driving forces for change and their implications for feminism within the academy. Overall, we hope to connect feminist discussions of the contemporary university to literatures which enhance their explanatory capacity and which raise issues for consideration which to this point have been somewhat overlooked.

We will begin by pointing to the main forms of governmentality which are constructing the life of the contemporary university and those who work within it. We will follow this discussion by outlining the preoccupations of the current feminist literature on the university, identifying the manner in which it attends to such matters and noting some limitations. This provides the stepping-off point for the introduction into the discussion of two bodies of literature which, to date, have not informed the feminist material. These are, first, the wider feminist literature on globalisation and, second, that on fast capitalism, knowledge workers and intellectual capital. We have grouped these under the generic title 'theories of the contemporary'. We conclude the paper by returning to the university to consider the implications of this literature for an understanding of the future of universities and of feminism in universities.

Governmentality and the 'now' university

The current pace of change in university education in Australia is 'white hot'. University education policies are entirely different from those which predominated in the 1970s and early 1980s. As a consequence, universities have been restructured and recultured. Beneath a welter of policy rhetoric the key messages are simple: universities are to cost the state less and to serve both the state and market forces more. It seems that the triumph of economics over university education is now complete.

This identity transformation has been achieved by three particular forms of governmentality – what Foucault calls the 'conduct of conduct'. The first is *rationalisation*. Reductions in government funding have led universities to 'downsize', to look for sources of 'flexibility' and for non-state sources of funds. Most universities seem to understand flexibility in both hierarchical and numerical terms. Rationalisation is seen to apply particularly to academic staff below the professoriate and to faculty support staff. Increasingly, older tenured staff are encouraged to retire or are made redundant. The aim is to casualise and sessionalise a larger percentage of staff. The work of the core labour market, however, is intensified – fewer people do more work. We are all on the run, working harder, faster, 'smarter'. The name of the game is lean production – unless we are talking of management levels, which apparently must be *upsized*.

The second strategy of change is *corporatisation*, key features of which include the application of business management principles to university management. University corporatisation usually involves the contradictory double moves of aggregation and disaggregation, decentralisation and recentralisation, and autonomy and accountability. Within centrally devised frameworks and budget responsibility, stress and crisis are passed down the line; however, the 'flattened hierarchies' still have a clearly hierarchical command structure within which accountability is either steeply upwards (Coleman 1995: 108) or outwards – to 'clients' via an increased emphasis on student assessment of teaching.

Individual academic work is subject to intensified performance 'appraisal' through performance indicators. This has particular implications for worker relationships. The more academics' inputs and outputs are measured, the more they are encouraged to understand themselves as autonomous workers and their colleagues as their competitors, at both an individual and a group level. As a result of dramatically increased work loads and a wider range of expectations, teaching, research administration, entrepreneurial activities, consultancies, etc., staff are split within themselves. They are also split from each other: management from worker, and core workers among each other and from casualised workers. To the extent that they existed, collegiality and trust are increasingly being replaced by cultures characterised by distrust and anxiety. Control is gained by edict, fear of reprisal and by the internalisation of the new discourses of governmentality.

Marketisation, the third strategy of governmentality in university education, proceeds hand-in-glove with corporatisation. Its modes include privatisation, commercialisation, commodification and residualisation (Kenway 1995). Under marketisation, user-pays schemes are multiplying and universities are going further and further afield for new sources of income. Academic entrepreneurs roam an increasingly wide range of 'developing' countries in search of the lucrative education export dollar. We now see a whole new set of developments: onshore, offshore and various partnerships, subsidiaries and subcontractors. Students now 'invest' in a university education. The payment of fees intensifies the notion of customer rights. This feeds into the corporate model and potentially shifts responsibility for learning from the student to the academic (Coleman 1995: 108).

Increasingly, too, universities are turning to business and industry as sources of revenue and relevance. These range from research sponsorship to dedicated chairs to the creation of specific programmes. The effect of this particular turn is that universities often seek to redefine themselves according to the preferences and needs of business and industry: vocationalisation and commercialisation are the twin peaks of this agenda. Most universities now have commercial arms. Further, universities now regularly 'benchmark' against each other with regard not just to 'productivity' but also with regard to income (fees and other sources) (BJ 1997). Income generation tends to be treated as a product in its own right: input = output. Merit is being redefined accordingly, for both academic staff and for managers. Teaching and research are coming to be regarded as *baseline* activities, and staff are also expected to add value by gaining various lucrative consultancies and doing other deals. Among the core academic staff, those who do not are almost implicitly seen as asset strippers – taking out their pay but not bringing in resources. Indeed, there is a definite sense that the university's 'core' workers are not its academic staff but its managers, marketers and its quality management/staff development staff: those who know how to Work Smart in the Real World.

Clearly, there is a great deal more to Australian universities than this. There are significant differences between them and the campuses of amalgamated universities. There are the so-called Real Universities, the Wanna-Bes, the Never-Will-Bes and the Don't Wanna-Bes. But whatever their differences, the logics that we have described have taken hold of them in one way or another (Healy 1997).

Gender issues

So what does the feminist literature have to say about all of this? Surprisingly little. When we turn to it we see a preoccupation with important and enduring concerns but little work which strongly connects these to the changes mentioned above. What are these concerns and what examples do we have of work which makes the connections to new modes of governmentality?

In the past five years or so, feminists have 'investigated the gap between [the] model of equality and academic fairness and the sexist reality of the academy' (Brooks 1997: 1). They have looked within the university at the operations and processes of power, as well as how academic women are located within, and experience, these processes. They have documented patterns of discrimination, disadvantage and differentiation for academic women (ibid.: 6) and their concerns have included:

- understanding and confronting biases that reflect male dominance in academic knowledge and practice (ibid.: 130). In the 1960s, Jessie Bernard divided faculty into teachers and 'men-of-knowledge'. Teachers, she argued, are instruments of communication; 'men-of-knowledge' are authors of knowledge. She observed that teachers are usually female; 'men-of-knowledge' are usually male (in Simeone 1987: 52);
- the difficulties for women academics of co-ordinating the demands of two 'greedy institutions' – university and family (Acker 1994: 126);
- the management of colleague relations from a minority or token position, leading to either invisibility or extra-visibility (ibid.: 127–8);
- the perception that women are mainly support workers and educational consumers, not educational decision-makers (Ramsay 1995: 91);
- the effects on notions of merit and thus on promotion of all the above (Allen and Castleman 1995: 20–30);
- experiences of setting up equal employment opportunities policies/initiatives and feminist approaches to educational reform (Arnot and Barton 1992: 50) and associated difficulties.

In general, this body of literature exposes the implications for university women of the 'chilly climate' of university cultures of exclusion, exploitation, discrimination, career limitations and cultural entrenchment. While some analyses are remarkably context-blind, others argue that current contexts make the 'chilly climate' even chillier for women, with:

- organisational micro-politics further undermining women and women's knowledge (Morley 1995: 272–4);
- experiences of alienation, frustration, overwork, and of being devalued, despite achievement and institutional commitment (Butler and Schulz 1995: 38–57);

- the debasement of women's place in the restructured organisation, that is, the decline in working conditions, rates of pay, tenure/contract, and the feminisation of teaching (Blackmore 1997b);
- enhanced opportunities for individuals and institutions to mobilise their 'politics of advantage' and so to overwhelm notions of gender equity (Blackmore 1997a: 93).

Further, some studies point to the importance of better understanding the gender implications of the current conjuncture in order that it may be better challenged in the interests of women (Acker 1994: 133). Others go so far as to argue that the time is ripe for feminist-inspired change. As Butler and Schulz say, given the current climate of uncertainty and massive change within higher education in Australia, it is an 'open moment' for women to transform the culture and structures of universities (1995: 55). Eva Cox calls for vision beyond equal employment opportunities and Women's Studies which involves a 'feminist redesign of the whole system' (1995: 69–70).

While we commend the fighting spirit of such views, we feel they are just a tad optimistic. Clearly the chillier climate of current times makes institutional redesign in the interests of gender justice even more difficult. But on a related but alternative tack, it is worth asking if there are specific implications here for *feminist* academics and *feminist* knowledge.

We find it surprising that there is so little feminist literature which seriously examines the implications of these new conditions for *feminists* and *feminisms*. Are feminist academics all so busy working smart, working fast, that there is no time to examine the contemporary conditions for the production of feminist knowledge and for feminist pedagogy? In what follows, we will identify some literature which provides a starting-point for such an examination. In so doing, we will point to some possible new lines of inquiry for feminism.

Theories of the contemporary

Let us consider the range of conceptual vocabularies associated with theories of the contemporary by doing a quick linguistic grab. There are sets of ideas which converge around 'age' themes and theses – 'the age of redefinition', 'the age of rage', ' the age of uncertainty', 'the age of anxiety' and 'the age of self-interest', 'the second media age'. There are those which converge around 'post' themes and theses: 'post-Fordism', 'post-nationalism', 'post-industrialism', 'post-modernism', 'post-colonialism', 'post-feminism'. There are those which converge around 'end of' themes and theses: 'the end of nature', 'the end of work', 'the end of society', 'the end of history', 'the end of Reason'. Then there are those which converge around 'new' themes and theses: 'new times', the 'new work order', the 'new media order'. There are those which converge around renaming society: 'risk society', 'network society', 'jobless society'. Others converge around renaming capitalism: 'fast capitalism', 'casino capitalism', 'informational capitalism'. Then there are the 'de-' and 're-' themes: 'de-territorialisation', 'de-traditionalisation', 'de-institutionalisation-', 'decentring' (e.g. of Europe and/or the West) and 'restructuring', 're-culturing', 'reconfiguration', and 're-imagining' (e.g. communities). Finally, there is the catch-all concept of globalisation. Predictably, the meaning of most of these concepts is explored and contested at length.

However, most analysts, from whatever broad theoretical orientation, agree on the necessity of adopting a global analytic which is sensitive to state and local articulations, which takes into account the powerful forces of recent relationships between capitalism and new information and communication technologies – techno-capitalism – and which is cognisant of their considerable and variable implications for different economies, policies, cultures and identities.

Feminists have written quite extensively on topics pertinent to the above, yet their work is not usually framed by such apocalyptic titles and it is often more mini-narrativist in its focus. However, there is a body of work which, while sensitive to the problems of meta-narratives, still addresses 'macro issues' despite their current unfashionableness in certain feminist circles. Very generally, it considers the reorganisation of the economy and political power through analyses of state restructuring and its association with globalisation. While this literature stresses big economic and cultural shifts, it also considers the ways in which these are read and rewritten nationally, locally and subjectively, thus offering accounts of the human dimensions and effects of big structural forces. Here we will mention feminist analyses of the state and restructuring and of globalisation.

Gender, the state and restructuring

The feminist literature on gender, the state and the politics of restructuring focuses on the following; recent changes ('structural adjustments') in the state/nation, and in public policy and services, the ways in which gender is inscribed within them, and their gendered effects (e.g. Edwards and Magarey 1995). It considers the shifting relationships between market, state and individual and between public and private; new forms of regulation; and redefinitions of citizenship within the state in contemporary times. It usually involves the identification and critique of the key features of neo-liberal economics and philosophy, their hegemonic manifestations in policy, and their implications for the welfare state and thus for women. The turn to the market is the guiding motif for many analyses which observe that, as a result of restructuring, more women are 'exposed to direct market forces (whether as workers, traders and consumers)' (Bakker 1996: 7).

In the process of documenting the shift to the 'minimalist state and the unfettered market', Brodie (1995) makes the case that the state is undergoing a paradigm shift in its forms of governmentality. This contention is borne out by much of the literature which points to the move away from notions of the universal provision of public goods and services, to minimised notions of public provision and minimised, individualised and, indeed, stigmatised notions of welfare (Fraser and Gordon 1994). It shows how many public services are handed over to the market and are thus both removed from the realm of political negotiation and redefined. The 'Nanny State' metaphor is a particularly gendered concept in which drawing attention to needs is defined as whingeing, and dependency is reinscribed as irresponsible (Sawer 1996). In contrast, we are offered the 'Stingy State' which justifies such withdrawals with arguments about scarcity and which, through policies of careful 'targeting', offers a safety net to fewer and fewer people. In such circumstances welfare and services become reprivatised and redomesticised; the family becomes needier and greedier.

This literature makes very clear the losses which the women's movement is incurring under the processes of restructuring. It points to: entitlements that are lost (equal access to public services such as universities); standards that are lowered (e.g. environmental and labour); the end of equity interventions (redistributive justice); and the subordination of social policy to economic policy. It also points to the erosion of people's belief in collective action, the promotion of individuality and the lessening of connection and community. For instance, Huws (1995: 334–5) argues that the whole concept of society is being rewritten from a disaggregated perspective. People are finding themselves making individual choices to 'protect' themselves, and at the same time inadvertently contributing to the disintegration of public infrastructures (ibid.). Some feminists argue that the move to individual and community reliance marks the end of claims-based politics; others argue that the state has been transformed, and that this requires the mobilisation of new political forms. For example, Brodie argues that restructuring 'alters the economic, public and the domestic; the very constitution of gendered political actors; and, ultimately, the objects of feminist political struggle' (1995: 23).

With regard to universities, there are many possible lines of inquiry arising from this broad theoretical perspective, yet, as indicated, only a few feminist scholars have taken these up. Those which could be further developed include: the construction of gender within the discourses of economic rationalism, human capital theory, neo-liberal theory and corporate managerial theory as they apply to universities; the gendered experiences of restructuring by differently located women workers and women students in the university; and the implications for education and equity claims within university policies and practices. However, while such potential lines of inquiry have their merits, given the dazzling array of theories of contemporary change noted above, it is clear that they require supplementation. It is pertinent, therefore, to mention a few things about the feminist literature, which adopts a global analytic.

Gender and globalisation

There are several overlapping strands to the feminist literature on economic globalisation. These include analyses of:

1 regionalisation and the role of supra-national organisations, global or regional, and their particular implications for nation-states and women;
2 global competition and transnational corporations and organisations *in situ*;
3 transformations and continuities in women's gendered subjectivities and membership as a result of global flows.

Let us take each in turn.

Some feminists who analyse globalisation take the argument about the changing nature of the state much further than those whose focus is 'structural adjustment'. Saskia Sassen (1996), for instance, focuses on changes to territoriality and sovereignty – key systematic properties of the state. She argues that, as a function of economic, non-economic and new legal practices associated with globalisation, 'sovereignty is also being unbundled. At the limit, this means "the State is no longer the only site of sovereignty and the normativity that accompanies it"' (Sassen 1996: 8).

Her point about sovereignty connects to those feminist analyses which consider the work of supra-national (regional and global, e.g. the European Union, World Bank, UNESCO, etc.) agencies, and their differential effects for different countries and the women within them (see, for example, Unterhalter 1996; Brodie 1995). But she also points to the opportunities which arise for new equity claims through international law.

Another set of this literature considers international and transnational capitalism and its implications for women's working lives in different countries. There is an interest here in comparative work on women's experiences across and within countries and in identifying who reaps the benefits and bears the costs of globalisation and regionalisation. Sassen (1996) identifies three stages to this particular work.

The first stage is part of the 'development' literature and examines the introduction and/or encouragement of cash crop plantings and wage labour, typically by foreign firms. This literature identifies how these development programmes depend on women subsidising the waged labour of men through their household production and subsistence farming. The subsistence sector and the modern capitalist enterprise are thus shown to 'be articulated through a gender dynamic that veiled this articulation' (ibid.: 9).

A second phase of scholarship examines the internationalisation of manufacturing production and the feminisation of the international proletariat that came with it. A key argument is that sending manufacturing off First World shores activates a disproportionately female labour force in poorer countries which had previously not been involved in the industrial economy (ibid.: 9, 10). This research examines the structural exploitations of Third World women by multi-national corporations in global factory/assembly lines and global 'sweat shops' (e.g. Fuentes and Ehrenreich 1983) and work practices in free trade or export processing zones. It also considers the international traffic in women, patterns of migration for the purposes of work, and migrant women workers who have moved to 'developed' countries and their search for work and workers' rights. Ironically, because of the gendering of the workplace, plus coercive economic conditions and policies which subtly encourage exploitation of women workers, highly skilled women workers are good selling points for Third World countries wanting to attract direct foreign investment (Mitter 1995: 7–8). This, however, does not necessarily enhance women workers' status or opportunities, internationally, within their own country or within their homes. Some of these studies also demonstrate the flow-on effects of 'global factory/assembly lines' in First World countries. They point to the difficulties for trade unions due to the disappearance of the assembly line in developed nations and the proliferation of part-time employment, self-employment, home work and small workplaces (Women Working Worldwide 1991; Probert 1995).

Sassen's third phase of scholarship on women and the global economy concentrates on 'transformations in gendering, in women's subjectivities, and in women's notions of membership' (Sassen 1996: 10). She mentions scholarship on: women immigrants, that which understands global economic processes via the key analytic category of the household and home, and scholarship on 'new forms of cross-border solidarity, experiences of membership and identity formation that represent new subjectivities, including feminist subjectivities' (ibid.).

Most recent feminist work on globalisation is particularly conscious of the 'uneven and fractured' (Bakker 1996: 19) process of both globalisation and identity formation within the webs of power that constitute what Grewal and Kaplan (1994) call 'scattered hegemonies'. It points to multiple identifications of race, nation, religion, class, gender, sexuality, to the importance of what Haraway (1991) calls 'partial and situated knowledges', and to matters of place, embodiment and experience. In many instances, it also draws on a version of standpoint theory to attend particularly to the views of those who are marginally located outside the privileges of geographic and institutional locations.

Despite the considerable range of this work, there seems to be a relative absence of sustained feminist accounts of the relationship between capitalism and new technologies and the changes in the economic, knowledge and management approaches which have arisen, in part at least, as a function of the application of new information and communications media.[1] Let us consider some of these.

Fast capitalism, knowledge workers and intellectual capital

Of interest here is a literature on 'fast capitalism' or techno-capitalism and the techno-scientific and management knowledge apparatus that sustains it. A particularly popular vocabulary in such work has arisen from cultural geography or, as Morley and Robins (1995: 26) say, 'social theories informed by geographic imagination'. This vocabulary includes such concepts as 'networks', 'flows', 'landscapes', 'spaces', 'places' and 'virtuality'. There is a fascination with new configurations of time and space, and with the spacelessness and placelessness of images, screens and machines and with virtual worlds. There is great interest in the porousness of borders and boundaries and in global flows of trade, foreign investment, wealth, culture, information, images, labour and people through tourism, migration, war and refugee status. There is a fascination with the 'fluid firm', with 'flexible' management and labour and with the technologies which permit such flexibility. On another hand, there is also a good deal of interest in the politics and importance of space and place, in fragments, segments, in the role of tradition, heritage, roots and, again, notions of home, and in 'torrid zones' – lawless places which are out of regulatory control. Take, for example, the scholarship of Castells (1996) and Lash and Urry (1994).

Castells' main focus is on the new techno-economic system which he calls 'informational capitalism' (1996: 18). He argues that capitalism is the mode of production and informationalism is its mode of development. Indeed, Castells goes further and makes the distinction between information society and informational society (ibid.: 21). To him, information involves the communication of knowledge and, as such, it has been critical to change in all societies. But information*al* society is a specific form of social organisation in which information generation, processing and transmission become the fundamental sources of productivity and power. Productivity and competitiveness depend on capacity to generate, process and apply efficiently knowledge-based information to all sectors of the economy, to agriculture, industry and service, and of course to the information processing too. He argues that we live in an informational society because of the new technological conditions emerging in this historical period. Further, it involves an increasing number of non-material products such as services, communication, information and entertainment (ibid.).

To Castells there is a reflective relationship between information technology and capitalism: they operate in a virtuous circle. Information technology has shaped capitalism and capitalism has shaped information technology. To him, technology is central to capitalism's rejuvenation and expansion and is the new material base to capitalism (ibid.: 17–22). It gives it its knowledge base and its global reach. As he indicates, production, consumption and circulation are now organised on a global scale, either directly or through networks or linkages. He makes the point, however, that an informational economy is different from a world economy due particularly to its capacity to work 'as a unit in real time on a planetary scale' (ibid.). Further, as Lash and Urry (1994) observe, with the increasing capacity of electronic networks, the processes of reproduction, circulation and consumption are able to occur in greater profusion at a much faster speed. They talk of flows of material and post-material objects which are moving at ever greater distances and at ever greater speeds – processes of 'speed up and stretch out'.

A feature of these changes which is most pertinent here is the rise of the so-called knowledge worker (Drucker 1995). While the notion of knowledge worker has not been fully theorised and debated in the literature we will uncritically stay with it for a while and return to it for further consideration in the final section.

As indicated, these times have seen the decline of manufacturing, the expansion of the service sector, and the rapid rise of the information sector and its increasing importance as a source of output, growth and wealth creation. Moving 'bits rather than atoms' (Negroponte 1995) costs much less, and therefore this represents the highest value-added sector. The talk is now less of human capital and more of intellectual capital – the brain-based worker/organisation (Burstein and Kline 1995: 274). What is required is people's knowledge and creativity with regard to applications and content, their capacity to manipulate, understand and make productive (commercial, exportable, transferable and licensable) use of symbols.

As materialist feminist Hennessy points out, the rise of the knowledge worker has significant implications for class formation and relations.

> As the terms of economic power veer more and more towards control over information, knowledge is being stripped of its traditional value as product of the mind, making it a commodity in its own right whose exchange and circulation helps multiple new divisions of Labor and fractured identities. Politically, the 'ruling class' is being reconfigured as a conglomerate of corporate leaders, high level administrators and heads of professional organisations.
>
> (Hennessy 1993: 10)

The reconfigured ruling class includes the glitterati set of the digerati set, the men at the electronic frontier – the digital entrepreneurs. Clearly these men hold many of the current levers of cultural and economic production. They lead to what Kroker and Weinstein (1994) call the new virtual class. In an era when all things digital capture increasing media coverage, their corporate battles and values have a particularly high profile and are constantly offered to us by the press as models of entrepreneurial inspiration. Rushkoff (1996) implies this is 'the revenge of the nerds'. For such digital entrepreneurs, particularly in the US, Europe and Japan and, to a lesser extent, in other parts of Asia, Latin America, Canada and Australia, all the world is a potential source of labour, custom and profit. They are creating a new digital world-order based on information flows.

In his recent book *Intellectual Capital*, Stewart argues that today's intellectual (knowledge) workers are strong and powerful in the labour force. Their work, working styles and requisite work conditions (informal project-oriented work groups assisted by technology, especially computers) undermine the centralised and hierarchical power structures and practices of Taylorism – those still widely used, especially in manufacturing industries (Stewart 1997: 183–5). While, in this neo-liberal information-based economy, employees have weakened job security and loyalty for employers, and while employers offer employees less security and loyalty, they depend more than ever on particular forms of human (intellectual) capital. According to Stewart, knowledge workers are needed by organisations more than the knowledge workers need the organisation (ibid.: 106). Interestingly, Stewart also argues that the most valuable parts of jobs have become the most essentially human tasks: sensing, judging, creating, building relationships (ibid.: 51), aspects which have often been regarded as 'female' in the past – subjective, intuitive – and of little worth, monetarily or otherwise.

Clearly, techno-capitalism has helped to effect new organisational and institutional forms and philosophies which, virtuous circle again, make these technologies central. One brand of management philosophy which is becoming hegemonic is what Gee *et al.* (1996) call 'fast capitalist texts'. These incredibly popular texts are written by a new slick breed of management gurus, the icon of which is Tom Peters, the 'liberation manager'.

In fast capitalist texts, we meet the fluid, flexible firm that supposedly thrives on disorganisation and chaos, responds immediately to any market stimulus, and replaces hierarchies and lines of management with self-starting, fast paced teams, doing 'highly meaningful' work in collaborative environments. Small is beautiful, groups are never stationary and all 'just do it'. The following remark from Peters is typical:

> 'I think I figured out why all these little businesses work. They've got to.' From that comment was born what I call the 'gotta unit' concept.
>
> A gotta unit is one of modest size, which may be living in a larger body but which routinely does the impossible, not because its members read books (even mine) on getting close to the customer, but for precisely the reason the mom-and-pop grocery store will do almost anything (and then some) to serve its neighbors in the surrounding

seven-block area. Without that effort, it goes out of business. Kaput. In other words, they do it, 'cause they gotta.

Implementing the gotta concept almost amounts to automating spunk – making it absolutely necessary for the unit to deliver a spirited response to every customer.

(quoted in Gee *et al.* 1996: 39)

With regard to the implications of the fluid firm for the power of knowledge workers, Gee *et al.* (1996) have a less benign view than Stewart. They argue that such texts and the management practices which flow from them offer a particularly partial view of the world of work, which brackets out not only bigger driving forces but also private and personal relationships, stable communities, shared histories and long-term commitments (ibid.: 40). Further, they have no apparent morality but are driven by consumers' desires (ibid.: 41).

It seems clear that the feminist globalisation literature on work, place, embodiment and experience, and migration flows would be complemented by a feminist analysis of flow and speed in networks of power, of the disembeddings and re-embeddings brought about by the collapsing of space and time and by studies of the upper circuits of capital, hyper-productivity, knowledge workers and, indeed, 'automating spunk'! But let us return to the university.

Back to the university

Clearly, universities have changed, and our concern here is with the implications of these changes both for the future of the university and for feminists and feminism. What do the theories of the contemporary outlined above suggest?

As a public institution, the fortunes of the Australian university are intimately tied to the fluctuations of the state. This is the case with regard to the state's guiding belief systems and its economy within the global and regional economy. To the extent that they continue to understand themselves as agencies of the state, universities can be expected to enhance the 'capacity building' work upon which the state is increasingly insisting. Predictably, as part of the productive infrastructure of the state, universities will increasingly gear their activities to supporting productivity gains, enhancing internal competitiveness and creating an ideological climate of support for such 'missions'.

However, as universities continue along the path of hyper-competitiveness and Continuous Improvement, technologisation and globalisation are becoming key features of the scenario. It is also thus predictable that universities will understand themselves as and take on the features of fluid firms and global corporations. Witness the following quotation from a promotional flier for a conference held at Royal Melbourne Institute of Technology in 1997:

> In the context of a rapidly internationalising global economy presenting new challenges for cultures, economies and technology, the world's universities are being faced with decisions about how they operate in a borderless world ... Easier movement of populations between countries, regional economic cooperation and new technologies are increasing competition to provide faster, better and more relevant education ... In effect, universities are reinventing themselves as dynamic service providers as well as traditional teaching, learning and research centres.
>
> (RMIT University 1997: 3)

Interestingly, the more universities see themselves as 'players' in global education techno-markets, the more their relationship to the particular territories and sovereignties of their origins becomes problematic. It may well be the case that in reinventing themselves internationally, universities move away from the state capacity building work which is expected of them. Perhaps they will orient themselves more towards regional interests, or perhaps local. At this stage such matters are unclear, but there are considerable tensions which are yet to be addressed, let alone analysed. These trends are having significant implications for knowledge production, academic work and academic workers, and thus for feminists and feminism.

Technologically supported lean production methods go hand in hand with the widespread business practices of subcontracting, outsourcing, offshoring, consulting, downsizing and customising. Indeed, the deterritorialised virtual university is a popular fantasy among university managers who, as we indicated at the outset, see themselves, not academics, as the core workers. It is possible that place-bound, classroom-bound workers will be increasingly marginalised as esteem and money flow increasingly to the top end of the corporate university – the internationally connected producers of the knowledge most valued in the corporate sector (knowledge workers) – and to those who manage and market that knowledge – smarter and faster.

And what are the implications for knowledge? Traditionally, universities were supported by society to pursue knowledge in a disinterested manner and to inform social progress (Filmer 1997). In addition, as Lingard (1997) argues, under the previous 'welfare economy', universities were implicated within public policies which involved some state intervention against the market and in the interests of social justice and the common good (Lingard 1997: 5). Further, historically, state funding and the state philosophies noted above ensured that universities had a certain autonomy and the authority to pursue knowledge according to their own designs.

Now, in contrast, there is less intervention from the state in the interests of justice and the common good, and instead the state underwrites the market economy (ibid.). Now, dependence on state funds and on new state philosophies has actually *compromised* universities' autonomy. The state expects universities to galvanise 'the economic potential of knowledge' (Symes, in McCollow and Lingard 1996: 16). University education has come to be seen as an industry, with attendant expectations of efficiency, utility and economic returns. Less and less is it seen as providing a public service with intangible social benefits, as a source of enlightenment, and as a contributor to the critical, cultural, aesthetic and liberal democratic sensibilities of the state. Specifically, new state influences have meant that academics are to become corporate and market professionals (McCollow and Lingard 1996: 12–16): in other words, 'knowledge workers'.

Knowledge workers are those 'who apply established intellectual and scientific skills in work geared to the ends laid down by the owners or controllers of large scale industrial and administrative complexes' (Sharp and White 1968: 15). In the general literature on knowledge workers, academics are seldom identified as such, even though generating various forms of intellectual capital is their stock-in-trade.[2] Certainly Drucker and Stewart ignore them. Nonetheless, as indicated, university academics are being reconstructed as knowledge workers, even if not all of them fit the description. Certainly, those academics who can function as conventional knowledge workers are most valued and rewarded by the university. They fit well Stewart's notion of a labour elite with bargaining power within the sector. A potential irony here is that universities' intellectual capital depends on the critical interrogation of knowledge from a range of points of view and in many different sets of interests. This contributes to the growth of knowledge, and without such critical friction knowledge may well stagnate and the university may have less to offer its 'clients'.

It would appear that universities are no longer expected or expect to pursue disinterested knowledge for its own sake and for the greater good. It should be noted, though, that the status of such knowledge remains ambiguous. One could speculate that if such knowledge is able to assist the university to achieve some aspects of its corporate goals then it would have no objection to it 'in principle'. However, one could also surmise that the university would not go out on a limb to protect such knowledge, and to the extent that it may be at cross-purposes with its corporate goals, it may well either let it languish or seek to repress it.

But, of course, many academics who remain in universities continue to hold views of knowledge as disinterested, for its own sake or for the common good or in the interests of what Giddens (1994) calls emancipatory and life politics. Stewart fails to take into account such workers with knowledge. Presumably, few corporate businesses include such workers in their stock of intellectual capital. Can they then be defined as knowledge workers? Should they be? Are they all now 'alternative' or 'oppositional' knowledge workers? Whose ends is their work geared towards? What happens to them in the new division of labour in academe? Let us pursue these questions a little with regard to feminist academics.

Feminist 'knowledge workers' in universities

As indicated, the university is remarkably absent from most of the feminist literature on contemporary global change. An associated absence is a feminist discussion of the changing nature of feminist workers and feminist knowledge in this current historical conjuncture. Given the not-too-bright picture painted earlier of women academics as workers within the conventional university, how are feminist 'knowledge workers' and feminist knowledge itself (within academia) going to hold up in the face of restructuring and globalisation and their underlying philosophies? Is there a need for a fourth wave of feminism?

As women, feminists will no doubt be drawn yet further into the vortex of the increasingly needy and greedy institutions of university and family, as welfare and service are reprivatised. Indeed, policies of reprivatisation are likely to intensify the emotional labour of feminists in the academy and elsewhere, as they struggle to undertake feminist work in conditions which are both increasingly hostile to it and increase the need for it. Feminism may thus be repositioned as a coping site for structural difficulties. In this sense, then, ironically, feminism might be seen to be nurturing restructuring within the university.

Historically, feminism has best flourished in those faculties not easily tied to economic utility. However, it is predictable that such faculties will be residualised in the corporate university. This could happen in one of several ways which include the possibilities of intensified teaching and marginalised research: a return to the days of women teachers and 'men of knowledge', perhaps.

This is a dangerous scenario, as knowledge production is crucial to keeping feminism alive and relevant. Indeed, as our discussion of contemporary changes indicates, a wild array of new lines of inquiry has emerged. Let us take some quick examples. Just as feminists reworked the notions of citizen and the state in the 1970s and 1980s, so they must now rework notions of the market, the global, national, regional and the local. Just as feminists reworked notions of politics and activism in the 1970s and 1980s, so too they must now rework such notions in alignment with new paradigms of governmentality, circumstances of the intensified individualism, the rise in significance of the 'third sector' (Rifkin 1995), non-government organisations (NGOs) and supra-national agencies and new configurations of time and space. Such reworkings will need to recognise not only the demonstrable limits of legislation and litigation at state and institutional levels but also their potential, as Sassen indicates, in international law. Further, just as feminists deconstructed and reworked the academic canons of the 1970s, 1980s and 1990s, so too must they now deconstruct those 'informational' canons which will predominate in the future. These include particularly those associated with screens and machines, bits, bytes and networks, digital entrepreneurialism and the management theories which are organic to it, and the tyranny of the virtuous circle between capital and technology.

While clearly, then, globalisation opens up very important lines for feminist research, it might well be the case that it simultaneously closes down feminists' opportunities to undertake such inquiry in universities. At this stage, it is not at all clear how feminism and which feminisms will survive the commercialisation and commodification of knowledge in the global intellectual/economic bazaar.

Given that the notion of knowledge as a basis of social progress is marginalised in the current climate, what price feminism? What economic utility is there for feminist knowledge which opposes economic rationalism and globalisation with all their attendant discriminatory and debilitating effects for women's economic, political, and citizenship rights? What economic utility is there for gender-inclusive models of scholarship and management?

Clearly, if feminism and feminists align themselves with social-democratic philosophies and against economic rationalism and liberal-individualist philosophies, feminist knowledge is not likely to be popular in universities desperately seeking resources and funding from radically conservative governments and from commercial sources. How many private sponsors are likely to provide funds to ensure that feminist knowledge remains in the academy, challenging mainstream disciplines with its calls for equity and inclusion in all facets of life? Indeed, are such sponsors likely to withhold funds to those universities which 'harbour' such uncomfortable knowledge?

The current conjuncture puts feminism in an awkward position for other reasons, too. Feminists helped to expose the interestedness of 'disinterested' knowledge and the gender, class, ethnic and sexual biases in notions of the common good. They showed how both could be connected to inequality and injustice. In a sense, then, they have always been oppositional knowledge workers within universities, challenging the tenets of established and 'critical' disciplines and practices. There is a paradox here for feminists.

While on the one hand many feminists have been very critical of the Enlightenment tradition within the university (for many different reasons), on the other hand they have been somewhat dependent on the historical association of universities with such traditions. Indeed, for the post-post-materialist feminist work which we have outlined, the Enlightenment notion is a vital factor of production. Another important factor, also as noted, is the notion that the university must have a certain critical distance from society, economy and culture for it to do its interpretative and critical work. Other important factors of production are the time and resources necessary for the leisurely pursuit of knowledge and the opportunity to develop rich pedagogies. All of these are at risk in the corporate university with its obsessions with speed and utility. It is not at all clear what meta discourses feminism has available to defend itself within the corporate university and the neo-liberal state and global economy. It cannot easily claim Enlightenment; has difficulty differently claiming utility; and the citizenship, needs, responsibilities and rights discourses that it once drew on so powerfully have been subsumed by market discourses of consumer citizenship.

We might well ask, at this point: are feminists able and do they want to become conventional knowledge workers and, through their universities, to be assimilated into the world of intellectual capital, buying into the exploitative, inequitable capitalist economy? Is there an alternative scenario for feminist knowledge workers in universities? This raises the always thorny but vitally important issues of feminist responsibility, accountability and authority.

Hennessy (1993) points to the responsibilities of the oppositional intellectual. Drawing on Stuart Hall, she talks of the 'alienation of advantage'; identifying the ways in which knowledge supports unfair advantage. This suggests that feminists have a responsibility *not* to become conventional knowledge workers. To Hennessy, the responsibility of the oppositional intellectual is to put a hegemonic system of knowledge in the service of counter-hegemonic projects and to help the non-dominant to develop counter-hegemonic knowledges. In a similar vein, Yeatman talks of subaltern intellectuals – those who develop an intellectual 'narrative which is ordered by metaphors of struggle, contest, forced closure, strategic interventions and contingent openings of public spaces for epistemological politics' (1994: 31). On matters of accountability she says,

> Subaltern intellectuals are positioned in a contradictory relationship to intellectual authority. As intellectuals and as evidenced especially when they are directing their intellectual claims upwards, as it were to the ruling elites of academy, they are drawn within the culture of intellectual authority and use its conventions unproblematically. At the same time, as subaltern intellectuals they are not only positioned as outsiders in respect of these ruling elites, which can foster a tendency to call into question the reliance of these elites for their status on intellectual authority, but they are positioned with loyalties and ties both to fellow subaltern intellectuals ... and to subaltern non intellectuals.
> (ibid.: 35)

Clearly such intellectuals are positioned across complex and contradictory lines of intellectual and political authority and accountability. In contemporary times, however, 'upward' lines of accountability within the university appear to be not so much to the ruling elites of intellectual authority as to the ruling elites of market authority. But who else are feminist academics accountable to and can their work be sustained by such groups? Yeatman suggests that feminist academics are also accountable to students generally and female and feminist students particularly, to women generally and women located in difficult circumstances particularly. Feminists in professional faculties are also accountable to service delivery practitioners (such as teachers, health and social workers) generally and oppositional service delivery practitioners particularly. In addition, as universities 'speed up and stretch out', other lines of accountability beyond the nation-state open up. Let us take one of many possible examples.

The feminist globalisation literature highlights the need for women world-wide, but especially in 'developing' countries, to be involved in education, training and 'development' if they are to move from the margins of the work force (Mitter and Rowbotham 1995). However, as Unterhalter (1996) points out, when their education is sponsored by economically rationalist international agencies such as the World Bank this may well reinscribe oppressive versions of femaleness. Clearly, there are opportunities for feminist work through such agencies as well as with a range of NGOs, including international labour organisations. Of course, as the post-colonial literature makes clear, the vexed question of authority arises in such contexts.

What is important, then, is to what end and how Western feminists practice their authority as intellectuals in international contexts, whether they make it problematic to themselves and to others, and whether and how they make themselves accountable, and to whom. Clearly, their position is highly ambiguous, but this does not mean that they should abandon their authority which, for various reasons and in various ways, can play a powerful supportive role for the non-dominant. Indeed, in some senses the feminist academic should 'hold onto her authority as an intellectual and place it in the service of the nondominant' (Yeatman 1994). Oppositional service delivery practitioners at all levels of politics to some extent depend on her authority and expertise for the legitimacy and development of their own projects.

Our conclusion, then, is that these times and the contemporary university raise a host of new issues for feminists in the academy where, at the same time, old problems endure and intensify. Feminism's survival will depend on how well it is able to engage both.

Notes

1 The few relevant accounts that we are aware of include Sassen (1996) on global cities, Haraway (1991) on the social role of science and technology, and Hennessy's (1993) chapter on techno-capitalism.
2 There is, however, an emerging literature by academics themselves about intellectual property. Linda Heron (1996), for example, discusses the prospects for

knowledge workers in the university, focusing on knowledge workers as 'professionals who connect clients with information' (1996: 26), and considers their interconnections with new information technology. Intellectual property rights are also being discussed, in the new technological and industrial context, in terms of protection and 'value', from copyright issues to 'ownership' to resource allocation issues (Spearitt and Thomas 1996). This literature is growing as technological developments raise ownership and authorship questions for published research.

References

Acker, S. (1994) *Gendered Education*, Buckingham: Open University Press.
Allen, M. and Castleman, T. (1995) 'Gender privilege in higher education: examining its dimensions and dynamics', in A.M. Payne and L. Shoemark (eds) *Women, Culture and Universities: A Chilly Climate?*, Sydney: University of Technology, Sydney, Women's Forum.
Arnot, M. and Barton, L. (eds) (1992) *Voicing Concerns: Sociological Perspectives on Contemporary Education Reforms*, Oxfordshire: Triangle Books.
Bakker, I.C. (ed.) (1996) *Rethinking Restructuring: Gender and Change in Canada*, Toronto: University of Toronto Press.
BJ (1997) 'UTS tops fee-paying students', *Campus Review*, 7 (24): 5.
Blackmore, J. (1997a) 'Disciplining feminism: a look at gender-equity struggles in Australian higher education', in L. Roman and L. Eyre (eds) *Dangerous Territories: Struggles of Difference and Equality in Education*, New York: Routledge.
Blackmore, J. (1997b) 'Level playing field? Feminist observations on global/local articulations of the re-gendering and restructuring of educational work', *International Review of Education*, 43 (5–6): 439–61.
Blackmore, J. and Angwin, J. (1996) *Educational Outworkers: Emerging Issues for Women Educators in the Restructured Tertiary Educational Labour Market*, Geelong: Deakin Centre for Education and Change.
Brodie, J. (1995) *Politics on the Margins: Restructuring and the Canadian Women's Movement*, Halifax: Fernwood Publishing.
Brooks, A. (1997) *Academic Women*, Buckingham: Open University Press.
Burstein, D. and Kline, D. (1995) *Road Warriors: Dreams and Nightmares along the Information Highway*, New York: Dutton.
Butler, E. and Schulz, L. (1995) 'Women and the politics of university work: an agenda for the organisation', in A.M. Payne and L. Shoemark (eds) *Women, Culture and Universities: A Chilly Climate?*, Sydney: University of Technology, Sydney, Women's Forum.
Castells, M. (1996) *The Rise of the Network Society*, Oxford: Blackwell Publishers.
Coleman, K. (1995) 'Women and corporate management in universities', in A.M. Payne and L. Shoemark (eds) *Women, Culture and Universities: A Chilly Climate?*, Sydney: University of Technology, Sydney, Women's Forum.
Cox, E. (1995) 'Gender privilege in higher education: examining its dimensions and dynamics', in A.M. Payne and L. Shoemark (eds) *Women, Culture and Universities: A Chilly Climate?*, Sydney: University of Technology, Sydney, Women's Forum.
Drucker, P. (1995) *Managing in an Age of Great Change*, Oxford: Butterworth-Heinemann.

Edwards, A. and Magarey, S. (eds) (1995) *Women in a Restructuring Australia: Work and Welfare*, St Leonards: Allen and Unwin.
Filmer, P. (1997) 'Disinterestedness and the modern university', in A. Smith and F. Webster (eds) *The Postmodern University? Contested Visions of Higher Education in Society*, Buckingham: SRHE and Open University Press.
Fraser, N. and Gordon, L. (1994) 'A genealogy of dependency: tracing a keyword of the welfare state', in P. James (ed.) *Critical Politics*, Fitzroy: Arena Publications.
Fuentes, A. and Ehrenreich, B. (1983) *Women in the Global Factory*, New York: Institute for New Communications/South End Press.
Gee, J.P., Hull, G. and Lankshear, C. (1996) *The New Work Order: Behind the Language of the New Capitalism*, St Leonards: Allen and Unwin.
Giddens, A. (1994) *Beyond Left and Right: The Future of Radical Politics*, Stanford: Stanford University Press.
Grewal, I. and Kaplan, C. (1994) *Scattered Hegemonies: Postmodernity and Transnational Feminist Practice*, Minneapolis, MN: University of Minnesota Press.
Haraway, D.J. (1991) *Simians, Cyborgs, and Women: the Reinvention of Nature*, London: Free Association Books.
Healy, G. (1997) 'Unis Inc.: prestige degrees, full fees', *The Weekend Australian*, 28 June, 1: 6.
Hennessy, R. (1993) *Materialist Feminism and the Politics of Discourse*, London: Routledge.
Heron, L. (1996) 'Knowledge workers or threatened species? A commentary', *Australian Universities Review* 1: 26–8.
Huws, U. (1995) 'The fading of the collective dream? Reflections on twenty years' research on information technology and women's employment', in S. Mitter and S. Rowbotham (eds) *Women Encounter Technology: Changing Patterns of Employment in the Third World*, London: Routledge.
Kenway, J. (1995) *Marketing Education: Some Critical Issues*, Geelong: Deakin University Press.
Kroker, A. and M. Weinstein (1994) *Data Trash: The Theory of the Virtual Class*, Montreal: New World Perspectives.
Lash, S. and Urry, J. (1994) *Economies of Signs and Space*, London: Sage Publications.
Lingard, B. (1997) 'The problematic coalition of markets and social justice', *Education Links* 54: 4–7.
McCollow, J. and Lingard, B. (1996) 'Changing discourses and practices of academic work', *Australian Universities' Review* 39 (2): 11–19.
Mitter, S. (1995) 'Beyond the politics of difference: an introduction', in S. Mitter and S. Rowbottom (eds) *Women Encounter Technology: Changing Patterns of Employment in the Third World*, London: Routledge.
Mitter, S. and Rowbotham, S. (eds) (1995) *Women Encounter Technology: Changing Patterns of Employment in the Third World*, London: Routledge.
Morley, D. and Robins, K. (1995) *Spaces of Identity: Global Media, Electronic Landscapes and Cultural Boundaries*, London: Routledge.
Morley, L. (1995) 'Open forum: an agenda for gender: women in the university', *European Journal of Women's Studies* 2: 271–5.
Negroponte, N. (1995) *Being Digital*, New York: Knopf.

Probert, B. (1995) 'The transformation of work: social, cultural and political contexts', in J. Spierings, I. Voorendt and J. Spoehr (eds) *Jobs for Young Australians*, Adelaide: Jobs for Young Australians Conference Organising Committee in association with Social Justice Research Foundation.

Ramsay, E. (1995) 'The politics of privilege and resistance', in A.M. Payne and L. Shoemark (eds)*Women, Culture and Universities: A Chilly Climate?*, Sydney: University of Technology, Sydney, Women's Forum.

Rifkin, J. (1995) *The End of Work: The Decline of the Global Labour Force and the Dawn of the Post Market Era*, New York: G.P. Putnam's Sons.

RMIT University (1997) 'The global university: a 21st century view', Second International Conference, RMIT University, Melbourne.

Rushkoff, D. (1996) *Cyberia: Life in the Trenches of cyberspace*, London: Flamingo.

Sassen, S. (1996) 'Toward a feminist analytics of the global economy', *Indiana Journal of Global Legal Studies* 4 (1): 7–25.

Sawer, M. (1996) 'Gender, metaphor and the state', *Feminist Review* 52 (Spring): 118–34.

Sharp, G. and White, D. (1968) 'Features of the intellectually trained', *Arena* 15: 30–3.

Simeone, A. (1987) *Academic Women: Working Towards Equality*, Massachusetts: Bergin and Garvey.

Spearitt, P. and Thomas, J. (1996) 'Academic intellectual property in a new technological and industrial context', *Australian Universities' Review* 1: 29–32.

Stewart, T.A. (1997) *Intellectual Capital: The New Wealth of Organizations*, London: Nicholas Brealey Publishing.

Unterhalter, E. (1996) 'States, households and the market in World Bank discourse, 1985–1995: a feminist critique', *Discourse: Studies in the Cultural Politics of Education* 17 (3): 389–402.

Women Working Worldwide (ed.) (1991) *Common Interests: Women Organising in Global Electronics*, London: Women Working Worldwide.

Yeatman, A. (1994)*Postmodern Revisionings of the Political*, London: Routledge.

Conclusion
Reflections on global feminisms

Kelly Coate

One of the (many) challenges of producing a book based on feminist movements globally is the fractured and disparate nature of feminisms in the late 1990s. We were interested in understanding how feminists define themselves and their commitments as we approach the millennium. Obviously it is impossible to put together a collection which encompasses all aspects of a global movement for change, but also it is impossible to make our own judgements about what is or is not a part of feminist activism. In our meetings about the conference and the book we often found ourselves discussing the idea of 'belonging': who feels as though they belong to a women's movement, who wants to belong, who is longing for a sense of identity through such a movement? We wondered about our own senses of be/longing: in spite of our different backgrounds (we grew up on three different continents), we are now working within the predominantly white middle-class privileged environment of the higher education system in the UK. We engage with the discourses coming out of this location and our identities are now partly constituted through these discourses, even though we may perceive ourselves to be oppositional knowledge workers within this system (see Chapter 10). The academy brought us together, our work within it gave us a sense of collective identities, and it also brought together the women who have contributed to this collection.

This concluding chapter is not meant to be about us as editors, but I have raised these issues in order to acknowledge the very powerful influence the academy has had on feminisms (and I mean to say it that way rather than the other way around). Florence Howe, one of the founders of Women's Studies in the States in the late 1960s, recently pointed out that as the national women's movements in the US and the UK have gradually lost a sense of collectivity and public visibility, there are burgeoning women's movements in non-Western countries which have gained their impetus from the integration of Women's Studies into the higher education system (Howe 1997). In other words, the trajectory is in the opposite direction: Women's Studies in higher education in the UK and US grew out of the national women's movements, whereas the women's movements in some non-Western countries have gained ground because of the visibility of women's political activism in the academy.

To claim that Women's Studies in the academy may be responsible for the growth of women's movements is perhaps contentious. There are many long-standing arguments against the development of Women's Studies in the academy. First, many feminist activists struggling across the globe have argued that women have only so much energy and so many constraints on their daily lives, and that what little is left over can be put to better use than within an elite and exclusionary institution which for so long has devalued women and their contributions to it. Second, the notion that what women are doing in the academy can be called feminist political activism is not without problems (see Chapter 8). There are certainly enough anti-feminist discourses in the academy (meaning, for a start, racism, sexism and homophobia), and even sometimes within Women's Studies, that some feel it is disingenuous to claim that women in the academy are improving women's lives. The values and ethics within higher education are often at odds with feminist projects. Finally, the academy is often portrayed as out of touch with women's lives: it excludes many women (not just physically but intellectually) and does not always engage with them in meaningful ways.

These arguments rest on a dichotomy, and it seems imperative to again reconsider the barriers feminists have constructed around 'the academy' and 'the real world'. For instance, Wangui, Suki and I may have a sense of belonging through a higher education institution, but corresponding with any sense of belonging is also a sense of others not belonging. We help to perpetuate this dichotomy. As indicated in Suki's introduction to this collection, we spent a great deal of time during the organisation of the conference trying to reach out to those on the 'outside'. We wanted everyone to feel they could belong. Lakhbir Virk, speaking at the conference, very powerfully argued that feminists in the academy do not reach all women with the knowledge they have, nor do they necessarily shape their agendas to meet their needs. This is undoubtedly true, and without undermining these criticisms I would hope we could still construct different discourses around feminists 'inside' and 'outside' the academy.

Feminism can no longer be spoken about in the singular, and any woman who does speak about 'feminism' is immediately asked what she means and who she is speaking for (see Chapter 9). Feminism is no longer a grand narrative (if it ever was), and with this fracturing of what once provided a sense of collectivism for many women come very challenging questions about who 'belongs'. This movement away from binary logic and dichotomous thinking (and essentialism) has often been defined as a postmodern project, yet it was arguably the feminists who got there first. The experience of editing this collection has led me to think through how legitimate academic discourses often presuppose dualistic logic. In particular, what is striking for me is how feminist discourses can transcend dichotomies in ways that encourage new understandings and new forms of analysis.

For example, rather than perceiving activism as taking place largely outside the physical boundaries of the university, it seems necessary to now understand the work of academic women as a significant part of the wider movement. Social movements gain their power to transform through the collective struggles of the organisations of which they consist. This has been true of the women's movement, yet it is rare to find an acknowledgement in histories of the second wave movement to the contribution of academic women's groups which formed over the past three decades (the British Sociological Association's women's caucus, the Women's Resources and Research Centre, the WSN, to name but a few groups in the UK). Women's informal study or reading groups at universities, national academic women's organisations, community 'consciousness-raising' groups, women's NGOs: these are all organisations which together constitute a social movement which has been the most enduring social movement to emerge from the 1960s. There are no groups on the 'outside' or on the 'inside': they all belong.

In thinking along similar lines, a seemingly dualistic discourse of the local and the global can also be challenged. For example, the women's groups in South Africa described by Gertrude Fester in Chapter 2 are in one sense a response to the very specific policies of the national government, yet the discourses from the global women's movement were a significant influence on their development. She is able to make connections between the local and the global which, although sometimes problematic, are fundamental to a women's movement which has indeed become a global movement. Suki Ali, participating in a panel session at the conference, reiterated what has perhaps become the new women's movement slogan in the 1990s: as feminists, we need to act *locally* and think *globally*. Postmodernist theorists have made much of the notion of space–time compression through new technologies, and as Kenway and Langmead illustrate in Chapter 10, feminist theorists need to urgently engage with these concepts. While they may not seem to have immediate relevance to the lives of, for instance, the Bedouin women in Tovi Fenster's chapter, the reality is that the so-called space–time compression is enabling feminist theorists in Western academies to make connections with the lives of women who were previously distanced both culturally and geographically. Feminist theorists must not only begin to engage with the new discourses identified by Kenway and Langmead through substantive critique, but also provide a sense of 'grounding' to some of the more abstract, fanciful, postmodern playfulness of predominantly male theorists. Do the 'flows' and 'landscapes' of the new technologies touch the lives of Bedouin women? Yet, in reality, as editors we could not have produced this book without modern technologies enabling us to email Israel, South Africa, Ireland and Pakistan. It was more difficult at times to reach each other in London on the telephone than to contact Diana and Jane in Australia. The notion of 'belonging' is being radically reshaped.

Feminist theories were initially inspired by the notion that the personal is political. Throughout the past three decades, feminists have continued to develop this fundamental challenge to the public/private dichotomy, creating a significant contribution to intellectual transformation. Debbie Epstein and Deborah Steinberg's account of their involvement with feminist political activism will no doubt resonate with many women, and in so doing illustrate again how the personal experiences of women inform our understandings of the larger context. In the same vein, many feminist theorists have argued for the inclusion of autobiographical narratives to reconstruct social theories. Both Elaine Unterhalter and Ronit Lentin rewrite historical narratives informed by their identities. The discourses of the academy have previously distanced themselves from women's lives through the grand narratives of history, and one of feminism's greatest contributions to theory has surely been a re-visioning of these narratives through women's personal accounts.

Thinking through, and challenging, dualistic thought is not unproblematic. Indeed, both feminism and anti-racist struggles have strategically relied on dichotomies for their strength: where would we be if we had not collectively organised through the dichotomous categories black and white, men and women? Yet as Suki's chapter so powerfully demonstrates, social justice discourses emerging in the 1990s need to somehow go beyond these categories while retaining their political edge. We need to learn from the ways in which younger generations are constructing their sense of 'belonging', using lessons from the past to inform our thinking. New alliances need to be formed. As Gertrude Fester's experiences in South African politics illustrate, dominant groups construct social categories in order to create inequalities and maintain their power. Only through an inclusive politics which recognises difference will these categories be challenged and transformation achieved.

Finally, as Tijen Uguris and Tovi Fenster both demonstrate, we need to acknowledge the differences within our own communities. Our communities can be a source of strength and a location for our politics, but again we need to recognise the dangers of allowing the dominant groups to define the parameters of these communities. As this book is published, and as we start the new millennium, we are greatly saddened to be reminded of these dangers through the tragedies in the Balkan war. It will be many years before the women who have had their lives destroyed in this conflict will be heard. A women's movement which thinks globally will need to create the spaces for their voices to be heard. This catastrophe has reopened old and deep wounds from history. There will be many women who will look to their devastated communities for the strength to rebuild them, and who will reach out to women globally for support. Are we, within a truly global women's movement, ready to forge new alliances based on an inclusive politics which listens to all women regardless of religion, colour, nationality, ethnic origin, sexuality, political orientation or physical ability? Who will write this history, and whose voices will be heard? These are the greatest challenges for the women's movement as the new decade begins: *we hope that you belong.*

Reference

Howe, F. (1997) 'Promises to keep: trends in Women's Studies worldwide', *Women's Studies Quarterly* 25 (1 and 2): 407–13.

Index

Abu Lughod, L. 76, 86
Abu Odeh, L. 74
Acker, S. 157, 158
activism: in India 28–9; in Pakistan 7–8
Africa Educational Trust (AET) 112–13, 116–19, 120–2, 123
African National Congress (ANC) 11, 15, 17–18, 23, 116–17; Women's League 12
African Rights 93, 99–100
Afshar, H. 73, 74
Agarwal, K. 33
Agarwal, T.D. 46
Agnew, V. 29, 31
Alcoff, L. 102
Alderson, P. 139
Algeria, massacres 97
Ali, S. 2, 145, 177, 178, 179
Allen, B. 99
Allen, M. 157
Alterman, R. 71
Alton Bill 128
Amos, V. 93, 136
Anthias, F.: and Yuval Davis (1989) 108, 122; and Yuval Davis (1992) 51, 55, 93, 108, 137, 146–7
apartheid 19, 25n, 111
Ardener, S. 73, 74
Arnot, M. 157
Arora, K. 40
Asylum Bill 128
Atlantis Women's Group 15
Australia, universities 3, 154–72
Azad Hind Fauj 33

Back, L. 145
Bakker, I.C. 159, 162
Bangladesh 98, 99
Bar, A. 75, 78

Barrett, M. 94
Barton, L. 157
Basu, A. 30
Bedouin: domestic level 78–80; employment among Bedouin women 84–5, 87–8; forbidden and permitted spaces 77–8; gendered planning and the modernity project 86–8; housing density 70, 79–80, 83, 86, 87; Israeli Palestinian women married to Bedouin men 83–4; middle-aged traditional Bedouin women 82; in the Negev 69–70, 77–8; neighbourhood level 80; planning of services 87; public and private space 75–7; regional level 81–2; settlements 71; town level 80–1; urbanised Bedouin women 82–3; women's clubs 85–6
Beller-Hann, I. 73
Bellville Gemeenskaporganisasie 15
Ben David, J. 70
Benjamin, J. 23
Benson, M. 116, 120, 121, 123, 124
Bernard, J. 157
Bernstein, H. 124; (1994) 112–17, 119, 120, 123
Bhabha, H. 109
Bhavnani, K. 57
BJ (1997) 156
Black Consciousness 12
Blackmore, J. 158
blackness 136
Blair, T. 128
Boland, E. 97
Boric, R. 97
Brah, A. 109, 119, 122
Britain: employment 57; households 57, 60; housing policies 49–50, 56–7;

mixed-race children 137–8;
Women's Studies 130, 176–7
Brodie, J. 160, 161
Brooks, A. 157
Brownhill, S. 53, 55
Bryan, B. 136
Burleigh, M. 98
Burstein, D. 164
Butalia, U. 96, 101–2
Butler, E. 157, 158
Butler, J. 12, 16

Campaign Against Sexual Abuse 19
capitalism 54, 58, 161, 163–6
Caplan, P. 34
Carby, H. 136
Castells, M. 163–4
Castleman, T. 157
catastrophe: definition 95–7;
feminisation of 97–100
Cealey-Harrison, W. 138
Chand 32
Charman, A. 23
Chen, K.-I. 109
Cherifati-Merbatine, D. 95
childcare 60
Clarke, V. 57
class: and blackness 136; community construction 52; divisions in society 50, 58; nationalist movement in India 28–9; planning aims 57; women's movement in Pakistan 6; women's movement in South Africa 13–14, 18–19
Clinton, B. 128
clubs, women's 85–6
Coate, K. 135
Cohen, R. 108
Coleman, K. 155, 156
Collins, P.H. 51, 59
Coloured Labour Preference Act 11
Commission for Gender Equality (South Africa) 11
Commission for Racial Equality (UK) 55, 135
community: concept of 50, 51–6, 137; gender and ethnicity 49–50
Congress Party 40
Connell, R.W. 96, 97
Connolly, P. 147
Convention of Traditional Leaders of South Africa (CONTRALESA) 21
Convention on the Elimination of All Forms of Discrimination Against Women (CEDAW) 21
Cosgrove, D. 73
Cosmopolitan 128, 129
Cox, E. 158
Cross, M. 54
Cullingworth, J.B. 57, 66n
Cultural Studies 127, 148
culture, definition 73
Cuntack, C.B. 36, 40

Dainik Jagron 29
Davies, H. 145
Davis, L. 97
de Lauretis, T. 94
Delbo, C. 92, 100, 101
Department of the Environment (1972) 58
development literature 161–2
Devi, G. 43–5
Devi, K. 31, 40–1, 46
Devi, M. 29
Devi, R. 33
Devi, S. 36, 37–8
Devi, T. 40, 45–6
diasporas 108–11, 115, 117–19
Dickerson, B.J. 93, 94
Dilimini, Z. 115
Dixit, U. 39–41, 46
Dos Santos, P. 113–14
Dowler, L. 96
dress 73, 76, 81, 83–4, 86
Drew, A. 23
Drucker, P. 164, 168
Du Toit, B. 117, 120, 124
Dumasi, J. 117, 119
Duncan, N. 51, 59, 62–3

Education and Training Sub-Committee 14
Edwards, A. 159
Egypt: Bedouin in 76, 86; dress 73, 74
Ehrenreich, B. 162
employment: Bedouin women 84–5; ethnic minorities in Britain 57
empowerment: concept of 50; identities and 56–8
Engels, D. 36
Enloe, C. 96
Epstein, D. 3, 131n, 139, 149, 179
Equal Opportunities Commission 135
equality 134–5
ethnicity: and community 55; and

housing 49, 56–7; concept of 137; ethnic conflicts 94
Evans, J. 135–6
exile 107–8

Fainstein, S. 72
Faludi, S. 128
family: familial sacrifice 34–6; household size 57; structure 60
famine 98
fasting 34–5
Federation of South African Women (FSAW) 15–16
Fein, H. 95
feminism: approach to community 53; approach to town planning 54; centralisation of 128–30; future of 1, 3; global 176–80; history 134–6; in the 1990s 126–7; in universities 169–72; Western and Third World 88
Fenster, T. 2, 70, 178, 179
Fester, G. 1, 178, 179
Filmer, P. 167
Fincher, R. 71
First, R. 124
Forsyth, A. 71, 72, 88
Foucault, M. 102, 155
Fouche, F. 23
Frankenberg, R. 142
Fraser, N. 60, 160
Friedman, J. 72
Fuentes, A. 162
Fugard, A. 121
funding 8
Funkenstein, A. 101

Gaitskell, D. 23
Gandhi, M. 31, 34
Gee, J.P. 165–6
gender: concept of 8; genocidal projects 96; and globalisation 161–3; housing policies 49; mobility between forbidden and permitted space 78–82; oppression 13; the state and restructuring 159–61; university issues 156–8; within context of modernist planning 70–2
Gender Studies 148
genocide 93, 94–5, 95
Giddens, A. 49, 63, 168
Gilroy, P. 109, 119
Ginsburg, N. 57

Ginwala, F. 119, 121, 124
globalisation 4, 161–3
Goldenberg, M. 96
Gordenker, L. 97
Gordon, L. 160
Goorha, U. 43–4
governmentality and the university 155–6
Greed, C.H.(1994) 50, 51, 54, 55, 57, 58, 60, 61, 63, 64, 66n
Grewal, I. 162
Grosz, E. 111, 122
Group Areas Act 13
Grunfeld, U. 94, 103
Guatemala, *La Violencia* 102
Gupta, S. 33
Gypsy women 98

Habermas, J. 72
Hague, E. 94, 96
Hall, S. 109, 136–7, 140, 171
Hansson, D. 23
Haraway, D.J. 162, 172n
Harding, S. 94, 138
Harvey, D. 52–3, 56, 71
Hassim, S. 14–15, 23
Havakuk, J. 79
Healey, P. 61
Healy, G. 156
Hennessy, R. 164, 171, 172n
Heron, L. 172n
Hcy, V. 146
Hill, D.M. 56
Hill Collins, P. 138
Hillman, S. 145
Hindu: respondents 29; revivalism 36–7
Hodgson, T. 112–13
Holocaust 103n; *see also* Shoah
home: concept of 108–11; image of 119–22
Hood-Williams, J. 138
hooks, b. 62, 127, 129
Horn, P. 23
housing: Bedouin settlements 69–70, 79–80, 83, 86; British policies 49–50, 56–7
Howe, F. 176
Humm, M. 135
Huws, U. 160

identity, identities: difference of, 136; and empowerment 56–8; language of 140; politics 136; and race 133–4

Ifekwunigwe, J.O. 138, 148
India 28–47; clandestine activities within the domestic sphere 43–6; constructive programme 32–4; domestic values 30–1; domestic voices 29–30; familial sacrifice 34–6; nationalist movement 28–47; partition 96, 102; women as mothers and nurturers 36–8; women as sources of strength and support 38–43
information technology 163–4, 178–9
Inkatha Freedom Movement 17–18
International Federation of Red Cross and Red Crescent Societies 95–6
Iran, veiling 73–4
Islam see Muslim culture
Israel: masculinised 94, 98–9; planning 70, 77–8

Jackson, P. 73
Jacobs, B.D. 56
Jagesh, J.P. 29
Japan 96, 99
Jayawardena, K. 22–3, 29
Jones, S. 66n

Kadalie, R. 23
Kailash, Lady 36
Kaplan, C. 162
Karl, M. 56
Kasrils, E. 117
Katz, I. 137, 148
Kaur, M. 29
Keith, M. 54
Kelleher, M. 94, 98
Kemp, A. 14
Kenway, J. 3, 156, 178, 179
Khan, N. 2
Kitson, N. 124
Kline, D. 164
knowledge workers 168
Kobayashi, A. 78
Kosmarskaya, N. 96
Kroker, A. 164
Kumar, Y. 32–3
Kuper, H. 64
Kymlicka, W. 54

Langmead, D. 3, 178, 179
language 16, 18
Lash, S. 163, 164

Laska, V. 98
Lefebvre, H. 63, 65
Lentin, R. 3, 93, 94, 99, 179
lesbians 2, 63
Levitan, E. 123, 124
Lewando-Hundt, G. 75, 79, 80
Ley, D. 71
liberation, women's and national 18–22
Linden, R.R. 94, 101
Lingard, B. 167, 168

McClintock, A. 22
McCollow, J. 168
McDowell, L. 58
MacIntosh, M. 149
McKay, I. 124
Macleod, A. 74
Magarey, S. 159
Magona, S. 118, 123, 124
Maharaj, M. 117
Maharathi 37
Mahila Mandal 33
Makhoere, C. 123, 124
Mandela, N. 114
Marcus, T. 124
market: forces 159–60; marketisation 156
Martins, M. 115, 121
Massey, D.: (1993) 51, 64; (1994) 49, 50, 51–2, 55, 60, 61, 63
Matrix 50, 60, 61, 62
Matthews, F. 115, 123, 124
Mauthner, M. 139
Mayall, B. 139
Maybin, J. 139, 148
Maynard, M. 149
Meir, A. 70
Melman, B. 74
Merck, M. 129
Mernissi, F. 73
migrants 108–11
Milton, S. 93
Ministry of Education (1995) 85
Ministry of Housing (1995) 69, 70, 77, 84
Misra, B. 37–8
Mitchell, D. 73
Mitra, P.C. 35
Mitter, S. 162, 172
mixed-race 133–4, 137–8; case studies 139–48
Mntabo, M.M. 117
Mohanty, C.T. 73, 93, 109

Mompati, R. 116
Moore, H.L. 12
Moore Milroy, B. 72
Morley, D. 163
Morley, L. 157
Morris, J. 57
Moser, C. 77
motherhood: discourse of suffering mother 94; organisation on basis of 23; women as mothers and nurturers 36–8
Mozambique 113–14
Muslim culture 72–7
Mvusi, L. 115, 119, 121

Nadin, V. 57, 66n
Naidoo, P. 117
narratives 101–2
National Assembly/Conference of Development Activists 6
nationalist movement, Indian 28–47
Nayak, A. 139
Nazis 96, 98
Negev, Bedouin in 69, 76–8, 86
Negroponte, N. 164
Ngcobo, L. 124
NGOs 5, 7–8, 169, 172, 178
Nkadimeng, G. 116, 120
Ntantala, P. 123, 124

oppression, triple 13–14

Pain, R. 74, 75
Pakistan 5–8
Palestinians 97
Palm, R. 74
Pan-Africanist Congress 11
Pandey, D. 34
Pandey, G. 47n
Pandey, S. 34–5
Parker, A.B. 63
Parmar, P. 93, 129, 136
patriarchy 22, 54, 58, 96, 135
Personal Narratives Group 92, 101
Peters, T. 165–6
Phillips, A. 54
Phoenix, A. 137
planning: beliefs and assumptions 58; feminist approach 54, 71–2; gender and culture within modernist 70–2; modernist 69–89; public/private dichotomies 60

Podbrey, P. 115, 117, 123
political ground 128
postmodernism 108
Pratt, G. 72
Pred, A. 74
Pringle, R. 58
Probert, B. 162
public and private space: definitions 72–3; dichotomy 50, 58–60, 72; forbidden and permitted spaces 72–8
purdah 31, 33, 35, 36, 40, 44
Purvis, J. 149

Quiney, A. 60

race: concept of 137; mixed- 134, 137–8, 139
Race Relations Act (1976) 55
racism: in Britain 137; children's approaches to 134, 143, 150; planning 58; problem of 2; South Africa 13
Ramsay, E. 157
Rao, U. 29
rape 99
Rape Crisis 15, 19
Rappoport, A. 70, 75, 76
Rattansi, A. 109
Reay, D. 140
Richardson, D. 135
Rifkin, J. 169
Ringelheim, J.M. 92, 94, 102, 103
Rittner, C. 93, 98
Robins, K. 163
Robinson, V. 135
Rodman, M. 51–2
Root, M.P.P. 137, 138
Rosenthal, G. 101
Rotenberg, R. 64
Roth, J.K. 93, 98
Rowbotham, S. 172
Royal Melbourne Institute of Technology (RMIT) 167
Royal Town Planning Institute (RTPI) 56, 65n
Rozario, S. 98, 99
Rushkoff, D. 165
Russell, D. 116, 123
Rwanda, genocide 93, 99–100

Sahgal, V. 34
Sancho, N. 99

Index

Sandercock, L. 71, 72, 88
Saptahik Press 30
Sassen, S. 161–2, 169, 172n
Sawer, M. 160
Schulz, L. 157, 158
Segal, A. 108
Segal, L. 149
Segal, R. 110
Serb policy 96, 99
Seth, K. 41
sexism 20
sexuality 62–3, 136, 150
Sexwale, B. 117, 121, 124
Shapiro, I. 54
Sharoni, S. 96, 99
Sharp, G. 168
Shoah 93, 94, 98–9
Shukla, D. 36
Sibley, D. 70, 75, 77, 80
Simeone, A. 157
Simmonds, F.N. 148
Singh, A.R. 31, 32
Singh, B. 39
Sinha, M. 35
Sinha, R.K. 35
Sinha, S.K. 35, 46
Slovo, G. 114–17, 123, 124
Slovo, R. 124
Slovo, S. 117, 124
Smith, D. 94, 101
Smith, S. 54
South Africa: building unity 14–18; diaspora identities 112–15; diaspora journeyings 118–19; emergence of South African feminism 22–4; exile and migration 107–23; exile community as family 115–18; gendered diaspora identities 107–8; housing 60; image of home 119–22; triple oppression 13–14; unity despite diversity 11–13; women, exile and migration 111–12; women's groups 1; women's liberation and national liberation 18–22; women's unity 11–25
South African Communist Party 11
South African Domestic Workers' Union (SADWU) 15, 17
Soviet Union 96
space: forbidden and permitted 69; in Israel 70; and place 50, 51, 61–5;
Spearitt, P. 173n
spinning *khadi* 30, 32–3, 45

Spivak, G. 109
Stanley, L. 100–1, 103, 138
state, politics of restructuring 159–61
Steinberg, D.L. 3, 131n, 149, 179
Stewart, T.A. 165, 168
Stree Dharm 34
Suri, R. 37

Tal, S. 85
Tamana, D. 19
Thapar, S. 37
Thapar, Sukhdev 39
Thapar-Bjorkert, S. 1, 3
Thatcher, M. 135
Third World 88, 93, 162
Thomas, J. 173n
Thorne, B. 149
Tillion, G. 99
Times of India, The 30
Tizard, B. 137
Tohidi, N. 73
Tong, R. 135
town planning 54, 60
Transvaal Women's Movement 21
Traweek, S. 101
triple oppression 13–14
Turner, J.F.C. 70

Uguris, T. 2, 179
United Democratic Front (UDF) 17, 19–21; Women's Congress 21
United Nations 5
United States (US), Women's Studies 176–7
United Women's Congress (UWCO) 13, 14–15, 20, 24
United Women's Organisation (UWO) 11–15, 18–19, 20, 24
unity, building 14–15
university: academic freedom 130; corporatisation 155; feminist 'knowledge workers' 169–72; forms of governmentality 154, 155–6; future 166–9; gender issues 156–8; inequalities 127; marketisation 156; rationalisation 155
Unterhalter, E. 124; (1996) 161, 172; Gaitskell and (1989) 23; Gaitskell and (1990) 23; and Maxey (1996) 107, 111–12, 118, 121, 123; (this volume) 3, 107, 179
Urry, J. 163, 164
Uttar Pradesh 28, 31

Valentine, G. 63, 74, 75
Vance, C.S. 149
veil 73–4, 76
Virk, L. 177

wa Goro, W. 177
Wajcman, J. 58, 60
Walker, A. 135
Walker, C. 15, 23
Week, The 30
Weinstein, M. 164
Weisman, L.K. 63
Weiss, R. 120, 124
Weiss, T.G. 97
Wells, J. 23
Western Cape Civic Association 20
White, D. 168
whiteness 141, 150
Wicomb, Z. 123, 124
Widdershoven, G.A.M. 101
widowhood 36
Williams, B. 108, 122
Williams, R. 51
Wilson, E. 50, 62
Winn, M. 57
Winship, J. 131n
Wise, S. 100, 138
Wolpe, A. 117, 121, 123, 124
Women Working Worldwide 162

Women's Action Forum (WAF) 5, 6
Women's Alliance (WA) 16–17
Women's Charter for Effective Equality 22
Women's Front (WF) 20
women's liberation 18–22
women's movement 6–7, 9–10
Women's National Coalition (WNC) 11, 17–18, 21–2
Women's Studies: in Australia 158; in Britain 130, 176–7; courses 135; mainstream 9, 130; political project 127; race 133–4; trends 2, 176–7; in US 176–7
Women's Studies Network (UK) Association 1, 178
World Bank 161, 172

Yeatman, A. 171–2
Yiftacheal, O. 70
Young, G. 93, 94
Young, I.M. 53, 54
Yugoslavia, former 96, 97
Yuval-Davis, N.: (1994) 49, 50, 51, 54, 55, 58; (1997) 54, 93; Anthias and (1989) 108, 122; Anthias and (1992) 51, 55, 93, 108, 137, 146–7

Zur, J. 102